Art and Technology in
Maurice Blanchot

Technicities
Series Editors: Ryan Bishop, Winchester School of Art, University of Southampton and Jussi Parikka, Aarhus University and FAMU, Prague

The philosophy of technicities: exploring how technology mediates art, frames design and augments the mediated collective perception of everyday life.
Technicities will publish the latest philosophical thinking about our increasingly immaterial technocultural conditions, with a unique focus on the context of art, design and media.

Editorial Advisory Board
Marie-Luise Angerer, Benjamin Bratton, Sean Cubitt, Daphne Dragona, Matthew Fuller, Yuriko Furuhata, Olga Goriunova, Yuk Hui, Jin Huimin, Akira Mizuta Lippit, Shaoling Ma, Claudia Mareis, Gunalan Nadarajan, elin o'Hara slavick, Robert Pietrusko, Tania Roy, Susan Schuppli, Christina Vagt, Geoffrey Winthrop-Young.

Published
Lyotard and the Inhuman Condition: Reflections on Nihilism, Information and Art
Ashley Woodward

Critical Luxury Studies: Art, Design, Media
Edited by John Armitage and Joanne Roberts

Cold War Legacies: Systems, Theory, Aesthetics
Edited by John Beck and Ryan Bishop

Fashion and Materialism
Ulrich Lehmann

Queering Digital India: Activisms, Identities, Subjectivities
Edited by Rohit K. Dasgupta and Debanuj DasGupta

Zero Degree Seeing: Barthes/Burgin and Political Aesthetics
Edited by Ryan Bishop and Sunil Manghani

Rhythm and Critique: Technics, Modalities, Practices
Edited by Paola Crespi and Sunil Manghani

Photography Off the Scale: Technologies and Theories of the Mass Image
Edited by Tomáš Dvořák and Jussi Parikka

The Informational Logic of Human Rights: Network Imaginaries in the Cybernetic Age
Josh Bowsher

Art and Technology in Maurice Blanchot
Holly Langstaff

China and the Wireless Undertow: Media as Wave Philosophy
Anna Greenspan

Reconfiguring the Portrait
Edited by Abraham Geil and Tomáš Jirsa

www.edinburghuniversitypress.com/series/TECH

Art and Technology in Maurice Blanchot

Holly Langstaff

Edinburgh University Press is one of the leading university presses in the UK. We publish academic books and journals in our selected subject areas across the humanities and social sciences, combining cutting-edge scholarship with high editorial and production values to produce academic works of lasting importance. For more information visit our website: edinburghuniversitypress.com

This book is freely available on a Creative Commons CC-BY-NC-ND licence thanks to the kind sponsorship of the libraries participating in the Jisc Open Access Community Framework OpenUP initiative.

© Holly Langstaff, 2023, 2025, under a Creative Commons Attribution-NonCommercial-NonDerivative licence

Edinburgh University Press Ltd
13 Infirmary Street,
Edinburgh, EH1 1LT

First published in hardback by Edinburgh University Press 2023

Typeset in 11/13 Adobe Sabon by
IDSUK (DataConnection) Ltd

A CIP record for this book is available from the British Library

ISBN 978 1 3995 1547 4 (hardback)
ISBN 978 1 3995 1548 1 (paperback)
ISBN 978 1 3995 1549 8 (webready PDF)
ISBN 978 1 3995 1550 4 (epub)

The right of Holly Langstaff to be identified as the author of this work has been asserted in accordance with the Copyright, Designs and Patents Act 1988, and the Copyright and Related Rights Regulations 2003 (SI No. 2498).

Contents

Series Editors' Preface — vi
Acknowledgements — vii
Abbreviations of Works by Maurice Blanchot — viii

Introduction — 1
   'One of the most difficult but important tasks of our time' — 2
   Technology — 5
   Politics — 9

1 Blanchot and Mallarmé: 'The double state of the word' — 17
   'The double state of the word' — 19
   Literary Autonomy and Foundation — 22
   Literature as Imposture — 31
   'But when is there literature?' — 35

2 An Inhuman Interruption — 46
   The History of Being — 48
   'Why Poets?' — 57
   Death: The Impossibility of Possibility — 63
   A Turning — 71
   Animals and Automation — 77

3 The Neuter and Modern Technology — 99
   La technique — 101
   Writing as techne and Modern Technology — 112
   The Neuter: Kafka and *The Last Man* — 127

4 Inorganic Writing — 146
   Fragmentary Writing and Technology — 147
   Nature Gone Haywire — 162

Conclusion — 172

Bibliography — 178
Index — 189

Series Editors' Preface

Technological transformation has profound and frequently unforeseen influences on art, design and media. At times technology emancipates art and enriches the quality of design. Occasionally it causes acute individual and collective problems of mediated perception. Time after time technological change accomplishes both simultaneously. This new book series explores and reflects philosophically on what new and emerging *technicities* do to our everyday lives and increasingly immaterial technocultural conditions. Moving beyond traditional conceptions of the philosophy of technology and of techne, the series presents new philosophical thinking on how technology constantly alters the essential conditions of beauty, invention and communication. From novel understandings of the world of technicity to new interpretations of aesthetic value, graphics and information, Technicities focuses on the relationships between critical theory and representation, the arts, broadcasting, print, technological genealogies/histories, material culture and digital technologies and our philosophical views of the world of art, design and media.

The series foregrounds contemporary work in art, design and media whilst remaining inclusive, in terms of both philosophical perspectives on technology and interdisciplinary contributions. For a philosophy of technicities is crucial to extant debates over the artistic, inventive and informational aspects of technology. The books in the Technicities series concentrate on present-day and evolving technological advances but visual, design-led and mass mediated questions are emphasised to further our knowledge of their often-combined means of digital transformation.

The editors of Technicities welcome proposals for monographs and well-considered edited collections that establish new paths of investigation.

Ryan Bishop and Jussi Parikka

Acknowledgements

I would like to thank those who have advised and supported me during the writing of this book. I owe considerable thanks to Leslie Hill for his excellent supervision and meticulous comments on drafts of the original thesis and later this book, and to Alex Corcos for his patient intellectual engagement with and belief in this project over several years. My family have encouraged me throughout this process: thank you Mam, Dad, Paul, Val, Ruth, Doddsy, Tom and James, and thank you Arlene, Paul and Grandma Nancy for ensuring I could do a masters degree. I am grateful to Liz Guild for encouraging me to undertake postgraduate study, and to Ian James for introducing me to the work of Blanchot, and for the supervisions that made me want to keep trying to say something about this subject. The comments of my examiners, Ian Maclachlan and Oliver Davis, were invaluable when preparing this book for publication. I have also greatly benefited from the advice and encouragement of colleagues and friends at various stages: Emma Campbell, Cathy Hampton, Marie Léger, Alexandra Lloyd, Patrick McGuinness, Douglas Morrey, Jane Sinnett-Smith, Susannah Wilson, Chantal Wright. I am grateful to the team at Edinburgh University Press for their guidance throughout this process and to the series editors and readers for their helpful comments on the manuscript. Finally, I would like to thank the Department of French Studies at the University of Warwick for funding my doctoral study and St Edmund Hall, Oxford, for institutional support during the last stretch of writing this book. A section of the fourth chapter previously appeared as 'Uncontrollable Mechanisms: Maurice Blanchot's Inorganic Writing' in *French Studies* (2019).

Abbreviations of Works by Maurice Blanchot

References to English translations of Blanchot are given in the text where these are available. Translations have been modified in places for reasons of consistency and accuracy.

AO	*Awaiting Oblivion*
BC	*The Book to Come*
BL	'The Beast of Lascaux'
DN	*Death Now: Chronicles of Intellectual Life, 1944*
DS	*Death Sentence*
F	*Friendship*
FP	*Faux pas*
IC	*The Infinite Conversation*
ID	*Into Disaster: Chronicles of Intellectual Life, 1941*
IMD	'The Instant of My Death'
LM	*The Last Man*
LS	*Lautréamont and Sade*
MD	*The Madness of the Day*
MH	*The Most High*
PW	*Political Writings: 1953–1993*
SL	*The Space of Literature*
SNB	*The Step Not Beyond*
TO	*Thomas the Obscure* [1950 version]
WD	*The Writing of the Disaster*
WF	*The Work of Fire*

Introduction

The accelerating development of modern technologies in the twentieth and twenty-first centuries raises some of the most urgent questions of our time. These developments call for new ways of thinking our relationship to nature, culture, history. In the twentieth century, a series of writers responded to this demand by thinking technology in the broadest sense. Martin Heidegger gives equipment a privileged status when he articulates how the human 'is' in a world in *Being and Time*, and subsequently develops this analysis into a critique of modern technology perceived as the final stage of a deep-rooted philosophical tradition dating back to Plato. Jacques Derrida prolongs but challenges Heideggerian thought, offering a broad definition of technics that begins with the possibility of repetition inherent to language and extends to challenge the presupposition of a nature or thought free from technics. And at the end of the twentieth century Bernard Stiegler identifies the storage of memories in technical artefacts as the origin of the human and the constitution of time as technics. Occupying a crucial but unacknowledged position in this lineage is the writer and literary critic Maurice Blanchot (1907–2003), for whom writing is the side of technology released from anthropocentric mastery.

If Blanchot's significance for a philosophy of technology is underappreciated, other aspects of his legacy today are more widely acknowledged. The enduring relevance of Blanchot in the twenty-first century lies in his commitment to a writing that presents a radical challenge to totalising philosophical and critical discourses and refuses traditional views of literature. He is a reference for a diverse range of writers and thinkers reconsidering the relationship between inside and outside in various contexts, from Assia Djebar to Bernard Stiegler.[1] His essays resist neat categorisation into literary criticism or philosophy, and his fictional works, belonging to no literary movement or group of the twentieth century, are distinctive by the fact that they contest their own limits and any label that might be applied to them. At the heart of Blanchot's writing is a concern for the limits of the work or the conditions that make writing possible, as such strong readers of

Blanchot as Derrida and Foucault have pointed out, and this paradoxical focus results in an idiom marked by its restless movement.[2]

Too often, however, Blanchot is associated with a version of literary autonomy or a mysticism which obscures or overlooks his engagement with the events and debates of his time, including his thinking of technology. This book situates Blanchot's fictional and critical work in the context of a thinking of art as techne – the Greek root of 'technology', meaning both craft and art – as it develops in and follows from the philosophy of Martin Heidegger. That Blanchot has been overlooked in this lineage might be explained in part by his aversion to the French term *technologie*, in place of which he consistently opts for the more ambiguous *technique* – technique, technology, technics in English.[3] Blanchot's choice signals an engagement with technology understood in more inclusive terms which implies no clear division or hierarchy between art and its so-called opposite.

'One of the most difficult but important tasks of our time'

Blanchot worked as a literary critic throughout his career and critical works from *Faux pas* (1943) to *The Writing of the Disaster* (1980) are largely made up of essays and fragments first published elsewhere in journals, reviews and newspapers. In 1959, prompted by a questionnaire sent by the independent leftist journal *Arguments*, Blanchot reflected on the purpose of literary criticism, which he writes is so often reduced to an intermediary task, bolstering the authority of the Academy and the press, and said to be lacking any substance of its own. On this last point he references Heidegger, who writes, in relation to the poetry of Hölderlin, that the task of interpretation is to yield to the pure affirmation of the poem. Blanchot does not contradict this point but suggests that it offers a richer conception of criticism than we might first assume, which also tells us something about literature: this self-effacement is already a trait of the literary work.

The reference to Heidegger highlights the importance of the German philosopher to Blanchot's critical approach and is anything but innocuous. Introduced to Heidegger's work in 1927 or 1928 by his close friend Emmanuel Levinas while they were both studying in Strasbourg, Blanchot describes the experience of reading *Being and Time* as 'a veritable intellectual shock' (PW 123).[4] Many recognisably Blanchotian motifs develop from his reading of Heidegger: an interest in Hölderlin and therefore the relationship between poetry and philosophy; the question of death and dying; the relationship between the artwork and truth; and more generally a desire to extricate thinking from metaphysics. Blanchot's engagement with Heidegger is extensive and sustained but also tense and adversarial. This essay on the purpose of criticism is no exception. According to Blanchot in the main body of the essay, Heidegger writes that in the noisy tumult of non-poetic language a poem is like a bell suspended in mid-air on which a light snowfall would be enough to make it chime. Blanchot suggests, 'Perhaps commentary is just a little snowflake making the bell toll' (LS 2), but admits in a footnote that he has changed the meaning of Heidegger's text and that for the philosopher all commentary is a disturbance that goes out of tune.[5] This critical strategy has the unusual effect of making Heidegger say what Blanchot thinks even in the correction: this discord is not a degradation of literature but an indication that criticism, disappearing into nothingness, expresses something essential about the literary work.

'Nevertheless', Blanchot continues in his essay, 'we feel sure that the image of snow is just an image and that we have yet even further to go' (LS 4). Just an image: this unassertive phrase says a lot about literature and its relationship to the world. For Heidegger, the poem does not treat language as a material at its disposal because poetry first makes language possible. The poet – Heidegger privileges the German language and Hölderlin in particular – is the vehicle of an impersonal force which speaks through them to found a world and a new beginning free from the rationality of Western metaphysics. Heidegger relies on language not becoming an object for itself in this poetic saying, but, in Blanchot's account, if the distinguishing feature of poetry is the expression of the essence of language, we are nonetheless returned to transitive language. The consequences for Blanchot are far-reaching: in taking itself as object, language reveals the lack that is essential to poetry or literature, and 'literature' withdraws from the world so that words become images rather than signs or values. The self-effacement Heidegger identifies in criticism is therefore already inherent to the poem, and it is why 'literature' in Blanchot, which is later replaced in his work by the more inclusive 'writing', moves beyond its own limits in an endless movement of outward self-reflection.

This view of literature differs from that offered by Blanchot's contemporary Jean-Paul Sartre, for whom to write is to name and unveil the world and to project an image of being in the world. According to Sartre, the writer is committed to the extent of being conscious of their involvement in the world and is under the moral imperative to disclose a reality to the reader in which the individual is a historically situated being who is committed to a quest for authentic freedom.[6] In a distortion of Sartre's account of morality, freedom and existence, Blanchot argues in several essays from the 1940s and 1950s that the 'truth' of the work cannot correspond to any worldly truth or political project: writing reveals the imaginary rather than the world and the writer cannot therefore be committed because they are not involved in the world as such.[7] Literature by its very definition is what Sartre would deem bad faith, which is not to say that the literary work is not revolutionary for Blanchot, but this never has as its starting point the world of work, objects and political parties. The radical contestation that begins with literature extends beyond its limits; and it is why Blanchot, reflecting on the purpose of criticism in 1959, can describe both criticism and literature in the following weighty terms:

> In this sense criticism – literature – seems to me to be associated with one of the most difficult but important tasks of our time, played out in a necessarily ambiguous movement: the task of preserving and of liberating thought from the notion of value, consequently also of opening history up to what in it is already freed from all forms of value in preparation for an entirely different – still unforeseeable – sort of affirmation. (LS 6)

Criticism, radicalising a feature already inherent in literature and thus including literature, does not give up any truth, and in doing so liberates thought from value and subservience to ruling powers. The stakes are high, as literature and criticism resist the notion of epochal change or narratives of the end of history told in the wake of the development of nuclear weapons in the mid-twentieth century. The final line of the above extract is reworked from an earlier review of Dionys Mascolo's book on communism: 'It is undoubtedly the task of our age to move toward an affirmation that is entirely *other*' (F 97).

Blanchot and Mascolo agree that the task of moving beyond value is shared by communism and art, but Blanchot goes one step further by suggesting that the artistic experience is more attentive to this task because recalling us to it 'in the realm that is proper to [art]'. He concludes the essay on Mascolo: 'A remarkable coincidence' (F 97). Blanchot is at once establishing and ironically displacing the congruence between art and communism because the revolutionary potential of literature – thought here in broader terms as 'the poetic work, the artistic work' – stems precisely from its not belonging to the world and extends beyond politics in the limited sense of the word.

The various contexts in which Blanchot writes and then republishes the later response to *Arguments* stress the wide reverberation of literature and criticism: the publication of the essay in 1959 came one year after Blanchot had protested against De Gaulle's controversial and, according to some, illegal return to power; and the essay was selected as preface to *Lautréamont and Sade* the year after the end of the Algerian War (Blanchot and Mascolo were jointly involved in drafting and distributing the 'Declaration of the Right to Insubordination in the Algerian War' also known as the 'Manifesto of the 121' in 1961), which was the same year that Blanchot learned the extent of Heidegger's political endorsement of Nazi rule.[8] Blanchot adds a footnote to his next book concerning Heidegger's explicit support for the November 1933 plebiscite withdrawing Germany from the League of Nations: 'with the aim of recommending a decisive vote in favour of National Socialism, it put in Hitler's service the *very* language and the *very* writing through which [. . .] we had been invited to participate in the questioning designated as the most lofty' (IC 451). *The Black Notebooks* have since shown that, even at a time when Heidegger was particularly critical of National Socialism, a specific antisemitism was emerging in his thought inscribed in the history of Being.[9] The disastrous consequences of this philosophical language emphasise the urgent need to clarify the distinction between Heidegger and Blanchot, which begins with their view of literature and extends to their treatment of the machine in modernity.

Technology

In 1953, the year Heidegger published 'The Question Concerning Technology' and the year Blanchot started as a monthly columnist for the newly relaunched *Nouvelle Nouvelle Revue française*, Blanchot argues that writing is one technique among others: 'the impersonal knowledge of the book [. . .] is bound to the development of technology in all its forms and it treats speech, and writing, as technology' (BL 9). In several essays published that year, Blanchot reflects on the relationship between art or literature and technologies, arguing that what we experience today in the name of modern technology could already be heard in the works of writers such as Mallarmé and Hölderlin (BC 202). This thinking of writing as techne comes to the fore in 1953 and is developed in essays with an explicit focus on nuclear weapons, space flight and the printing press in the 1960s, but was already implied in earlier critical and fictional work which is marked by a close engagement with Heidegger.

Heidegger has been described as the single most influential twentieth-century philosopher of technology,[10] for whom modern technology threatens to transform everything into a calculable resource to be exploited, and art is the saving power that will provide the foundation for a new beginning. 'But where danger threatens | That which saves from it also grows [*Wo aber Gefahr ist, wächst | Das Rettende auch*]'.[11] This quotation from Hölderlin leads Heidegger to conclude that where technology rules, so too techne as art has a chance and a role to counteract it.

Heidegger famously argues that the essence of technology is nothing technological and that modern technology should be distinguished from its Greek root techne: the latter is a bringing-forth which allows Being to come into unconcealment, while modern technology is a challenging-forth which transforms everything, including Being, into a resource to be exploited. Modern technology is a continuation of metaphysics by other means. The danger is that we will have lost our openness to Being and to the possibility of historical transformation, and it is for this reason that Heidegger turns to poetry as the saying through which we can once again think Being. Techne is a mode of poiesis, writes Heidegger, and the essence of art is poetry because it is in language that beings are founded and Being takes hold of us.[12] The reduction of nature to an object for metaphysical calculating rationality was perhaps the reason why, in the aftermath of the Second World War and despite his politics, about which relatively little was known at the time, so many readers in France considered Heidegger to be the crucial contemporary thinker.

Blanchot follows Heidegger in the view that writing is a sort of technique or techne, but never appeals for salvation from the menace of technology in the modern era. There is no evidence of technophobia in Blanchot. His thinking of the impossibility of an authentic relationship to death and dying and his emphasis on the abyssal non-foundations of literature, in contrast to the Heideggerian appeal to a foundation that will provide the ground for a new beginning in the desolate time that is modernity, disrupts Heideggerian thought. Levinas notes as much: 'Does Blanchot not give art the role of uprooting the Heideggerian universe?'[13]

Blanchot is conspicuous by his absence in most responses to the Heideggerian critique of modern technology; however, one telling instance of how he has set the agenda for later thinkers is the use of his work by Bernard Stiegler in *Technics and Time*.[14] Stiegler wants to specify the way technics constitutes our experience of time differently in different epochs; he argues that historical epochs and the collective forms of time consciousness which define these epochs are constituted in and through technical systems and prostheses. The impersonal knowledge of which Blanchot writes in 'The Beast of Lascaux' is used several times by Stiegler as evidence that writing as technics is a tool for memory.[15] Only humans have access to the memory deposited in technical systems or artefacts, but Western philosophy has accorded technicity secondary instrumental status when it is in fact constitutive of the human (this is the focus of Stiegler's critique of Heidegger). Stiegler undoubtedly sees in Blanchot a thinking of writing as techne: he lists Blanchot and Walter Benjamin as two thinkers who recognised that the question of repetition is a question of technics.[16] The centrality of Blanchot to this appeal to think the originary technicity of the human is further underscored by the use of an extract from the first of Blanchot's two essays on nuclear weapons – in which anonymous interlocutors discuss the possibility of knowing for certain whether we are at a turning point in history – as epigraph to the general introduction to *Technics and Time*.[17]

The use of Blanchot to suggest that we have crossed into a new age is, however, misleading. Stiegler frames his philosophical project as a remembering of the forgotten technicity of the human, a task which is becoming ever more pressing with the development of digital communications media: our experience of time in the age of writing had been linear, but our consciousness, constituted as it is by technics, risks becoming industrialised in an age when geographical situatedness and temporal delays are annihilated by real-time media. Blanchot is sceptical of the Heideggerian claim, which Stiegler adopts while critiquing other aspects of Heidegger's thought, that there are different epochs of Being that can be identified and addressed as such; his objection is that to do so with any certainty it is necessary to withdraw from Being, which then implies that the epoch cannot be delimited. When Stiegler cites Blanchot on the impression of a turning in Herodotus and in the experience of modern technologies – defined by Blanchot in this essay as 'collective organization on a planetary scale for the purpose of calculated planning, mechanization and automation, and lastly atomic energy' – he uses the argument of one interlocutor as evidence that our experience of time has been fundamentally changed in the age of modern technology: 'What hitherto only the stars could do, man now does. Man has become a star [*astre*]. This astral era now commencing can no longer be contained within the bounds of history.' (IC 266).[18] But the quotation from Blanchot is taken out of context because the interlocutors continue their discussion: there is something insurmountable for thought in both writing and the experience provoked by the development of the atomic bomb. Writing is a forgetting or interruption of the present for Blanchot; modern technologies have the same effect, but these are more easily recuperated by the ruling class and capitalist ideology.[19]

The distinction between the two conceptions of writing as a tool for memory and as a means of contesting our historical assumptions reveals how Stiegler fundamentally misreads or misuses Blanchot. Stiegler argues that writing gives time, and as such is the origin of the human; but for Blanchot it is writing without horizon that inscribes the horizon, and for this very reason exceeds and precedes any horizon. The difference is emphasised towards the end of the first volume of *Technics and Time* where Stiegler quotes extensively from Blanchot to argue that writing exemplifies the question of invention or the beginning as paradox; at stake here is the inaugural moment of the human in tool use, understood as a process of exteriorisation with no pre-existing interiority.[20] Stiegler argues that writing in Blanchot is a forgetting of the self, but that it also means a 'conversion', 'one that never forgets, however, the outside-of-itself: it is not a return to self but a moving-outside into effects (of writing), a moving toward the world'.[21] The stress on writing as a tool for memory means that Stiegler has to twist Blanchot, who would not agree with this characterisation of the outside as instrumentality. Stiegler directs us in a footnote to those essays 'on use' in *The Space of Literature* – we can speculate that he has in mind a passage from 'Rilke and Death's Demand' (cited elsewhere in *Technics and Time*) in which Blanchot considers conversion in the world and in the imaginary:

> Thus we see that the conversion, the movement toward the most interior, work [*œuvre*] in which we transform ourselves as we transform everything, has something to do with our end –, and this transformation, this realisation of the visible into the invisible for which we are responsible, is the very task of dying that has until now been so difficult for us to recognise, which takes effort [*qui est un travail*], yet effort certainly quite different from that which we put into making objects and projecting results. (SL 141)

Blanchot writes in the above extract that this conversion has something to do with our end, but the dash following this statement indicates something that cannot be articulated or recalled. For Stiegler, the technical embodies the problematic of human finitude, and death makes the constitution of the human possible via the process of exteriorisation. In Blanchot, however, the unachievable task of writing is associated with the unachievable task of dying because in both one is dispossessed of one's self and no longer faces the thing as object. The transformation described by Blanchot is not a simple change of form, the concretisation of consciousness in the technical artefact, but a deconstruction of the will which outplays the sovereign subject. It is why Blanchot as early as 1949 can describe analysis as a machine that is not easily stopped (LS 66).

In Blanchot's account of the relationship between art and technology, the technical is irreducible to history, which it contests, thus allowing him to recognise in both writing and modern technologies (radio, cinema, the telephone, the atomic bomb, the printing press and space flight) the potential to challenge our worldly perspective. By refusing to think in terms of different epochs of Being, Blanchot welcomes the uncertainty of an unknowable future and foretells neither devastation nor salvation. Fear felt in the face of an uncertain future does not translate into simple technophobia for Blanchot, but responsibility for someone or something which is radically unknowable and not limited to the human.

Politics

Blanchot started his career as a literary critic and political journalist in the 1930s, when he wrote for publications such as the liberal-conservative *Journal des débats*, the fiercely anti-Nazist *Rempart*, and the short-lived, nonconformist, right-wing nationalist broadsheets *Combat* and *L'Insurgé*. In these early articles he expresses a nationalist position that is also firmly anti-Hitler, anti-Nazism and in favour of decisive military action to deter German expansion. Several scholars have claimed that Blanchot in the 1930s was close to a certain kind of French fascism. Recent research has demonstrated the opposite.[22] The parallel too often drawn between Blanchot and Heidegger is based on a misunderstanding of Blanchot's politics. Michel Surya, for instance, writes that the two thinkers shared similar political views for a long time and that both subsequently tried to hide, or refused to acknowledge the full extent of, this earlier political commitment. Seeing little difference between the two, Surya argues that Blanchot's criticism of Heidegger after he became aware of the extent of his adherence to National Socialism must be applied in turn to Blanchot himself.[23] While Heidegger's own language was corrupted and devalued by his politics, Blanchot never committed his language to any political party and, even as he lamented the weakness and corruption of French parliamentary democracy, he was fiercely opposed in equal measure to Nazism, fascism and Stalinism.[24]

The disagreement between Blanchot and Heidegger begins with their view of literature, criticism and language, and extends to their analysis of technology in modernity. Jean-Luc Nancy – who played an influential role in reassessing Blanchot's politics, albeit in controversial and disputed fashion – has suggested that Blanchot in this decade, by dint of his Catholic familial background, shared with Catholicism a hatred of modernity which is a symptom of malaise in and of civilisation.[25] Blanchot wrote of France weakened by bad government and failing democracy and called for a spiritual, national revolution in his political journalism of the 1930s. There is such a plea at the end of a review from 1932 of Henri Daniel-Rops's *Le Monde sans âme* [The World without Soul], where Blanchot also clarifies that the fault with the modern decadent world does not lie with the machine: we see the machine as characteristic of our time and we deem it responsible for all progress, wonder and disorder, but it is vain to think that the machine is the cause of our ruin. What is much more threatening, Blanchot writes following Daniel-Rops, is that the materialism responsible for our current disarray is nothing new.[26]

The misuse or misunderstanding of the machine is most dangerous in the context of Soviet Russia – Blanchot is critical of Daniel-Rops for overlooking this point in his study – where it is used to offer a sort of sham spirituality based on the refusal of material ownership. Blanchot argues that, like capitalism, Soviet Russia promises material happiness but, in offering this happiness to all, binds the aspirations of the individual to the collective and puts the individual to work for a system that relentlessly pursues an impossible goal. The machine is made indirectly responsible for a dream that offers nothing higher than material value when it is in fact aligned with the order, precision and uniformity of Blanchot's spiritual revolution:

> What is formidable about the machine is its very perfection, the precision of the material order to which it submits and where no fault remains. We hesitate to condemn the machine because it excludes the slapdash and the inexact, it has no weakness, and it does not allow any disorder to remain from which the mind could hope to profit by making itself the master of it.[27]

The machine denies the incalculable disorder of materialism perpetuated by Marxism and Stalinism in a striking rejection of any attempt to blame the machine for the troubles of modern times; this is evidence that, from a very early stage in his career as a journalist, Blanchot did not condemn modernity or mechanisation, as Nancy suggests, but saw in it the potential for change. Blanchot is thus very far from Heidegger's condemnation of modern technology as the final phase of Western metaphysics.

What interests Blanchot about all technologies from the late 1940s onwards is the revolutionary potential for uncontrollable mechanisms – from the literary or critical machine to the telephone – to interrupt our worldview and prepare the way for that entirely different affirmation which often appears in the form of an oblique inhuman interruption. The machine persists as a faulty rather than perfectly functioning mechanism in Blanchot's work from this point; it is closely associated with the work of criticism, which produces inexact copies of the literary work rather than a precise and silent replica. This is not a degradation of the poetic as Heidegger argues, but an open-ended metamorphosis that allows a vibrant and vagrant writing unconstrained by the limits of literature, criticism and philosophy. Here the difference between Blanchot and Heidegger is most marked. Heidegger famously establishes a hierarchy between human, animal and stone because only the human has access to world as a system of meanings through language and tools. Derrida later vehemently challenges Heidegger's anthropocentrism, but the inhuman interruptions of Blanchot's fictional and critical writing indicate that he was already aware of the implications of this aspect of Heideggerian thought from an early stage of his career. These inhuman figures have been largely overlooked until now because their appearances are oblique and fleeting, but this book argues that they are an indication of that radically other affirmation heard in literature but also all other technologies.

For example, in the essay on Lautréamont from 1949 which his 1959 thoughts on the purpose of criticism later prefaced, Blanchot considers the significance of the inhuman figures that flood *The Songs of Maldoror*, resulting in 'a metamorphosis wherein the limits of [Lautréamont's] person and the chains of his human reality are shattered' (LS 162). A reading of Blanchot attentive to this experience bears little resemblance to the unflattering and inaccurate reputation with which he has been lumbered by certain critics. Take, for instance, the account of Blanchot given by the contemporary novelist Marie Darrieussecq, for whom Blanchot represents the intellectual authority and academic severity from which she felt excluded while studying at university, not least because the feminine is deemed to be almost entirely absent in his work (an experience not shared by the author of this book).[28] Darrieussecq associates Blanchot with the despondent lifelessness of the same academic authority from which he sought to distance criticism in 1959. This book demonstrates that there is something much more to this writing than a cadaverous and bitter outlook. It emphasises the unknowable affirmation revealed in writing as techne, and in all other technologies, and demonstrates that this affirmation often takes the shape of an inhuman interruption.

Art and Technology in Maurice Blanchot begins by tracing the development of Blanchot's view of literature in opposition to everyday language in a series of essays written in the 1940s and early 1950s on the poet Stéphane Mallarmé. When the relationship between art or literature and the everyday or the utilitarian becomes one of slippage rather than opposition, the linguistic hierarchy imposed by Heidegger collapses and we are left with a vibrant and shifting literature that contests its own limits. The second chapter explores the disagreement between Blanchot and Heidegger through a comparison of their respective readings of Rilke. It demonstrates that Blanchot engages with the Heideggerian concept of world in order to reveal its cracks: inhuman figures in Blanchot signal the disruption of the hierarchy established by Heidegger between human, animal and stone, and unruly hands reveal a disobedient technology which challenges the limit of the human. In essays from the 1950s, Blanchot engages in more explicit terms with technology, and Chapter 3 examines the relationship between writing and modern technologies to explore how we might hear in all forms of techne something new and unexpected. The chapter culminates in a reading of *The Last Man* informed by Blanchot's reading of Kafka; it demonstrates that writing for Blanchot cannot be enclosed within anthropocentric or anthropological mastery, which it challenges in the name of the other to which it gives voice. Between 1965 and 1980 there is no mention of the term *technique* in Blanchot's writing; the final chapter shows that rather than a condemnation of technology, the suppression of the term reveals that technology is everywhere implied. Fragmentary writing is a sort of powerless power or a wayward inorganic proliferation that outplays the human. This chapter considers the role that an affirmative refusal plays in resistance and in the undoing of the subject, and the various forms this refusal takes in Blanchot's work, from a stag beetle to mounds of rubble.

Writing for Blanchot is increasingly – as the chronological approach taken here will demonstrate – a sort of disobedient technology beyond the control of the human which, sharing the interruptive quality with all other technologies that withdraw us from the world of work and tools, allows an excess that outplays the limits of literature, criticism and the human. A reading of Blanchot focused on his thinking of the relationship between art and technology presents a writer who is actively engaged in the events and debates of his time and whose work continues to be relevant in the twenty-first century.

Notes

1. See references to Blanchot in Assia Djebar, *Ces Voix qui m'assiègent: ... en marge de ma francophonie* (Paris: Albin Michel, 1999), pp. 62–3, 195, 229. For example: 'Blanchot is not a woman and is not, like me, Arab. He is a writer, that is all. I mention him here, however, to outline something like a sky for my writing' (p. 63, my translation). Bernard Stiegler's use of Blanchot in the articulation of his philosophy of time and technics will be examined later in the Introduction.
2. See, for example, Jacques Derrida, *Parages*, trans. Tom Conley, James Hulbert, John P. Leavey and Avital Ronell, ed. John P. Leavey (Stanford, CA: Stanford University Press, 2011); and Michel Foucault, 'Maurice Blanchot: The Thought from Outside' (1966), trans. Brian Massumi, in *Foucault, Blanchot*, by Michel Foucault and Maurice Blanchot (New York: Zone Books, 1987), pp. 7–58.
3. Compare Richard Beardsworth and George Collins's note on the translation of these terms in Bernard Stiegler, where they opt for 'technique(s)' [*une technique/des techniques*], 'technics' or 'the technical' [*la technique*], 'technology' and 'technological' [*la technologie, technologique*]. Bernard Stiegler, *Technics and Time*, 3 vols (Stanford, CA: Stanford University Press, 1998–2010), I: *The Fault of Epimetheus*, trans. Richard Beardsworth and George Collins, p. 280 n. 1.
4. References to existing English translations of Blanchot are given in parentheses throughout; some translations have been modified. Almost all of Blanchot's critical writing was first published in journals and later collected in critical works; the original publication date of essays is indicated throughout.
5. For Heidegger's comment, see the preface to the 1951 edition of Martin Heidegger, *Elucidations of Hölderlin's Poetry*, trans. Keith Hoeller (Amherst, NY: Humanity Books, 2000), pp. 21–2.
6. See Jean-Paul Sartre, *What is Literature?*, trans. Bernard Frechtman (London: Routledge, 1993).
7. See, for instance, Maurice Blanchot, 'The Novels of Sartre' (1945) and 'Literature and the Right to Death' (1947/8), in *The Work of Fire*, trans. Charlotte Mandell (Stanford, CA: Stanford University Press, 1995), pp. 191–207, 300–44. The later essay and the disagreement with Sartre will be discussed in Chapter 1.
8. The connection between the 1953 essay on Mascolo and the 1959 response to *Arguments* is noted in Leslie Hill, *Blanchot politique: sur une réflexion jamais interrompue* (Geneva: Furor, 2020), p. 372. For his response to De Gaulle's return to power and the Algerian War of Independence, see Maurice Blanchot, 'Refusal', 'The Essential Perversion' and the 'Declaration of the Right to Insubordination in the Algerian War [Manifesto of the 121]', in *Political Writings*, trans. Zakir Paul (New York: Fordham University Press, 2010), pp. 7–17.
9. See Peter Trawny, *Heidegger and the Myth of a Jewish World Conspiracy*, trans. Andrew J. Mitchell (Chicago: University of Chicago Press,

2015). Heidegger perceives modernity as a threat to German rootedness and Jewish people belong to this threat in their uprooted, mathematical, technicised state; they have forgotten what only the German people can remember: Being.
10. Arthur Bradley, *Originary Technicity: The Theory of Technology from Marx to Derrida* (Basingstoke: Palgrave Macmillan, 2011), p. 17.
11. Friedrich Hölderlin, 'Patmos', in *Poems and Fragments*, trans. Michael Hamburger (London: Routledge and Kegan Paul, 1966), pp. 462–77 (pp. 462–3).
12. See Martin Heidegger, 'The Question Concerning Technology', trans. William Lovitt, in *Basic Writings*, ed. David Farrell Krell, rev. edn (London: Routledge, 1993), pp. 311–41.
13. Emmanuel Levinas, 'Le Regard du poète' (1956), in *Sur Maurice Blanchot* (Montpellier: Fata Morgana, 1975), pp. 9–26 (p. 25) (my translation).
14. See Bernard Stiegler, *Technics and Time*, I: *The Fault of Epimetheus*, pp. 1, 15, 89, 108, 219, 234, 252, 262, 264–6, 285 n. 11, 286 n. 8, 289 n. 6, n. 9; II: *Disorientation*, trans. Stephen Barker (2008), pp. 31–2, 132; III: *Cinematic Time and the Question of Malaise*, trans. Stephen Barker (2010), p. 110. A further quotation from Blanchot is given in the short introduction of the first volume of *Technics and Time* which is not included in the English translation: '[The danger] is not in the unwonted development of energy and the domination of technology [*la technique*], it is first of all in the refusal to see the change of epoch and to consider the meaning and direction [*sens*] of this turning' (IC 270); quoted in Bernard Stiegler, *La Technique et le temps* (Paris: Fayard, 2018), p. 17. Texts by Blanchot referenced in *Technics and Time* include 'Literature and the Right to Death' (1947/8) in *The Work of Fire*, *When the Time Comes* (1951), 'Death as Possibility' (1952) and 'Rilke and Death's Demand' (1953) in *The Space of Literature*, 'The Beast of Lascaux' (1953), 'On a Change of Epoch' (1960) in *The Infinite Conversation*, and *The Unavowable Community* (1983).
15. Stiegler, *Technics and Time*, I, pp. 219, 234, 252, 262; II, p. 31. Stiegler does not cite 'The Beast of Lascaux' in the first volume but it is listed in the bibliography and it seems likely that he has this essay in mind when referring to Blanchot, technics and 'impersonal knowledge'.
16. Ibid., I, p. 219.
17. 'Do you accept this certainty: that we are at a turning?
   – If it is a certainty, then it is not a turning. The fact that we may be witnessing a change of epoch (if such exists) surely also affects the certainty with which we might define that change, making both certainty and uncertainty equally inappropriate. We are never less able to circumvent [*contourner*] ourselves than at such a moment: the discreet force of the turning is first and foremost that' (IC 264). See Stiegler, *Technics and Time*, I, p. 1.

18. For the reference to Blanchot on Herodotus, see Stiegler, *Technics and Time*, I, p. 89.
19. See, for instance, Maurice Blanchot, 'The Conquest of Space' (1964), in *Political Writings*, pp. 70–2; and Maurice Blanchot, 'The Great Reducers' (1965), in *Friendship*, trans. Elizabeth Rottenberg (Stanford, CA: Stanford University Press, 1997), pp. 62–72. These essays, and the essay on nuclear weapons, will be discussed in Chapter 3.
20. For an overview of Stiegler's argument in *Technics and Time*, see Bradley, *Originary Technicity*, pp. 120–42; and Ian James, *The New French Philosophy* (Cambridge: Polity, 2012), pp. 61–82.
21. Stiegler, *Technics and Time*, I, p. 266.
22. Jeffrey Mehlman claimed to have discovered evidence of Blanchot's antisemitic past in 'Blanchot at Combat: Of Literature and Terror', *MLN* 95, no. 4 (1980): 808–29. These claims were renewed in a special issue of *Lignes: Les Politiques de Maurice Blanchot: 1930–1993*, ed. Michel Surya, Revue Lignes, 43 (Paris: Lignes, 2014), in which Blanchot is accused of fascism in articles by David Amar, François Brémondy, Michel Surya and David Uhrig. Most recently, Leslie Hill has provided a thorough and comprehensive reading of Blanchot's political articles from the 1930s in *Blanchot politique* which sets them in their specific historical and political contexts and challenges the association of Blanchot in the 1930s with fascism, Nazism and antisemitism.
23. Michel Surya, *L'Autre Blanchot: l'écriture de jour, l'écriture de nuit* (Paris: Gallimard, 2015), p. 24.
24. See Kevin Hart, 'Foreword: The Friendship of the No', in Blanchot, *Political Writings*, pp. xi–xxx; Christophe Bident, *Maurice Blanchot: A Critical Biography*, trans. John McKeane (New York: Fordham University Press, 2019), pp. 88–90; and Leslie Hill, *Blanchot: Extreme Contemporary* (London: Routledge, 1997), pp. 21–44.
25. Jean-Luc Nancy, *Maurice Blanchot: passion politique, lettre-récit de 1984 suivie d'une lettre de Dionys Mascolo* (Paris: Galilée, 2011), p. 40. Nancy's disagreement with Blanchot begins with the latter's response to his essay 'La Communauté désœuvrée' (1983); for an extended version of the original essay by Nancy, see *The Inoperative Community* (1986), trans. Peter Connor, Lisa Garbus, Michael Holland and Simona Sawhney (Minneapolis, MN: University of Minnesota Press, 1991); for Blanchot's response, see *The Unavowable Community* (1983), trans. Pierre Joris (Barrytown, NY: Station Hill Press, 1988). Nancy returns to this debate in 'The Confronted Community' (2001), trans. Amanda Macdonald, *Postcolonial Studies* 6, no. 1 (2003): 23–36; and in *The Disavowed Community* (2014), trans. Philip Armstrong (New York: Fordham University Press, 2016). Leslie Hill sets out this debate and examines how Nancy misreads Blanchot in *Nancy, Blanchot: A Serious Controversy* (London: Rowman and Littlefield International, 2018).

26. Maurice Blanchot, 'Le Monde sans âme' (1932), in *Chroniques politiques des années trente: 1931–1940*, ed. David Uhrig (Paris: Gallimard, 2017), pp. 74–88 (p. 80).
27. Ibid., pp. 79–80 (my translation).
28. 'To live, it was necessary for me to reject. After Blanchot, I was no longer obliged to adhere to this cadaverous and infernally solemn writing.' Marie Darrieussecq, 'Blanchot blafard', in *Blanchot*, ed. Éric Hoppenot and Dominique Rabaté, Cahiers de l'Herne, 107 (Paris: Herne, 2014), pp. 284–5 (my translation).

Chapter 1

Blanchot and Mallarmé: 'The double state of the word'

The Greek term techne refers to both what is understood today by technology and what we call art, poetry or literature. To oppose art and the utilitarian is to imply that there are two states or varieties of language: the one reserved for artistic, poetic or literary expression and the other given over to utilitarian communication and subject to a contrasting logic, economy or set of conventions that more clearly belong to what we know as modern technology. This division maps on to the distinction made by Heidegger between truth as a fundamental mode of revealing by which the world is disclosed, and truth as agreement between word and thing in functional language. The reduction of truth to mere correspondence in Western philosophy has dangerous consequences for Heidegger because it leads to the treatment of everything as a resource to be exploited in the era of modern technology. It is in this context that Heidegger appeals to poetic language as a more fundamental mode of revealing through which we might remember our ontological mode of existence and begin anew. Poetic language and functional language are therefore modes of techne, but the former is more originary because it provides the foundation for human existence. What at first seems like an innocuous distinction between two modes of language, and two modes of techne, has profound implications.

Blanchot subscribed with very little apparent qualification to the Heideggerian view of poetry in the early 1940s, but by the end of the decade he refused to see art as embodying any sort of truth. This stems from his own experience as a novelist and from his role as critic whose task, if they are to communicate the truth of the literary work to the public, requires there to be something particular about the work that sets it apart from the everyday.

The question of techne far exceeds the narrow realm of the literary or the aesthetic, and touches more widely on the relationship between writing, politics and philosophical thought in general.

Writing in the early 1940s, when the chief editorship of the once independent *Nouvelle Revue française* (*NRF*) had been transferred from Jean Paulhan to the collaborationist Pierre Drieu La Rochelle, under whose editorship Blanchot refused to publish in the *NRF*, it seems likely that Blanchot sought to shield the literary domain from being compromised by collaboration with the Nazis. Essays from this time reveal a writer and literary critic profoundly changed by the events of the late 1930s and the unconstitutional dissolution of the Third Republic in July 1940. Blanchot later told Roger Laporte that he was present when the Assemblée nationale voted overwhelmingly in favour of Philippe Pétain as leader of the newly installed Vichy regime: 'My decision was immediate. It was refusal. Refusal before the occupying forces of course, but refusal no less obstinate with regard to Vichy, which in my view represented what was most degrading.'[1] He goes on to explain that his life at this time was divided into writing of the day and writing of the night: a dichotomy was imposed between journalism and literature (he completed *Thomas the Obscure* in May 1940, and *Aminadab* was published in 1942), and so the latter was, at the start of the 1940s, a refusal of the everyday world of war and politics.

The call for literary autonomy is often associated with the collaborationist right but it was not solely their prerogative: Paulhan – the pre- and post-war editor of the *NRF*, founding member of the Comité national des écrivains and of *Les Lettres françaises*, a member of the Resistance, and a close associate of Blanchot – was a vocal opponent of the politicisation of the literary and the call for a committed literature by writers such as Sartre and Camus.[2] The circumstances in which Blanchot promoted literary autonomy during the war were very different to those in which Sartre was writing directly after the Liberation, and these changing political circumstances provide some explanation for the considerable shift in Blanchot's thought during this decade, which is not to say that he moved from literary autonomy to a committed literature, but that this led him to question the very possibility of literature.

In his criticism from the 1940s one of Blanchot's most persistent points of reference is the poet Stéphane Mallarmé, in whose work he identifies a writer similarly grappling with the question of the status of language as techne in both senses of the word: as an essential naming which reveals or founds human existence and as a tool for everyday communication. This chapter examines the distinction between poetic and everyday language made by Mallarmé when he described 'the double state of the word', before considering how Blanchot's reading of Mallarmé developed over the course of the 1940s. Blanchot is often seen as committed to a belief in this double state of language.[3] This might have been the case at the beginning of the decade, but the distinction between the essential and the everyday collapses as order, foundation and truth in literature give way to instability, suspension and imposture. The relationship between the aesthetic language of art and the utilitarian language of technology becomes one of slippage rather than opposition for Blanchot by the 1950s. This slippage has far-reaching consequences for the relationship between literature and the world, and it allows a broader conception of literature that does not exclude technology.

'The double state of the word'

At the end of the nineteenth century Mallarmé, prompted by the crisis of poetry represented by free verse and the prose poem, famously identified a difference between essential and immediate language: put simply, the former is characterised by a necessity that shields it from the contingency of the everyday. Poetry was no longer restricted to verse following the advent of the prose poem, and so, with the traditional formal distinction undermined, Mallarmé sought characteristics to distinguish between the two forms of language; in so doing, he set the agenda for writers and writing about literature for generations to come. The extent to which Mallarmé perceives an uncomplicated distinction between essential and immediate language is, however, up for debate: 'An undeniable desire of my time is to distinguish between two kinds of language as though according to their different attributes [*comme en vue d'attributions différentes*]: taking the double state of the word [*la parole*] – brute and immediate here, there essential.'[4] This view is seemingly attributed to the Symbolist poets of his time, and the use of *comme* in the original French makes this a somewhat hypothetical statement. Blanchot will later pick up on this hesitancy. The reading of Mallarmé as it develops in Blanchot's critical work provides an insight into the evolving relationship throughout the twentieth century between the aesthetic and the technical.

Mallarmé demonstrates that free verse has unsettled traditional expectations of poetry in 'Crisis of Verse' and that the effects of this new form are the fragmentation of language and a violent rupture within language. This 'crisis' within poetry may be seen as symptomatic of the broader crisis of modernity; it is akin to a revolution, but one much more subtle than that of 1789: 'we are witnessing, in this fin-de-siècle, not – as it was during the last one – a revolution, but, far from the public square: a trembling of the veil in the temple, with significant folds, and, a little, its rending'.[5] This revolution will not take place on the streets but in literature, which has become a temple, inheriting a quasi-holy function following the failure of religion. In a godless world and in the aftermath of the 1870 Franco–Prussian War, this was a time of crisis but also a time of hope for Mallarmé, who believed that literature could fill the void left by modernity with its own idea: 'What good is the marvel of transposing a fact of nature into its vibratory near-disappearance according to the play of language, however: if it is not, in the absence of the cumbersomeness of a near or concrete reminder, the pure notion.'[6] Literature will not replace like for like, it will not provide humanity with a concept by which to understand the world, as would be the case in immediate language. Instead, literature will provide an indeterminate idea, one that is difficult to grasp, that sets itself apart from the world and is based in the non-realistic.

Replacing what had been lost in modernity required a structure that would unite the fragmentary in a time of transition and crisis. Roger Pearson stresses Mallarmé's desire throughout his work to 'lay a verbal pattern over the void of a godless universe'.[7] Free verse is evidently not as free as some of Mallarmé's contemporaries might have wished it to be and it is no accident that some similarities remain for Mallarmé between free verse and previous forms: 'some kind of regularity will last because the poetic act consists of seeing that an idea can be broken up into a certain number of motifs that are equal in some way, and of grouping them; they rhyme; as an external seal, the final words are proof of their common measure'.[8] Mallarmé, here and throughout 'Crisis of Verse', points to the benefits of this form but also to its limitations, arguing that free verse is descended from other more structured and traditional forms of poetry.[9] The underlying structure that persists in free verse unifies the fragmented idea and gives the poem orderliness. This structure and basis in the non-realistic are characteristics of the modern myth as deployed by writers such as James Joyce in *Ulysses*, T. S. Eliot in *The Waste Land* and Guillaume Apollinaire in 'Zone'. Myth provides ahistorical order when there is no order and when history has failed, a state observed by Stephen Dedalus: 'history [. . .] is a nightmare from which I am trying to awake'.[10]

The pure idea that sets essential language apart from ordinary language is a meticulously structured linguistic construction without reference to the world of things. 'I say: a flower! And, out of the oblivion where my voice casts every contour, insofar as it is something other than the known bloom, there arises, musically, the very idea in its mellowness; in other words, what is absent from every bouquet.'[11] Mallarmé is not referring to a particular flower or a knowable bunch of flowers; this idea is detached from primroses, tulips or daffodils and all the associations with, for instance, springtime which might be evoked in the day-to-day use of the word by a musicality, a system of references between words that exist in isolation from the world of objects. Pearson notes how in the French word 'flower' [*fleur*] there is an echo of 'hour' [*l'heure*] and 'lure' or 'trick' [*leurre*], and so the idea that arises musically from this word might include temporality and unreliability rather than a flower's traditional value as a symbol of transient beauty associated with the object in the world.[12] It is the syntax of poetry, its rigorous construction, even in free verse, that renders the most utilitarian words rich and strange: 'As opposed to a denominative and representative function, as the crowd first treats it, speech, which is primarily dream and song, recovers, in the Poet's hands, of necessity in an art devoted to fictions, its virtuality.'[13]

Some might argue that Mallarmé's reference to 'the crowd' here and elsewhere in this essay introduces a political dimension that demonstrates disdain for common, vulgar, mass society, but the masses to whom Mallarmé refers are most likely the *nouveaux-riches* middle class who deal with numbers and currency ('a denominative and representative function') rather than the working class. His politics were anarchistic rather than aristocratic: 'I know of no other bomb than a book.'[14] He gave the work of art a political effectiveness, but in doing so distanced the work from the real, by insisting on its resistance to usefulness or functionality. He writes elsewhere that the poet will 'Give a purer sense to the words of the crowd.'[15] There is hope for Mallarmé that poetry will be the vehicle for revolution.

Mallarmé recognises that the language of the poet is characterised by a necessity which sets it apart from the real ('of necessity in an art devoted to fictions'). The struggle between necessity and contingency is a central concern of the modern novel, and this is why Blanchot will later use Mallarmé as a reference point when reading Melville, Joyce and Lautréamont. This struggle is famously played out in *A Throw of the Dice Will Never Abolish Chance*, in which Mallarmé uses the image of a shipwreck hanging over an abyss and the motif of metaphysical gaming to paint a picture of contingency and risk which the mind tries to control by finding pattern and purpose in this experience.[16] Malcolm Bowie describes this as 'a splendidly organised and overspilling portrait of contingency'. Bowie continues: 'The "impossible" chance-abolishing thought is present as a permanent temptation to which minds are subject and, in the final, culminating pages, as the only hope worth retaining amid chaos and dissolution.'[17]

This poem reveals that thought necessitates chance, and so the divide in language between order and chaos, mind and world, necessity and contingency, the essential and the immediate, does not appear quite so impermeable – an impermeability that might be said to be reflected more broadly in Mallarmé's work, which tested the boundaries between poetry and narrative prose, as well as traditional genres such as lyric and drama.[18] The divide between the aesthetic and the technical is not, then, as clear-cut as it might first appear for Mallarmé, and we will see how a reading of this slippage plays out in Blanchot's literary criticism during the 1940s.

Literary Autonomy and Foundation

Reading Mallarmé in the early 1940s, Blanchot is interested in the way he purifies words in order to restore an inventive force to them. In his first article to appear after a year-long hiatus in April 1941, Blanchot expresses profound admiration for Mallarmé, 'a man who, in total and obscure solitude, was able to hold sway over the world through the pure exercise of an absolute power of expression' (ID 11). And in another essay that year, Blanchot likens the task of the artist to the creation of a world: everything depends on an internal order, a network of necessities all submitted to the force of invention; men obey the law of poetic order in this universe (ID 32). This world or universe exists autonomously beyond the boundaries of the everyday where Blanchot works as a journalist, and it is achieved through the poetic expression of Mallarmé, who is described at the end of 1941 as the poet who was 'capable of creating everything while expressing almost nothing' (FP 102). Others might come close, but Mallarmé is the name Blanchot employs to signal the most glorious creative ambition which ensures that poetic language is separated from functional use.[19]

Blanchot commits in essays from 1941 to a distinctly Mallarméan literary autonomy which is characterised by a structure and basis in unreality and not confined to poetry or prose. The struggle between the poetic and the everyday defines Herman Melville's *Moby-Dick*, which Blanchot describes in a review of Jean Giono's French translation in terms of myth: the structure of the novel – its perpetual abstract digressions that interrupt and distract the reader from the story – and its basis in the non-realistic – a world of tempests and foam rather than solid visible objects – ensure its status as myth. This is not a struggle against the whale but against a mythic force, to which the everyday world is destined to succumb:

Sometimes his officers try to pull him back up the slope down which they are all slipping; they tell him: let's stop, go back, put an end to this foolish trip so that we can rest and enjoy the pleasures of dry land; but of course no one really believes these platitudes [*paroles de la vie banale*]. Ahab is now merely a witness of an invisible order in which he is subjected to the commands of something nameless, unfathomable, supernatural; in the struggle which he believes himself engaged in, he is but the destitute and tragic servant of the terrible unforgiving sovereign. (FP 242)

The officers on board speak of earthly pleasures, but this world is disappearing from beneath their feet as they are delivered alongside their captain to another invisible place. The comparison is made to *The Songs of Maldoror* where language says everything in place of the world, attracting the reader, who is comparable to these sailors, into its wake and obliging total obedience (FP 243). *Moby-Dick* enacts a struggle between the literary and the everyday, and the name of Mallarmé, cited at the beginning of the essay, overshadows this project.

In his early criticism the reference to 'myth' is a coded rejection of literary realism, and it is in these terms that Blanchot praises Melville for writing a novel that aspires to be the written equivalent of the universe; Poe, Nerval, Lautréamont and Joyce also wrote books which help us to understand Mallarmé's lofty ambition to 'raise a page to the power of the starry sky' (FP 239).[20] Blanchot traces a line from the romantics to the modernists in the essay on Melville, and at the heart of this literary genealogy is the name of Mallarmé, whose work acts as a passage between the two movements and exemplifies the defiance towards reality and the structured unity which lends these other texts their mythic quality. The work might be fragmented, as is the nature of the artwork in modernity, but a union in the non-realistic endures thanks to this overarching structure: 'Interminable anecdotes burst forth and catch our attention, distracting us from our object, and now and then the recollection of an eternal design rises like a cloud above these anecdotes' (FP 242).

A shift in Blanchot's reading of Mallarmé and his view of literature is prompted by closer engagement with Heidegger in the early 1940s, for whom the view that poetry is detached from world in an imaginary realm makes it seem like the most innocent of occupations, when it is in fact concerned with the founding of Being – Heidegger is here paraphrasing Hölderlin. According to Heidegger, the poetic act is the originary event when the ontological ground is laid for the disclosure of beings in history and when language gives us the horizon against which we appear as beings-in-the-world, and so it is, as Hölderlin famously writes, poetically that man dwells on the earth.[21] Language therefore serves comprehension only because poetry is foundational: 'a naming of being and of the essence of all things – not just any saying, but that whereby everything first steps out into the open, which we then discuss and talk about in everyday language'.[22] For obvious political reasons the name Heidegger appears only once in essays written by Blanchot during the Occupation, but his critical stance during this period is very close to that of the German philosopher; so close, in fact, that Blanchot is able to lift phrases and expressions from the essays on Hölderlin and apply them in turn to Mallarmé.[23]

The Heideggerian view of the primacy of poetic over functional language is unambiguously repeated by Blanchot in 'Is Mallarmé's Poetry Obscure?' (1942), a review of Charles Mauron's *Mallarmé l'Obscur* in which Mauron provides a line-by-line and word-by-word explanation of each poem in an attempt to offer an approximate sketch of the network of relations that constitute the poetic work. Blanchot is critical of Mauron's systematic approach, which takes for granted that every poem has an objective meaning that can be expressed by a prose translation and accessed by rational thought (FP 108). He points to the original and irreducible structure of the poetic work – where there are no insignificant or accidental details, which is non-transferable and cannot be expressed otherwise because what the poem signifies coincides exactly with what it is – which leads Blanchot to a markedly Heideggerian view of the division between these two modes of techne: 'in the poetic act language stops being an instrument and reveals itself in its essence, which is to found a world, to make possible the authentic dialogue that we ourselves are, and, as Hölderlin says, to name the gods' (FP 109). Rather than offering itself as the 'written equivalent of the universe', the poetic act is now described as an originary event, a point Blanchot repeats one year later in 'Mallarmé and the Art of the Novel' (1943) when he clarifies, in a revision of his earlier comments, that language cannot be reduced to instrumentality: 'The mistake is to believe that language is an instrument that man uses in order to act or in order to manifest himself in the world; language, in reality, uses man in that it guarantees him the existence of the world and his existence in the world' (FP 167).[24] Poetic language founds human reality – Blanchot is here using Henry Corbin's controversial French translation of *Dasein* as 'la réalité humaine'[25] – and it is far from the instrumental language put to use in practical life (FP 167).

Myth, the motif that dominates Blanchot's earlier discussion of *Moby-Dick*, nonetheless remains a central concern of 'Mallarmé and the Art of the Novel' because it is one way of resolving the struggle between necessity and contingency, and the aesthetic and the technical. In the opening paragraphs, Blanchot quotes a letter in which Mallarmé explains that he aspires to a structured and calculated book shielded from the everyday, which fulfils the duty of the poet by providing an Orphic explanation of the earth (FP 165). The conception of creation offered in Mallarmé's letter is so broad that no genre of literature is excluded and the writer of prose is similarly obliged to maintain the linguistic hierarchy and the necessity of the artwork in modernity; Blanchot references Novalis, Hölderlin and Joyce as examples of this struggle, but one could also cite Flaubert and Gide, for whom it was an unavoidable aporia. The relationship between the artwork and chance happenings of the everyday is under closer scrutiny here than it was in earlier essays: not only was Mallarmé's letter only brought to our attention by chance, but the requirement for the work to have a meaning for others is an accident which the novelist must accept as an external constraint, while still trying to ensure that the book is as absolute and as necessary as possible, and it seems that the writer of prose – who is more accustomed to structuring their work around the world in which we live and does not think to separate their language from that tarnished by everyday use – is only by accident attentive to what they write (FP 170). The task of the novelist is to found a world by granting the text its own law and by containing the text within itself so that it does not lapse into the hazardous everyday, which is perceived as a constant threat to the strict limits of the novel.

This threat is acknowledged by Heidegger, who argues that mistaking the essential for the everyday is 'the danger of dangers', because the slippage between these two modes of techne results in the forgetting of Being which is characteristic of modernity.[26] Blanchot borrows this phrase in an amendment to 'Mallarmé and the Art of the Novel' for its publication in *Faux pas* (1943), where he adds that this 'supreme danger' drives to silence, 'by the exercise of an intelligence caught in infinite labours and by the rigour of a mind that keeps finding chance', the creator who rejects any impure or inauthentic form (FP 168). Blanchot had explained in 'The Silence of Mallarmé' (1942) that this silence achieved through a methodical arrangement of words is 'a pure intellectual act, capable of creating everything while expressing almost nothing' (FP 102); this is not the mere keeping quiet of functional language but a silence that allows us to retain hope of that chance-abolishing thought about which we necessarily know nothing. It is a silence negotiated by Mallarmé's biographer Henri Mondor, who is praised by Blanchot for hiding nothing of the poet's work while maintaining his reader in a state of pure ignorance.[27]

The question of what it means for the poet or novelist to write in the wake of Mallarmé, and of what it means for the critic trying to say something about this mode of creation, had been raised by Blanchot in a 1941 review of Jean Paulhan's *The Flowers of Tarbes, or Terror in Literature*, where there is early evidence of the shift in Blanchot's view of literature which would play out over the course of this decade. Paulhan identifies a shift from a pre-Revolutionary classicism – Rhetoric – in which linguistic commonplaces were a necessary part of communication and expression, and literature was a matter of submission to the rules and traditions of genre, to a post-Revolutionary romanticism – Terror – in which accepted literary forms were abandoned in the search for authentic and original thought.[28] The former gives priority to language over thought while the latter prioritises thought over language, named the Terror thanks to this belief in the purity of thought and this mistrust which verges on hatred of words.[29] Paulhan reveals the futility of the Terrorists' project: seeking to affirm the precedence of thought and to rid their language of all commonplace, they demonstrate an excessive concern with that very language. Through the metaphor of the garden in Tarbes – where visitors prohibited from taking flowers from the garden find ways around this interdiction by claiming to have brought their own flowers in – Paulhan questions how we are to tell whether authors intended their words to be read as commonplaces or as original thoughts. His solution is to turn back to Rhetoric; he argues that we must submit to the authority of commonplaces if we are to free ourselves from such a preoccupation with language: visitors to the garden are now forbidden from entering without carrying flowers so that they do not think to gather more.[30]

Blanchot demonstrates how Terror flips to Rhetoric and vice versa as both try to express authentic thought: literature cannot be deemed Terror or Rhetoric with any certainty because both share a common goal. The Rhetoricians aim to express thought in a manner that does not draw attention to discourse, writes Blanchot, so that the words vanish as they are pronounced. The Terrorists, he continues, seek to express themselves in a language that is not an instrument of expression and where expression does not bring along the wear and tear of everyday life. 'The writer's mission, in both cases, is therefore to make an authentic thought – truth or secret – known, one that an excessive attention to words, especially to words frayed by everyday use [*mots usés de tous les jours*], could only endanger' (FP 79).

While heavily paradoxical, Paulhan's account of literary language is nonetheless controllable: the ambiguity at the heart of the relationship is resolved as the writer seeks mastery of words by accepting commonplaces. Blanchot's move in his review is to radicalise this account to reveal that literature escapes everything one can say about it. He refers to these commonplaces as 'monsters of ambiguity' because they are at once transparent and clear while also being characterised by a double meaning that is not fixed or understood (FP 78). Such monstrous ambiguity governs the distinction of literature from everyday language: Terror rejects all commonplaces in the search for authentic expression, but any such expression, once expressed, becomes a commonplace like any other. On this Blanchot draws attention to what it means to write in the wake of Mallarmé: while the poet restored the power of creation to words – seeming to invent or to discover them anew – for those who follow him and similarly seek to rid language of its functional aspects, these terms are already corrupted by use (FP 80). Terror therefore becomes another name for literature and reveals its impossible conditions:

> It is a fact: literature exists [existe]. It continues to exist [être] despite the internal absurdity that inhabits it, divides it, and makes it strictly inconceivable. In the heart of every writer there is a demon which pushes him to strike dead all literary forms, to become aware of his dignity as a writer insofar as he breaks with language and with literature; in a word, to call into question in an inexpressible way what he is and what he does. (FP 80–1)

It is for this reason that Paulhan concludes his study: 'In fact, let's just say I have said nothing.'[31] This is not a throwaway remark to be ignored, because it reveals the secret of Paulhan's text, which is that it articulates, through these unresolvable paradoxes, the impossible foundations, the void or the abyss, that constitute literature. This idea is repeated by Blanchot in relation to Mallarmé only a few months later: 'this silence, this fact of having remained silent in the midst of so many words, may seem like the very secret whose existence was not supposed to be revealed to us' (FP 106).

Blanchot's essay on Paulhan has proved controversial, with more than one critic reading it in the context of his political shift between the 1930s and the 1940s. Jeffrey Mehlman reads the dismantling of the 'terroristic imperative' as an 'encoded farewell to plans for French fascism': this is evidence of a withdrawal of literature from Blanchot's political engagement of the 1930s.[32] Gerald Bruns considers this 'politics of refusal' in slightly different terms, arguing that this is less a renunciation of violence than a relocation of it within the ongoing currents of Blanchot's thinking: terror, violence and anti-rationalism remain basic features of Blanchot's poetics. Working from Zeev Sternhell's understanding of fascism as an ideological revolt against modernity which had substantial appeal in France in the 1930s, Bruns situates Blanchot within this tradition without labelling him a fascist as such.[33] According to Bruns, Blanchot is a 'last Romantic', perhaps someone 'who has just never been modern'.[34] Elsewhere in this study, quoting the following passage from 1964 but omitting what comes after 'to make possible a non-transitive speaking whose task is not to say things', Bruns claims that early German Romanticism is the tradition in which Blanchot would most likely situate himself.[35]

> One can indeed say that in [Novalis's] texts we find the expression of the non-Romantic essence of Romanticism and all the most important questions that the night of language will help to generate in the day: that to write is to create a work of language [*qu'écrire, c'est faire œuvre de la parole*], but that this work is worklessness [*cette œuvre est désœuvrement*], and that to speak poetically is to make possible a non-transitive speaking whose task is not to say things (and to disappear in what it signifies), but to say (itself) by letting (itself) be said [*mais de (se) dire en (se) laissant dire*], yet without making itself the new object of this language without object (for if poetry is simply a language that claims to express the essence of language and of poetry, we return, and only slightly more subtly, to the use of transitive language – a major difficulty by which we will eventually identify the strange lacuna within literary language which is its own difference and as if its night; a night somewhat terrifying, comparable to what Hegel thought he saw when gazing into men's eyes). (IC 357)[36]

The omission of the concluding lines of this passage by Bruns produces a distorted reading of Blanchot as a writer for whom literature is characterised by self-reflexive autonomy. In the lines that follow Blanchot shows that transitive and non-transitive language are one and the same once they adopt a fundamental teleology, such as the expression of authentic thought, and this exposure to the lacuna at the heart of literary language, the nothing of which Paulhan writes, turns writing endlessly outwards. This is night not as Hegel understood it – the pre-subjective and impersonal basis for self-conscious subjectivity and historical time – but that other night which is irreducible to the day–night binary because it puts history and world in parentheses. The aporetic logic is Mallarméan: necessity necessitates chance, depriving literature of any secure and stable foundation, and the beginning of this view of literature was evident in the early essay on Paulhan. Rather than a coded farewell to fascism or a revolt against modernity, the early review of Paulhan's *The Flowers of Tarbes* reveals that literature, contesting its own limits, is never autonomous.

The realisation that the literary work is always under threat from the everyday leads Blanchot to the view that any founding law cannot belong to the text itself.[37] This repudiation of the view of poetry as foundation, plus the expanded understanding of poetic creation in 'Mallarmé and the Art of the Novel', coincides with the publication of Blanchot's first novel *Thomas the Obscure* in 1941. The opening pages of this novel, as Thomas swims in the sea and struggles with an implacable sense of danger, echo the sense that poetic language is pressed on all sides by a threat which pushes it towards complete necessity; but indicated here is also the beginning of a departure from a Heideggerian view of poetic language as Thomas hangs above a watery abyss:

> Then he noticed that his limbs, whether from fatigue or for an unknown reason, gave him the same feeling of unfamiliarity as the water in which they flailed. Every time he reflected on the disappearance and reappearance of his hands in a state of total indifference to the future – with a sort of unreality he had no right to know – he was willing to believe that he would experience unforeseeable difficulties when it came to getting out of this bind. He was not discouraged. The sense of danger was quite unrelated to the discomfort he felt because of this situation. What did he have to fear? Yet his position did not improve with this realisation, because although he could have remained indefinitely in the water, or in this strange element that had taken its place, there was something intolerable about swimming this way, aimlessly, with a body whose only use – he now realised – was to make him think that he was swimming.[38]

Thomas exists in a world marked by its unreality and strangeness: the water is an unfamiliar element where he is pure consciousness; he swims only in his imagination; his body is alien to him and seems to melt into the surrounding water or whatever element – the language of this fiction – has replaced that water. In an earlier version of the novel, written between 1931 and 1937, the emphasis in this much more concise opening scene is on the inexhaustible power of the sea and Thomas's growing physical fatigue, which prompts him to return to the safety of the beach where the crashing of the waves continues to ring in his ears in place of the usual sound of passing coaches.[39]

The ability of Thomas to remain in this state indefinitely and the indifference of his hands to the future, in the version of the novel published in 1941, suggests a suspension of time which is indicative of the phenomenological epoché as it is conceived by Husserl. Husserl sought to break with unfounded but deep-rooted assumptions about the structure and meaning of experience; he did this by placing the world within parentheses, by taking nothing for granted, not even the existence or non-existence of the world presupposed in metaphysics, and by progressing from the certainty of the transcendental phenomenological Ego to establish certainties via a rigorous scientific method which worked from the intuited-real and not the mathematical-ideal, which he considered an error of the sciences since Galileo.[40]

The stress on certainty found in Husserl is not, however, reflected in the passage from *Thomas the Obscure* quoted above, where the narrator hangs above a watery abyss and comments that there is something unbearable about this state in which he is estranged from himself. This opening scene indicates a shift from the foundation of a world in literature to the suspension of world altogether, and it was articulated in clear terms by Blanchot thirty years later when reflecting on the opening lines of the later 1950 edition of *Thomas the Obscure*: 'it – the sea [il – la mer]'. Literature is an uprooting force and what results is disunity and fragmentation rather than any unified structure.

> ♦ Writing as a question of writing, a question that bears the writing that bears the question, denies you this relationship with being – understood primarily as tradition, order, certainty, truth, all forms of rootedness – that you once received from the past history of the world, that domain you were called upon to manage in order to fortify your 'Ego' [*ton 'Moi'*], although this had seemingly been split asunder [*fissuré*] since the day when the sky opened to reveal its emptiness.
>
> Try as I may I cannot picture the person who was not me and who, without wishing it, began to write, writing (and then realising it) in such a way that as a result the pure product of doing nothing introduced itself into the world and into his world. This went on 'at night'. During the day, there were acts of the day, everyday words, everyday writing, statements, values, habits, nothing that counted and yet something one dimly had to call life. The certainty that in writing he was putting this certainty into parentheses, including the certainty of himself as a subject of writing, led him slowly, but also immediately, into an empty space whose void (the barred zero, like a heraldic device) in no way prevented the twists and turns of a lengthy itinerary. (SNB 2)

Blanchot pushes the logic behind the phenomenological epoché to the limit in this fragment, as brackets open on to brackets, which open on to further brackets, in a movement that endlessly undermines the possibility of certitude. In suspending the everyday world in this way, the writer becomes unfamiliar to himself or herself and so the certainty of the night, the certainty that they write, is undone. The same workless logic evident in the early review of Paulhan that interrogates the distinction between Terror and Rhetoric here undoes the possibility of writing. Foundation gives way to suspension in the development of Blanchot's thought over this period, which is not to say that the stress returns to pure consciousness, because the subject who writes is effaced in this process.

Literature as Imposture

Blanchot's engagement with Heidegger on Hölderlin therefore significantly informs his reading of Mallarmé and others during the 1940s, but not in an unchanging and uniform way. The radical undecidability of literature will soon challenge the view that poetic language can be differentiated from instrumental language, with implications for the critic whose task it is to comment on the work. We have seen that the distinguishing feature between aesthetic and technical language for Heidegger maps on to the difference between truth as a mode of revealing which founds a world and truth as mere correspondence between thing and idea, associated with metaphysical representation and modern technology. Later in the 1940s, Blanchot would accuse literature of imposture because it claims to offer up some truth but does not engage in work in the world and so cannot respond to worldly criteria; the epigraph to *The Most High* (1948) says as much: 'I am a trap for you. Even if I tell you everything; the more loyal I am, the more I will deceive you: it's my frankness that will catch you.' 'Please understand: everything that you get from me is, for you, only a lie, because I am the truth.' The hierarchy between the essential and the everyday, the aesthetic and the technical, becomes unstable and impossible to maintain with the realisation that literature will always deceive and never give up any truth.

This is a danger that Heidegger had already identified: language can be deceptive because it might express the essential, but it also preserves beings as such in the work and so equally expresses the common or the everyday: 'Thus language must constantly place itself into the illusion which it engenders by itself, and so endanger what is most its own, genuine utterance.'[41] According to Heidegger, the 'danger of all dangers' is the slippage from Being to beings by which we mistake Being for a being like any other, and the subsequent forgetting or loss of Being which is characteristic of modernity. Blanchot similarly recognises that the essential may lie in the simplest of phrases; he writes in 1943 that the literary word can act as a trap because it can appear simple, clear and innocent when it is in fact concerned with the founding of all being (FP 166), and that it is the novelist's and the poet's task to ensure that the essential does not lapse into the banal by maintaining this hierarchy (FP 168).

The traditional task of the critic to present works in more accessible terms, and to draw a meaning or truth from these works, leaves them susceptible to the trap set by literature; this became more pressing for Blanchot after the publication of *Faux pas* in 1943, his first volume of collected essays, and in the years following the Liberation when writers such as Sartre were calling for a literature that would reveal some truth about the world. The danger of the slippage between essential and everyday language is articulated in 'The Myth of Mallarmé' in 1946, which responds to the treatment of Mallarmé's work by his close confidant Paul Valéry. At the centre of this essay is the idea that Mallarmé's thought cannot easily be reduced to the unity and simplicity of a doctrine, which is, in Blanchot's view, precisely what Valéry attempted. Valéry is focused on method – take, for example, the reduction of the distinction between poetry and prose to the difference between dancing and walking, or two forms of language that follow different rules[42] – but Mallarmé, Blanchot argues, is interested in the means only in view of the end, which is the creation of a poetic language. The distinction between the poetic and the functional, which had once seemed so clear-cut, is now attributed to Mallarmé rather than stated by Blanchot and is much more precarious than Valéry would have us believe: 'Mallarmé believed in the existence of two languages, one essential, the other crude and immediate. That is a certainty that Valéry will reassert and that has since become very familiar to us. Why? That is less obvious' (WF 29).

These reflections on the difficulties of criticism are nothing new. Blanchot had considered his own role as literary critic in the 'Prière d'insérer' – an editorial note on a loose sheet of paper slipped between the pages of a book – of *Faux pas*. The critic's task is difficult, perhaps even impossible, as they attempt to expose the secret of the work without falling foul of the trap set by literature:

> Every book of any importance hides a secret which elevates it above what it would otherwise be. The critic, swept along by the duty to make new publications known to readers, moves towards this secret while it pulls away from him. His progress [*marche*] is therefore sluggish and difficult. If sometimes it seems that the goal is close, this is nothing more than a misstep [*faux pas*].[43]

The critic might appear to approach the essential concealed in the work, but this is never truly the case; they are bound by their duty to communicate the appearance of new works to the public, to articulate these useful facts in everyday language, and so the possibility of a meta-language becomes increasingly complicated by the contradictory aims of this task. An essay from 1944 develops this point when Blanchot, reviewing Paulhan's study of Félix Fénéon, claims that criticism is even more out of reach than the novel or poetry. It is, Blanchot writes, not at all certain that criticism exists. A discussion then proceeds from a consideration of the double state of language: literature protests the abuse of words in everyday language by destroying discourse, ruining practical words to render them useless; in literature, language is the victim of a sort of sacrifice and the writer hopes that this destruction will raise banal language to the status of the sacred. Blanchot argues that the critic should be no different in their treatment of language – they should not deal in understandable simplifications but must work within the same destructive medium as the poet or novelist – and that their status as critic should be perpetually in doubt: Paulhan is, after all, able to identify only one 'critic' from the last one hundred years (DN 13)!

The realisation, through a reading of Mallarmé, that the destruction characteristic of literature is also a defining feature of everyday language leads Blanchot to the view that literature is radically undecidable. Mallarmé is struck by the capacity of language in all its forms to be both meaningful and abstract: in order to function as language – to be understood in different contexts – language must negate or destroy the presence of the thing it names. The hierarchy maintained between the aesthetic and the technical in earlier essays is suddenly inverted: 'If poetry exists, it is because language is an instrument of comprehension' (WF 30). Blanchot turns to the famous example of 'I say: a flower!' to show that in both forms of language the presence of the thing is negated or destroyed; what differentiates between the two is that the poet does not replace this absence with an ideal presence or truth, and therefore does not reduce language to a question of knowing or of learning (WF 30–1). The absence created by the destruction of the thing becomes the defining characteristic of the poetic, but it is clear from the 'common word' that this absence is readily filled by the idea of a presence, and so the poetic must maintain what Blanchot variously refers to as an unstable image, the art of movement, a perspective of parentheses, a more evasive reality in which everything must vanish in turn, 'a series of fugitive and unstable nuances, in the very place of abstract meaning whose emptiness it claims to fill' (WF 31). The 'reality' founded by essential language is unstable and unachievable: the rigid structure and solid foundations of Mallarmé's text have disappeared. While differences remain between the two forms of language, they are not dialectically opposed: 'the essential language that does not exclude prose [. . .] is poetry, and implies verse' (WF 33). The poetic is instead presented as the radicalisation of instrumental language.

The danger of a slippage is now inherent to poetic language rather than some external factor from which the poet, novelist and critic can shield the work. While everyday language destroys the world by reducing it to an abstraction, poetic language goes one step further and destroys this abstraction by the sensual tracing of the word: in order to create such absence, poetic language calls out to a form of presence which denies the presence of anything other than words themselves. The danger of a slippage between absence and presence is clear: 'the sensuality of language here carries it away, and the word dreams of uniting itself with the objects whose weight, colour, and heavy, dormant aspect it also possesses' (WF 38). If poetry retains one defining feature it is as an art of movement that does not allow its unstable images to solidify. What matters in Mallarmé is literature as the epochal suspension of world:

> [Language] is a sort of consciousness without subject; separated from being, it is detachment, contestation, the infinite power to create emptiness and to place itself within absence [*un manque*]. But it is also an embodied consciousness – drawn to the material form of words, to their sonority, to their life – which gives the impression that this reality opens up some path toward the obscure basis [*fond*] of things. Perhaps that is an imposture. But perhaps such trickery is the truth of every written thing. (WF 42)

The first aspect of literary language described here, impersonal and separated from the world, is informed by the phenomenological epoché. The second aspect of literary language is the material form that literature requires in order to create this void; this presence deceives us, leads us to believe that the literary will give up a truth when in fact it only deals in creating a void and does not work in the world. The epochal view of the world presented to us by literature, in which the world is constituted rather than constitutive, implies that there is something beyond world which literature cannot include – 'But "up there" does not concern us: it is, on the contrary, the singularity and wonder of language to give creative value, a startling power, to the nothingness [*rien*], the pure emptiness [*vide pur*], the oblivion [*néant*] that it approaches without ever attaining' (WF 40–1) – and so the traditional way of seeing the work of art as giving truth is undermined.

Blanchot writes that the fate of poetry is tied to imposture thanks to the 'scattered trembling of a page'; Valéry calls this a feeling or nascent thought, but it would be more accurately described according to Blanchot as 'a still suspended meaning, of which we hold only the empty outline' (WF 41). Literature creates an emptiness, and Valéry is at fault for attempting to fill this void with sensibility because seduced by the material form of words, which are only one aspect of poetic language.

'But when is there literature?'

The literary becomes an experience of its own limits, and its relationship to the everyday appears unstable as dialectical opposites are undermined, and any sort of truth – truth as correspondence or truth as revealing – becomes inaccessible in literature. Blanchot argues again in 'Literature and the Right to Death' (1947/8) that literature is imposture but, in a statement far from the critical position he adopted at the beginning of the decade, he states that such fraudulence is precisely what makes it interesting: 'if literature coincides with nothing for just an instant, it is immediately everything, and this everything begins to exist: what a miracle!' (WF 302). This focus on the trickery innate to literature stems in part from Alexandre Kojève's reading of Hegel which had appeared earlier the same year. Kojève, interpreting Hegel, states that it is only by working in the everyday world that man realises himself objectively as man; the intellectual, in contrast, does not engage in work in the everyday world and therefore fails to negate and to transcend himself, and remains a 'natural being' cut off from society. Any attempt by the intellectual to pit his ideal universe against the world is therefore deception, fraud, imposture.[44]

This view of literature as imposture contradicts the account of literature offered by Sartre, who argues that the writer can have an engaged relationship with the world. In 1947 Sartre stated unequivocally: 'To speak is to act; anything which one names is already no longer quite the same; it has lost its innocence.'[45] For Sartre, literature is engagement in the world because speaking inevitably changes the world through the process of naming and thus revealing. For Blanchot in 'Literature and the Right to Death', literature is not the gradual mediated transformation of the world over a period of time as Sartre claims it is, but the immediate negation of the world in its totality which results in the unreal or the epochal suspension of the world. It is for this reason that literature is imposture and does not correspond to worldly criteria: 'As for the task that is the world, literature is now regarded as more of a nuisance than a serious help' (WF 339). Literature is what Sartre would deem bad faith, whereas for Blanchot what distinguishes all literature is the impossibility of avoiding such imposture.

There is little discussion of a divide within language in Blanchot's essay. Literature eludes a single definition, and characteristics that might once have been associated with functional language are now related to one of the slopes (*pentes* and *versants*) of literature identified by Blanchot. The first slope is associated with the destructive and communicative function of language: literature negates things so that they might be known and communicated. On the second slope, however, literature is concerned with the reality of things and destroys the abstract idea we have of them to make way for their unknown and silent existence. The second slope inevitably turns back to the first, which is why, if anything defines literature, it is the refusal to fall resolutely on either side of this arête, to have a clearly functional or aesthetic purpose, which results in an endless oscillation between these two states (WF 330). The focus has shifted from an opposition between the necessity of the poetic and the contingency of the everyday to the ambiguity common to all language: 'This initial double meaning, which is the basis of every word [*ce double sens initial, qui est au fond de toute parole*]' (WF 344).

Blanchot and Sartre might share the reference to ambiguity, but it leads them in two very different directions. Sartre argues that the poetic attitude considers words as things rather than signs; the treatment of the word as sign in prose ensures that words can be manipulated, mastered and used to act in the world: 'For the ambiguity of the sign implies that one can penetrate it at will like a pane of glass and pursue the thing signified, or turn one's gaze towards its *reality* and consider it as an object.'[46] Ambiguity is a way of raising questions in the audience's mind about good and bad courses of action, thereby prompting a dialectical understanding of action in the real world. Denis Hollier argues that the existential heroes of Sartre's work are failures in that they all fall victim to bad faith, a view which confirms Blanchot's view that 'good' faith in art is impossible.[47] Ambiguity in Blanchot reflects a state that is prior to the world and to the possibility of any horizon, and is not restricted to prose but is a feature of all language:

> Literature is language turning into ambiguity [*qui se fait ambiguïté*]. Ordinary language [*langue courante*] is not necessarily clear, it does not always say what it says; misunderstanding is also one of its paths. This is inevitable. Every time we speak, we make words into monsters with two faces: reality which is physical presence and meaning which is ideal absence. But ordinary language limits uncertainty. It solidly encloses the absence in a presence, it puts *a term* to under-

standing, to the indefinite movement of comprehension; understanding is limited, but misunderstanding is limited too. In literature, it is as if ambiguity is abandoned to its excesses by the opportunities it finds and exhausted by the range of abuses it can commit. (WF 341)

A considerable conceptual shift has taken place for Blanchot over the course of the 1940s. The poet and the novelist (and Ahab) turned aside from the everyday to found another world in the essay on *Moby-Dick*; the everyday was the norm and the literary was the abnormal journey. By 1949 what is normal has been inverted; literary ambiguity is more inclusive because excessive or unlimited, and the literary cannot have a solid opposing relationship with the everyday now that ambiguity is everywhere, and so literature is marked by instability.

Husserl had shown that given with language is the possibility of suspending familiar assumptions, and so the epochal worldview of literature which Blanchot had explored in *Thomas the Obscure* is treated as the norm in essays published after the Liberation precisely because it is more inclusive. 'Unreality begins with the whole', Blanchot states, and he goes on to argue that literature stands neither in the world nor beyond it, but at its very limit, which it precedes and constitutes: the imaginary is the world 'grasped and realised in its entirety by the global negation of all the individual realities contained in it, by their disqualification, their absence, by the realisation of that absence itself, which is how literary creation begins' (WF 316). Literature is a power without foundation, because the work of art simulates being while providing only the absence of being; 'this initial double meaning which is the basis of every word' instigates an oscillation between presence and absence at the origin of the work, which results in what Blanchot in *The Space of Literature* will call 'worklessness' [*désœuvrement*]. Blanchot looks to Levinas and the force of the *there is* to name this state: 'this anonymous and impersonal flow of being that precedes all being, being that is already present in the heart of disappearance, that in the depths of annihilation still returns to being, being as the fatality of being, nothingness as existence: when there is nothing, *there is* being [il y a *de l'être*]' (WF 332).[48]

The *there is* stands outside history, time, world and the dialectic posited by Hegel and supported by Kojève; it is the lack of foundation from which all beings and things originate, and it is comparable to what Bataille had previously referred to, using an anti-philosophical paradox, as 'unemployed negativity'.[49] From a Hegelian perspective, unemployed negativity is a self-contradictory nonsense: Hegel resolves contradictions by sublating them into dialectical thought. Rodolphe

Gasché remarks that paradox is essential in Blanchot, it is a necessary but insufficient condition for the happening or chance of literature, and that none of the contradictions staged by Blanchot in 'Literature and the Right to Death' is ever resolved because the condition for any such solution must be what makes it impossible. Literature is this solution premised on its own impossibility: 'The opposite pulls between which writer and work find themselves do not lend themselves to a reconciliation. No causal, mechanical, logical or dialectical solution can be conceived. And yet, the work *is*, in its very underivableness from the insurmountable ordeal, the *impossible solution* of that conflictual situation.'[50]

When the conceptual ground has shifted to such an extent that literature is the norm, we move from art to world and not vice versa, as Ahab did for Blanchot in 1941 aboard his ship. The beginnings of this shift were evident in 'Mallarmé and the Art of the Novel', when Blanchot declared, in agreement with Heidegger, that the poetic precedes and founds the world and is constitutive of human existence and experience. The danger of a slippage – evident from his early reflections on the role of criticism – has inevitably been played out: no essence or truth is available in poetic language, which is now only imposture.

The double state of language is therefore untenable for Blanchot by the 1950s. Literature, if any such thing can be defined, aims for absence, remains attached to some form of presence and is governed by an oscillating worklessness. Blanchot writes in 1952 that silence defines both states of language according to Mallarmé, and repeats the view of language that had been developing in his work since 'The Myth of Mallarmé'. Crude, raw or natural language negates the reality of things in the world of tasks and ends: words disappear into their usage in this language of pure exchange. The language of thought has more in common with the everyday than we might at first assume; aiming for the pure idea, it also returns us to the world of tasks (SL 37–42). The world might be suspended in 'essential' language, but words nonetheless retain their capacity to disappear:

> Writing never consists in perfecting language in use [*qui a cours*], in making it purer. Writing only begins when it is the approach to that point where nothing reveals itself, where, at the heart of dissimulation, speaking is still but the shadow of speech, a language which is still only its image, an imaginary language and a language of the imaginary which no one speaks, the murmur of the incessant and interminable which one has to *silence* if one wants, at last, to be heard. (SL 48)

The work of art might appear to silence the world in a way that everyday language does not, but it only pretends to split itself from all presence and being. Yun Sun Limet identifies a continuity and coherence in Blanchot's reflections on language from the 1930s to the 1980s in which there is a continued distinction between the literary and the everyday. Limet argues that Blanchot thinks silence as double throughout his career: a sort of literary silence which speaks while imposing a different sort of silence on the noise of the everyday world, ensuring the limits of literature.[51] The idea that there is a more profound silence, to be distinguished from the trivial 'keeping quiet' of the everyday, is dismissed by Blanchot in 'Mallarmé's Experience', where he remarks that there is no way of telling the difference between 'the silent nullity of ordinary language [*la parole courante*]' and the 'accomplished silence of the poem' (SL 48). Silence, as that capacity of words to disappear, is attained neither in 'common' nor 'essential' language and unworks any linguistic hierarchy. The impoverished language that is never silenced is the only proof we have of the literary and looks more like the banal – Blanchot would later write about Beckett's work in such terms.

Mallarmé remains an important reference for Blanchot from the 1950s onwards, but the name is now associated with the question of the absence of the work and fragmentation rather than any dichotomy between the aesthetic and the functional. This is not to say that Blanchot denies a double state of language, but that he refuses any dividing line between two opposing forms:

> By means of a violent division, Mallarmé separated language into two almost unrelated forms: raw language [*langue brute*] and essential language [*langage essentiel*]. This is perhaps true bilingualism. The writer moves toward a speech [*parole*] that is never already given: speaking, waiting to speak. He makes his way by drawing ever closer to the language [*langue*] that is historically intended for him, a proximity that nonetheless challenges, sometimes gravely, his belonging to any native tongue [*langue natale*]. (F 148)

The division of language which neatly delimited the poetic and the everyday, poetry and prose, was violent, forced and unsustainable. The two forms of language do not stand in a stable opposing relationship to one another; both exist in perpetual flux as they shift and overlap without any binding or separating relationship, in what Blanchot, writing in 1971, deems to be true bilingualism. The crisis that Mallarmé sought to negotiate in *Crisis of Verse* again comes back to haunt Blanchot in 1984: '[Poetry], exhausting all definition, launches me [. . .] towards a definitive crisis due to the indefinite which it incessantly provokes.'[52] Mallarmé reached out to the distinction between the poetic and the everyday when the boundary between poetry and prose became confused. Blanchot recognises that this crisis cannot be resolved, as all boundaries within language – between poetry and prose, the essential and the everyday, fiction and criticism, the aesthetic and the technical – are indeterminable because constantly shifting.

The authoritative self-referential distinction which meant that literature was characterised by myth and necessity in 1943 was impossible by the 1950s: literature cannot be defined in contradistinction to everyday language, to the real, to chance, now that it has become an unanswerable question in which differences infinitely proliferate. During this period, it becomes a question for Blanchot of when one starts thinking about literature, or of how to police the boundaries between literature and politics. Autonomy can take on various guises depending on the circumstances, and the sort espoused by Blanchot at the beginning of the 1940s, when the text gives itself its own law, is very different from the autonomy from political appropriation supported in 1945, with the admission that literature is not action in the world but only ever imposture. When the limits of literature are challenged, as they were for Blanchot during the Occupation and in the years following the Liberation, the radical non-essentiality of art and literature is exposed: 'the profound labour of literature which seeks to affirm itself in its essence by ruining distinctions and limits' (SL 220).

This is why the question of literature is also the question of techne (the Greek term encompassing technology and art); and it is why, as later chapters will demonstrate, it is significant that Blanchot chooses to use the French term *technique* and not *technologie* to refer to techniques, methods, modern instruments and machines, and to writing that precedes, exceeds and therefore necessarily includes these technologies. Blanchot anticipates what Derrida would later argue in *Of Grammatology* (1967): writing functions according to a logic of the supplement which is an indication of abundance that is also proof of a deficiency, lack, absence; this is a sort of originary prosthesis unworking the opposition between nature and culture, or nature and technology.[53] Blanchot's account of literature in essays from 1946 onwards had already shown that literature is nothing essential. In the place of literature, there is only doubt, uncertainty, a question: 'literature is the sort of power [*puissance*] that takes account of nothing. But when is there literature?'[54] We will see in Chapter 2 that the shift in emphasis or understanding in Blanchot has significant implications for his relationship with Heideggerian fundamental ontology and the possibility or impossibility of an 'authentic' relation to death and dying.

Notes

1. Blanchot, 'Lettre de Maurice Blanchot à Roger Laporte du 22 décembre 1984', in Nancy, *Maurice Blanchot: passion politique*, p. 59 (my translation).
2. Hadrien Buclin considers how the political right became associated with literary autonomy during and after the Occupation, and he associates Blanchot with this position. He argues that it was in this climate that, opposed to the notion of a 'pure literature', Jean-Paul Sartre in *Les Temps modernes* and Albert Camus in editorials for *Combat* called for a committed literature. See Hadrien Buclin, *Maurice Blanchot ou l'autonomie littéraire* (Lausanne: Antipodes, 2011), pp. 17–32.
3. See, for instance, Antoine Compagnon, *Literature, Theory, and Common Sense*, trans. Carol Cosman (Princeton, NJ: Princeton University Press, 2004), p. 82; Mark Hewson, *Blanchot and Literary Criticism* (London: Continuum, 2011), pp. 37–65; and Buclin, *Maurice Blanchot ou l'autonomie littéraire*, pp. 9–16.
4. Stéphane Mallarmé, 'Crisis of Verse', in *Divagations*, trans. Barbara Johnson (Cambridge, MA: Belknap Press of Harvard University Press, 2007), pp. 201–11 (p. 210) (translation modified).
5. Ibid., p. 201.
6. Ibid., p. 210.
7. Roger Pearson, *Mallarmé and Circumstance: The Translation of Silence* (Oxford: Oxford University Press, 2004), p. 8.
8. Mallarmé, 'Crisis of Verse', in *Divagations*, p. 206.
9. Rosemary Lloyd presents the correspondence between Mallarmé and his peers on these issues and their articulation in 'Crisis of Verse', in *Mallarmé: The Poet and His Circle* (Ithaca, NY: Cornell University Press, 1999), pp. 189–95.
10. James Joyce, *Ulysses* (Oxford: Oxford University Press, 1998), p. 34.
11. Mallarmé, 'Crisis of Verse', in *Divagations*, p. 210.
12. Roger Pearson, *Stéphane Mallarmé* (London: Reaktion, 2010), pp. 141–2.
13. Mallarmé, 'Crisis of Verse', in *Divagations*, pp. 210–11.
14. Stéphane Mallarmé, 'Sur l'explosion à la chambre des députés', in *Œuvres complètes*, ed. Bertrand Marchal, 2 vols (Paris: Gallimard, 1998–2003), II, p. 660. Blanchot, loosely quoting Mallarmé – '*There is no explosion but a book*' – relates the book as explosion to a fragmentary writing which contests everything, including itself. The explosion, simultaneously unveiling and destroying, is the book to come which never arrives: '[the book] points to itself as the violence that excludes it from itself, the convulsive [*fulgurant*] refusal of the plausible: the outside in its fractured becoming [*en son devenir d'éclat*]' (WD 124).
15. Stéphane Mallarmé, 'The Tomb of Edgar Allan Poe', in *Collected Poems and Other Verse*, trans. E. H. Blackmore and A. M. Blackmore (Oxford: Oxford University Press, 2006), pp. 70–1 (translation modified).

16. See Stéphane Mallarmé, *A Dice Throw at Any Time Will Never Abolish Chance*, in *Collected Poems and Other Verse*, pp. 136–81.
17. Malcolm Bowie, *Mallarmé and the Art of Being Difficult* (Cambridge: Cambridge University Press, 1978), pp. 133, 128.
18. See Pearson, *Mallarmé and Circumstance*, pp. 27–41.
19. Compare, for instance, Blanchot on Lautréamont in 1941, who is described as striking dead all work content with the imitation of reality, placing us in the presence of a world that no usual experience allows us to approach (FP 173); Lautréamont's project is similar to that of Mallarmé but the language employed by Blanchot in this review is never quite as superlative: 'As unique as this seems, there is nothing in this movement [the moment of invention] that must be regarded as the personal exactingness of an overly original author' (FP 176).
20. Blanchot is loosely quoting Valéry on *A Throw of the Dice*: 'He has undertaken, I thought, *finally to raise a printed page to the power of the midnight sky*.' See Paul Valéry, 'Concerning *A Throw of the Dice*: A Letter to the Editor of *Les Marges*', in *The Collected Works of Paul Valéry*, ed. Jackson Mathews, 15 vols (Princeton, NJ: Princeton University Press, 1957–1975), *VIII: Leonardo, Poe, Mallarmé*, trans. Malcolm Cowley and James R. Lawler (1972), pp. 307–16 (p. 312).
21. Martin Heidegger, 'Hölderlin and the Essence of Poetry', in *Elucidations of Hölderlin's Poetry*, p. 53. The quotation from Hölderlin: 'Is God unknown? Is He manifest as the sky? This rather I believe. It is the measure of man. Full of acquirements, but poetically, man dwells on earth. But the darkness of night with all the stars is not purer, if I could put it like that, than man, who is called the image of God.' Hölderlin, 'In lovely blueness . . .', in *Poems and Fragments*, pp. 600–5 (p. 600).
22. Heidegger, 'Hölderlin and the Essence of Poetry', in *Elucidations of Hölderlin's Poetry*, pp. 51 65 (p. 60). This was originally given as a lecture in 1936 and first published in French translation by Henry Corbin in 1938.
23. The only explicit reference to Heidegger in essays first published during the war comes in 'The Myth of Sisyphus' (1942): 'From Husserl to Heidegger, from Kierkegaard to Jaspers to Chestov, [Camus] identifies a whole family of minds whose influence on our time is obvious and who have all made some face of absurdist thought appear. It is not enough to say that these philosophers have blocked the way to reason; not only have they left the reasonable universe in ruins, they have made these very ruins their domain, made exile their home [*patrie*] and – in contradiction, paradox, emptiness and anguish – they have embroiled man's reality in a situation where it can only exist as an enigma and as a question' (FP 55).
24. This subtle but important shift is stressed by Leslie Hill in 'Blanchot and Mallarmé', *MLN* 105, no. 5 (1990): 889–913.

25. For the French translation of *Dasein*, see Martin Heidegger, 'Hölderlin et l'essence de la poésie', trans. Henry Corbin, in *L'Approche de Hölderlin*, trans. Henry Corbin et al. (Paris: Gallimard, [1963] 1973), pp. 39–61. Derrida describes this rendering into French of *Dasein* – later adopted by Sartre – as a 'monstrous translation'. See Jacques Derrida, 'The Ends of Man', in *Margins of Philosophy*, trans. Alan Bass (New York: Harvester Wheatsheaf, 1982), pp. 109–36 (p. 115).
26. Heidegger, 'Hölderlin and the Essence of Poetry', in *Elucidations of Hölderlin's Poetry*, p. 55.
27. On this essay, Blanchot's response to Mauron and his reading of Mallarmé's silence, see Michael Holland, 'From Crisis to Critique: Mallarmé for Blanchot', in *Meetings with Mallarmé in Contemporary French Culture*, ed. Michael Temple (Exeter: University of Exeter Press, 1998), pp. 81–106.
28. See Jean Paulhan, *The Flowers of Tarbes, or Terror in Literature*, trans. Michael Syrotinski (Urbana, IL: University of Illinois Press, 2006).
29. For a useful summary of Paulhan's argument and Blanchot's response, see Michael Syrotinski, 'How is Literature Possible?', in *A New History of French Literature*, ed. Denis Hollier (Cambridge, MA: Harvard University Press, 1989), pp. 953–8.
30. Paulhan, *The Flowers of Tarbes*, p. 92.
31. Ibid., p. 94.
32. Jeffrey Mehlman, *Genealogies of the Text: Literature, Psychoanalysis, and Politics in Modern France* (Cambridge: Cambridge University Press, 1995), p. 92.
33. Gerald L. Bruns, *Maurice Blanchot: The Refusal of Philosophy* (Baltimore, MD: Johns Hopkins University Press, 1997), pp. 23–33. See also Zeev Sternhell, *Neither Right Nor Left: Fascist Ideology in France*, trans. David Maisel (Princeton, NJ: Princeton University Press, 1986). Sternhell writes: 'Maurice Blanchot, who was to become in post-war France a famous writer and literary critic, provided a perfect definition of the fascist spirit in claiming that it is a synthesis between a left that forsakes its original beliefs not to draw closer to capitalist beliefs but to define the conditions of the struggle against capitalism and a right that neglects the traditional forms of nationalism not to draw closer to internationalism but to combat internationalism in all its forms' (p. 223).
34. Bruns, *Maurice Blanchot: The Refusal of Philosophy*, p. xv.
35. Ibid., pp. 148–9.
36. Hegel as quoted by Kojève: 'This is the night we glimpse when looking into a man's eyes: through this gaze we plunge into a night that becomes *terrible* (*furchtbar*); the night of the world presents itself (*hängt entgegen*) to us.' Alexandre Kojève, *Introduction à la lecture de Hegel: leçons sur la 'Phénoménologie de l'esprit' professées de 1933 à 1939 à l'École des Hautes Études*, ed. Raymond Queneau (Paris: Gallimard, 1947), p. 674 (my translation). The section from which this quotation

is taken, 'L'Idée de la mort dans la philosophie de Hegel' [The Idea of Death in Hegel's Philosophy'], is not retained in the abridged English translation of Kojève's text.
37. The same applies to genre, as Jacques Derrida shows in 'The Law of Genre', trans. Avital Ronnell, in *Parages,* pp. 217–49. Derrida argues that in order for art to declare itself as art, there has to be something in its presentation that was not part of the genre: 'this supplementary and distinctive trait, a mark of belonging or inclusion, does not properly pertain to any genre or class. The re-mark of belonging does not belong' (p. 228).
38. Maurice Blanchot, *Thomas l'Obscur* (Paris: Gallimard, [1941] 2005), p. 26 (my translation). Sections of this passage are retained in the abridged 1950 version of the text; see Maurice Blanchot, *Thomas the Obscure,* trans. Robert Lamberton (Barrytown, NY: Station Hill Press, 1988), p. 8.
39. See Maurice Blanchot, *Thomas le Solitaire,* ed. Leslie Hill and Philippe Lynes (Paris: Kimé, 2022), pp. 11–12.
40. See Edmund Husserl, *The Crisis of the European Sciences and Transcendental Phenomenology: An Introduction to Phenomenological Philosophy,* trans. David Carr (Evanston, IL: Northwestern University Press, 1970). For an introduction to Husserl's philosophy, see Dermot Moran, *Husserl's Crisis of the European Sciences and Transcendental Phenomenology: An Introduction* (Cambridge: Cambridge University Press, 2012). For Husserl's influence on Blanchot, see Leslie Hill, *Maurice Blanchot and Fragmentary Writing* (London: Continuum, 2012), pp. 51–60.
41. Heidegger, 'Hölderlin and the Essence of Poetry', in *Elucidations of Hölderlin's Poetry,* p. 55. *Blendwerk,* translated as 'deception' in the English edition, is given in Corbin's French translation as 'vide sonore' [sonorous emptiness] (p. 47).
42. 'Prose and poetry are therefore distinguished by the difference between certain links and associations which form and dissolve in our psychic and nervous organism, whereas the components of these modes of functioning are identical. This is why one should guard against reasoning about poetry as one does about prose.' Paul Valéry, 'Poetry and Abstract Thought', in *The Collected Works of Paul Valéry,* VII: *The Art of Poetry,* trans. Denise Folliot (1985), pp. 52–81 (p. 71).
43. *Prière d'insérer, Faux pas* (Paris: Gallimard, 1943) (my translation). The author of this passage is not indicated, although the style suggests that it may have been written by Blanchot.
44. Kojève, *Introduction à la lecture de Hegel: leçons sur la 'Phénoménologie de l'esprit',* pp. 106–9; this section is not retained in the abridged English translation. Several critics have noted the influence of Kojève on this essay: see, for instance, Rodolphe Gasché, 'The Felicities of Paradox: Blanchot on the Null-Space of Literature', and Christopher Fynsk, 'Crossing the Threshold: On "Literature and the Right to Death"', in

Maurice Blanchot: The Demand of Writing, ed. Carolyn Bailey Gill (London: Routledge, 1996), pp. 34–69, 70–90. Leslie Hill argues that Jean Hyppolite's *Genesis and Structure of Hegel's Phenomenology of Spirit* and his translation of Hegel are just as important to Blanchot as Kojève's work. See Hill, *Maurice Blanchot and Fragmentary Writing*, pp. 254–6 n. 9.
45. Sartre, *What is Literature?*, p. 12.
46. Ibid., p. 6.
47. See Denis Hollier, *The Politics of Prose: Essay on Sartre*, trans. Jeffrey Mehlman (Minneapolis, MN: University of Minnesota Press, 1986).
48. Blanchot here cites Levinas. See Emmanuel Levinas, *Existence and Existents*, trans. Alphonso Lingis (The Hague: Martinus Nijhoff, 1978). See Chapter 2 for a discussion of Blanchot's engagement with Levinas in the context of their responses to Heidegger.
49. Georges Bataille, 'Letter to X, Lecturer on Hegel', in *The College of Sociology, 1937–1939*, ed. Denis Hollier, trans. Betsy Wing (Minneapolis, MN: University of Minnesota Press, 1988), pp. 89–93.
50. Rodolphe Gasché, 'The Felicities of Paradox', in *Maurice Blanchot: The Demand of Writing*, ed. Gill, pp. 34–69 (p. 42).
51. Yun Sun Limet, *Maurice Blanchot critique: essai* (Paris: La Différence, 2010), pp. 49–60, 118.
52. Maurice Blanchot, 'La Parole ascendante ou sommes-nous encore dignes de la poésie?' (1984), in *La Condition critique: articles 1945–1998*, ed. Christophe Bident (Paris: Gallimard, 2010), pp. 381–90 (p. 381) (my translation).
53. See Jacques Derrida, *Of Grammotology*, trans. Gayatri Chakravorty Spivak (Baltimore, MD: Johns Hopkins University Press, 1976).
54. Maurice Blanchot, 'Allow me to reply briefly ...' (1992), trans. Michael Holland, in *Blanchot's Epoch*, ed. Leslie Hill and Michael Holland = *Paragraph* 30, no. 3 (2007): 43.

Chapter 2

An Inhuman Interruption

From the outset of his career as a journalist and literary critic, having been introduced to *Being and Time* by his friend Emmanuel Levinas in the late 1920s while studying in Strasbourg, Blanchot was reading Heidegger in the original German. The previous chapter demonstrated the debt owed to Heidegger in essays such as 'Is Mallarmé's Poetry Obscure?' and 'Mallarmé and the Art of the Novel', and that from the mid-1940s onwards there is increasing distance between Heidegger and Blanchot, as the latter undermines the possibility of a linguistic hierarchy between poetic saying and instrumental language. Nonetheless, the philosophy of Heidegger remains a fundamental starting point from which to understand aspects of Blanchot's later writing concerning, for instance, death and the neuter, as well as his reading of poets such as Mallarmé, Hölderlin and Rilke.

Allusions to Heidegger in Blanchot's essays of the early 1940s often go unreferenced, but their significance should not be overlooked. Blanchot develops an understanding of poetic language in this period that incorporates the Heideggerian view of poetry as foundation, truth as a mode of revealing, and language as the house of Being. The influence of Heidegger, particularly his 1936 lecture 'Hölderlin and the Essence of Poetry', is clearest in those essays on Mallarmé, originally written for the *Journal des débats* and later reworked for publication in *Faux pas*, in which the conception of poetic language presented is so close to that articulated by Heidegger that Blanchot is able to lift phrases directly from the former's lecture and apply them in turn to his reading of Mallarmé. Blanchot implicitly revisits Heidegger in these essays because the German philosopher has become 'the thinker most deeply and purposefully engaged in articulating philosophically the question of the foundational nature of language in general and poetic language in particular, and in challenging the inherited presuppositions of aesthetic theory as such',[1] which is also to say that Heidegger's turning was not simply a matter of philosophical interest for Blanchot, but was clearly linked to his own early career as a novelist. In this chapter we will see that Blanchot engages critically with Heidegger in essays written in 1953, the year that Heidegger published 'The Question Concerning Technology' and when Blanchot became a regular contributor to the *Nouvelle Nouvelle Revue française*, exploring how Heidegger relates such ideas to death, technology and the privileging of the human over the animal, and how these broader concerns are adopted, rejected or displaced in Blanchot's writing.

Blanchot engages with the Heideggerian concept of world precisely in order to show its cracks, insofar as what writing does for Blanchot is to suspend what constitutes world. In *Being and Time*, world refers to the familiar environment in which the human being [*Dasein*] dwells; it is 'a system of purposes and meanings that organises our activities and our identity, and within which entities can make sense to us'.[2] Worldliness is the privilege of *Dasein*; non-human entities can be described as belonging to or within the world, but they are never in the world. The phenomenology of Being-in-the-world appears to open up the possibility of originary technicity because the instrument or the tool is the means by which *Dasein*'s fundamentally ontological mode of existence is disclosed to it.[3] In later Heidegger, world becomes more explicitly historical and no longer refers to beings as a whole. Richard Polt, with some reservations, compares the relation between world and earth to the tension between culture and nature: culture arises from nature and tries to understand that from which it arises, but nature, or earth, tends to reassert itself in its mysterious power, affirming the limits of our understanding.[4]

Heidegger has been accused of reducing or excluding technics from thought, of giving residual ontological priority to physis over techne, of presiding over a naturalisation of technology rather than a technicisation of nature.[5] By comparing the treatment of the poet and prose writer Rainer Maria Rilke by Heidegger in 1946 and Blanchot in 1953, in particular Rilke's conception of the Open, a limitless region beyond metaphysical representation in which life and death are unified and to which the animal has privileged access, this chapter will reveal a work compatible with ecological thought, not because Blanchot romanticises nature and condemns the effects of technology, but because the technical is found to be always already inhabiting the natural. The aporetic relation between nature and culture, or nature and technology, or nature and history, means that, while being opposed, they are also mutually implicated, so that the one is always already contaminated with the other.

The History of Being

It is usually assumed that there is a shift in Heidegger's thought after the publication of *Being and Time* in 1927, signalling his abandonment of fundamental ontology for the history of Being. In this turning the stress shifts from the analytic of *Dasein* to a thinking of Being where art and language loom large. The English translator of his essays on Hölderlin notes that poetry is mentioned only twice in *Being and Time*.[6] A reading of Hölderlin therefore plays an important role in this turning, as Heidegger delivered a series of lectures in the mid-1930s not long after his resignation as Rector at the University of Freiberg in 1934, a position he acquired through his connection to the Nazi party, which is to say that the turning has political, as well as philosophical, significance. In these lectures, Heidegger repeatedly affirms the view of poetry as the foundation of Being:

> The poet names the gods and names all things with respect to what they are. This naming does not merely come about when something already previously known is furnished with a name; rather, by speaking the essential word, the poet's naming first nominates the beings [*das Seiende*] as what they are. Thus they become known *as* beings. Poetry is the founding of being in the word [*Dichtung ist worthafte Stiftung des Seins*].[7]

Dichtung is difficult to translate accurately in English; in German it refers to poetry in the sense of lines of verse, but can also be translated as fiction, literature, or the works of an author. The term therefore refers to a broader artistic category that is not fully encapsulated by 'poetry' in its normal usage. This reversal of the traditional hierarchy between ordinary language and poetic language, with its roots in German Romanticism, renders *Dichtung* the origin of beings, and so poetry, as a broad fictional and artistic category, becomes the mode through which a people can access its common origin: Being. The focus on the ability of the poet to reveal Being through language is characteristic of Heidegger's writing after the so-called turn.

In later work, Heidegger understands Being as essentially historical. In 'The Origin of the Work of Art', an essay which, although first published in 1950, was drafted in the 1930s and so belongs to the same period as 'Hölderlin and the Essence of Poetry', he writes: 'The artwork opens up, in its own way, the being of beings. This opening up, i.e., unconcealing, i.e., the truth of beings, happens in the work. In the artwork, the truth of beings has set itself to work.'[8] Heidegger is here referring to a fundamental mode of revealing that is prior to objective truth and more primal or original than mere correspondence between thing and idea. The work of art is where truth happens; it is where beings are brought into unconcealment in the Open – the clearing that allows beings to stand revealed in time – while the work withdraws into its inexhaustible materials – the sculptor's stone, the painter's paint, or the poet's words. The Open will figure prominently later in this chapter, as divergent readings of this region as it appears in the work of Rainer Maria Rilke – on the one hand as a false Open that is simply an inversion of the traditional metaphysical view, on the other hand as a mystical moment of confrontation with the outside, a fusion between the inner world of feeling and the outer world of animals – highlight the displacement of thought that occurs between Heidegger and Blanchot.

Truth happens in the artwork in the strife between what Heidegger calls 'earth' and 'world'. It was earlier noted that in *Being and Time* world refers to the familiar environment in which *Dasein* dwells. In this later essay, world can similarly not be objectivised and is only available to the human: the stone is described as world-less, plants and animals belong to 'the hidden throng of an environment into which they have been put', and it is only humans who possess a world because they stay in the openness of beings thanks to their use of equipment. Heidegger writes: 'In its reliability, equipment imparts to this world a necessity and proximity of its own. By the opening of a world, all things gain their lingering and hastening, their distance and proximity, their breadth and their limits.'[9] This definition of world remains largely unchanged from *Being and Time* with the exception that world takes on a historical and collective dimension, which Polt summarises as expressing 'a particular community's way of understanding itself at a particular juncture in history'.[10] World is what gives meaning to everything that we do as a historical people in 'The Origin of the Work of Art'.

Equipment is said to 'impart to this world a necessity and proximity of its own' because it is through equipment that we access world. It is for this reason that Heidegger elsewhere places such importance on the hand, writing in *What is Called Thinking?* that thinking is a handiwork (to be distinguished from the useful activity which cuts the hand from the essential).[11] A comparable hierarchy is evident in the opening pages of 'The Origin of the Work of Art', which are dedicated to a consideration of the distinction between mere thing and a piece of equipment. Equipment 'frames' its material as ready for use, reducing material to its usefulness. Something different happens in the work of art: the 'thingliness' of the thing is re-presented in the work in a way that does not reduce the thing to equipment and materiality to usefulness. Heidegger writes that the depiction of a pair of unworn shoes in a painting by Van Gogh reveals the world of the peasant woman who owns them:

> A pair of peasant's shoes and nothing more. And yet.
> From out of the dark opening of the well-worn insides of the shoes the toil of the worker's tread stares forth. In the crudely solid heaviness of the shoes accumulates the tenacity of the slow trudge through the far-stretching and ever-uniform furrows of the field swept by a raw wind. On the leather lies the dampness and richness of the soil. Under the soles slides the loneliness of the field-path as evening falls. The shoes vibrate with the silent call of the earth, its silent gift of the ripening grain, its unexplained self-refusal in the wintry field. This equipment is pervaded by uncomplaining worry as to the certainty of bread, wordless joy at having once more withstood want, trembling before the impending birth, and shivering at the surrounding menace of death. The equipment belongs *to the earth* and finds protection in the *world* of the peasant woman. From out of this protected belonging the equipment itself rises to its resting-within-itself.[12]

The closing lines reveal that earth is the foundation on which world is built. Earth is that elusive element into which the work sets itself back, allowing the materiality of the work to come forth and ensuring that the work cannot be objectified: 'Earth is the coming-forth-concealing. Earth is that which cannot be forced, that which is effortless and untiring. On and in the earth, historical man founds his dwelling in the world. In setting up a world, the work sets forth the earth.'[13] Truth happens in Van Gogh's painting not because this is a representation of some being that was once present, but because the equipmentality of the equipment, which is to say the Being of beings, is opened up. This essay demonstrates that truth is more than revealing (*aletheia*), it is also concealment. The eventfulness of the work and its otherness which cannot be objectified reflect the mode of revealing and concealing that is truth according to Heidegger.

The painting by Van Gogh discussed in 'The Origin of the Work of Art' was the subject of correspondence between Heidegger and Meyer Schapiro, who contests the claim that these are the shoes of a peasant woman, using Van Gogh's correspondence to argue that the shoes depicted in the painting that he determines to be the subject of Heidegger's essay (it is ambiguous in 'The Origin of the Work of Art') are those of the painter from the time when he had moved to the city.[14] Derrida contests such identification in his analysis; prioritising the double over the single he refutes the assumption made by both that the shoes form a pair and can be attributed to a subject. In binding the shoes together as a pair, Heidegger and Schapiro bind them to the law of normal usage: 'This was a condition of their doing justice to the truth they thought they owed in painting.'[15] Detached from one another, these shoes are then doubly detached on two further levels: on one level detached because defunct (unworn) and non-functioning (they are painted objects out-of-work because in a work); on another level detached in themselves (they are unlaced) and detached from the feet (the owner is absent).[16] Such excessive doubling cannot be reduced to 'mimetologism', nor can it be thought in terms of the conflict between earth and world which is an opposition that 'sutures'. This doubling is an interlacing that moves in and out of the frame like the laces threading the eyelets of the shoes, in so doing it defies the distinction between the real shoes and the shoes of the painting, so that we are tempted to tie the laces tightly around the ankle of a subject such as Van Gogh (Schapiro) or the peasant woman (Heidegger). 'All this system of interlacing edges detaches the being-product from its subjective scope whilst simultaneously baiting (inducing and luring) the reattachment of the said subjective scope.'[17] The distinction between reality and the painting is not effaced by this lacing, but defied and doubled. Consequently the painted shoes are spectral; they are never self-identical, but always doubled and open to the other. Derrida challenges the claim that truth happens in the work of art by thinking these shoes, and the feet on to which they fit, in the plural.

The discussion of reliability in Derrida's essay contests the pre-originary ground of Heideggerian thought and reveals that the product presupposes this condition of its possibility, which suggests that the tool is always already implicated in the pre-originary. The foundation of Heidegger's existential analysis, *Dasein* and then later Being, is always already contaminated by the technical. Derrida writes that what is reliable demands confidence, faith or credit. He continues: 'In this case, the credit is anterior to any symbolic contract forming the object of an agreement signed (explicitly or not) by a nameable subject. It is not cultural any more than it is natural.'[18] The doubling of the shoes therefore shows that one cannot claim a pure nature. Later in this chapter, we will see how Blanchot similarly contests what Heidegger's thought takes for granted, namely the possibility of an authentic relation to death, and how his fiction and criticism is haunted by hands that, always plural, signal the contamination of nature by the originary involvement of an automatic technology.

In 'The Origin of the Work of Art', Heidegger refers to several art forms (sculpture, painting and poetry) but privileges poetry as the essence of all art, because it is in language that beings are for the first time brought into the Open: 'Building and plastic creation [. . .]

are an always unique poeticizing within the clearing of beings which has already happened, unnoticed, in the language.'[19] Proof of this statement relies on the presumed worldly poverty or worldlessness of the inhuman: 'Where language is not present, as in the being of stones, plants, or animals, there is also no openness of beings, and consequently no openness either of that which is not a being or of emptiness.'[20] Blanchot and Derrida would both later contest this dogmatic division which privileges the human over all other beings. For Heidegger writing after the turn, however, human beings are privileged because they have language which is the 'house of Being' and the home in which human beings dwell. The poet acts as guardian of this home by bringing Being into language and preserving it there through their saying, a showing that is prior to language and speaking, which is also to say that language withdraws in this saying.[21]

In the early 1940s Blanchot took from Heidegger the idea that language has a more essential function in poetry ('in the poetic act language stops being an instrument [...] language is not only an accidental means of expression'); the view of poetry as foundation ('[language] reveals itself in its essence, which is to found a world'); and the claim that language is the house of Being in which the human dwells ('the authentic dialogue that we ourselves are') (FP 109).[22] In order to do so, Blanchot did not need to rearticulate the German's thought, but to translate this point into French and apply it in turn to Mallarmé, the French counterpart to Hölderlin.

Hölderlin remained an important figure for Heidegger from 1934 to the end of his life – he selected verses from Hölderlin's poetry to be read aloud at his burial. The poetry of Hölderlin is of such significance because it fulfils the proper task of the work of art as it is understood by Heidegger: in his poetry, the poetic founding of Being is achieved, which involves the establishment of a time and space between the gods and humans, in which humans can mourn the flight of the gods, endure their absence and prepare for the arrival of the new god.[23] Modernity for Heidegger is a time of distress, the dying days of the age of metaphysics when the gods have fled, and Hölderlin's poetry, more so than that of any other poet, offered the West the chance to turn away from this time, to found the inception of another history. According to Heidegger, metaphysics substitutes for a proper understanding of Being a concern with beings in general; in metaphysical representation everything is objectivised, and consequently in the age of metaphysics Being has withdrawn. It is through the event that is Hölderlin's saying – a showing that conceals, holds something back, prevents the totalisation that is rampant in metaphysical representation – that we can once again appropriate Being as our own in this other history.

The poet in Heidegger's account is associated not only with the poetic and philosophical overcoming of the age of metaphysics but also with the happening of a political event: through Hölderlin's mythic saying, German Being comes to be constituted as such, and the possibility of a new historical dwelling on earth is revealed.[24] Since the end of the First World War Hölderlin had been seen by some as the German national poet, and in the 1940s his poetry would be used by the Nazi party to inspire troops on the Eastern front. In this period Hölderlin's reputation was consequently transformed from that of 'an incurable dreamer and romantic whose utter inability to cope with life's demands might serve as a warning to impressionable young minds', to a nationalist icon, proto-fascist and source of inspiration for German troops.[25] Heidegger's own turn to Hölderlin followed his resignation as Rector of the University of Freiburg in 1934 which, it was noted earlier, was a position he had acquired through his connection to the Nazi party.

Philippe Lacoue-Labarthe relates Heidegger's turn to Hölderlin to the need to rectify his National Socialism (Heidegger attempts to differentiate between his own brand of Nazism and that of Hitler), but sees an essential affinity between the two positions: both inherit the Romantic project of establishing a new mythology which is connected to the founding of a people. The primal scene binding Romanticism, myth, religion and philosophy for Lacoue-Labarthe, with implications for Heidegger's reprise of Hölderlin, is the famous 'Oldest Systematic Programme of German Idealism' with its endorsement of a 'new religion' or 'new mythology'.[26] For Heidegger, the inception of the other history is the task of the German people in the time of distress: through their unique affinity with ancient Greece this people can recollect the primal event and appropriate Being once again through the poet's – Hölderlin's – saying. This recollection is patriotic or political in that it restores the German people to earth as their homeland. Heidegger does not explicitly state that he is concerned with founding a new mythology; Lacoue-Labarthe nonetheless argues that the poem for Heidegger is theological – it is concerned with the gods even when they are absent – as well as foundational, rendering myth the only possible translation of *Sage*:

> Nothing, then, assures us that *Sage* is anything other than myth in the most prevalent sense of 'mythology' – particularly if we keep in mind both the convoluted strategy pursued by Heidegger in relation to Nazism and the *apophansis* of fundamental ontology. The Poem is

originary, both as language and as poetry, to the extent that it is, in a direct and immediate way, the myth by which a people is 'typed' in its historical existence. The origin is properly mythical or, if you prefer, the beginning requires the forceful emergence of a 'founding myth'.[27]

Lacoue-Labarthe's argument is both forceful and compelling, though some have found it controversial. Why, it may be asked, should Heidegger employ *Sage* and not *Mythos* if indeed what he seeks to communicate here is the poem as myth? One possible reason is that Heidegger seeks to distance himself from Alfred Rosenberg, one of the principal ideologues of the Nazi party and author of *Der Mythos des 20 Jahrhunderts*. *Mythos* is closely associated with Nazi ideology and so Heidegger opts for a more Germanic word with its roots in Old Norse. *Sage* thus conveys a mythological moment in Heidegger's reading of Hölderlin which Lacoue-Labarthe finds extremely problematic, given its role as the founding moment of national identity and its subsequent connection to a 'disastrous politics'.[28]

Sage is a bringing-forth that does not objectify, what Heidegger refers to in 'The Origin of the Work of Art' as techne. There are two versions of techne at stake for Heidegger: techne as art and foundation, revealing while sheltering the mysterious [*Dichtung*]; and techne as modern technology and threat, commanding all into unconcealment and uprooting us from earth [*Technik*]. The former is more originary than the latter, rendering modern technology a form of art corrupted – the result of the unbridled totalisation and objectivity of metaphysics which reduces the whole of nature to a stockpile of resources.[29] Techne as art and foundation is the saving power in the time of distress and the counterweight to modern technology; it provides the mode of dwelling for the German people who are able to resist the rootlessness attributed by Heidegger to the technical. Heidegger seeks to distinguish between these two modes of techne, just as he tries to distinguish between his own politics and that of the Nazi party; however, as Lacoue-Labarthe argues, even if *Sage* is a more authentic and more originary version of techne, even if Hölderlin is more patriotic than Hitler, in the end the distinction does not survive scrutiny: modern technology and National Socialism are the logical extensions of this mythology.[30]

When Blanchot is engaging with the idea of poetry as distinct from instrumental language, because revealing the essence of language, which is to act as foundation for world and to offer shelter for Being, drawn from his reading of Heidegger on Hölderlin, there are therefore underlying motifs involving techne as *Sage* and politicised saving power that are not explicitly discussed in essays from the early

1940s. It is interesting to note that it is in his essays on Mallarmé that Blanchot regularly draws upon Heidegger on Hölderlin. Just as Hölderlin remained a contentious figure in post-war Germany, fought over by right-wing and left-wing critics such as Heidegger, Theodor Adorno and Bertolt Brecht, Mallarmé occupied a similar position in France: right-wing figures such as Maurras condemned him as the last and most dangerous, irrational, 'barbarian' romantic, while others on the right such as Brasillach struggled to reconcile the poet who revived a national tradition with the writer who challenges the unity of the French language.[31] Mallarmé and Hölderlin are both implicated in their own respective national traditions, and so, although Blanchot does not explicitly demonstrate that he is aware, which he surely must have been, of Heidegger's politics in the early 1940s, the use of Mallarmé as a parallel to Hölderlin in essays written for the pro-Vichy *Journal des débats* suggests that a nationalist agenda may have influenced Blanchot's preferred choice of poet.[32] The nationalist status of Mallarmé for Blanchot is evident in an essay for the *Journal des débats* from 1941, where he is cited as a poet (belonging to a lineage running from Maurice Scève to Paul Éluard) who embodies what is most essential about the French literary tradition: 'There can truly be few literatures in which a poet [. . .] could have been capable of conceiving the project for a book that would truly be the equivalent of the absolute.' This project is described as the 'torment and glory' of Mallarmé (ID 33).

There is, on the other hand, an important distinction to be drawn between Heidegger and Blanchot that casts doubt over the above assertion. The poetry of Hölderlin in Heidegger's account represents foundation. This is also the case for Blanchot reading Heidegger on Hölderlin in the early 1940s; but the selection of Mallarmé, the poet whose shipwreck hangs above the abyss in *A Throw of the Dice*, undermines the possibility of poetic foundation and propels Blanchot's view of poetry in the direction of the bottomless abyss and endless self-reflexivity. There is, of course, a parallel between Heidegger's use of Hölderlin and Blanchot's use of Mallarmé, but there is also radical dissymmetry. This stems from the important distinction between Heidegger as thinker and Blanchot as writer and critic.

In the opening two chapters of the 1941 edition of *Thomas the Obscure*, as Thomas swims in the sea and then gropes his way into a dark cave, Blanchot depicts a language reflecting on itself and distanced or detached from a worldly horizon; the watery grave and black fissure in which Thomas finds himself in chapters one and two respectively become bottomless, fathomless, as the narrative develops into an experience of language itself in the absence of all worldly objects: 'The night soon seemed to him darker, more terrible than any other night, as if it had really emerged from a wound of thought that no longer thought itself, of thought taken ironically as object by something other than thought.'[33] The bottomless abyss which defines the literary experience is possible because language can refer to itself, undoing the certainty of the thinking subject and holding it, like Mallarmé's shipwreck, above the abyss: 'like a boat adrift, in the water that gave him a body with which he could swim'.[34]

Heidegger's *Sage* relies on language not becoming an object for itself. As the house of Being, language brings beings forth in the poet's saying in a way that preserves the otherness of Being, protecting it from the rampant totalisation of metaphysical representation and providing foundation. This understanding of language, with its emphasis on foundation, demonstrates a desire for comprehension and the totality and unity of an absolute. For Blanchot, as writer and critic putting literature into practice and intervening in philosophy from a place irreducible to it, the fact that language can refer to itself is what makes literature possible.[35] Literature lies beyond this desire for comprehension and, in referring to itself, unworks itself into utter ambiguity, dispersing all meaning. The absence of foundation highlights the dispersal at the heart of the literary project.

The difference between these two perspectives is emphasised in a 1946 review of Heidegger's commentary on 'As When on a Holiday . . .'. Blanchot begins by stressing the way in which Heidegger interrogates every word and every comma of Hölderlin's poem, demanding from each isolated element a full answer; this is framed as an encounter between the vocabulary of autonomous philosophical reflection and a poetic language which points to itself as what does not yet exist and is always 'to come' (WF 112). A comparison is drawn between the impoverished language of Hölderlin's poetry, which has no object other than itself, and the grammatical and lexical richness of Heidegger's German, in which words seem to carry within themselves a hidden truth – there is a hint here that Blanchot is aware of the political implications of Heidegger's analysis when he notes the 'dangerous power words draw from the play of their structure' (WF 114). Blanchot homes in on the use of the term 'the Open' in both Hölderlin's poem and Heidegger's commentary to name the movement of opening that allows all that appears to appear. Both poet and philosopher agree that the being who wants to see must first meet the Open – Heidegger writes that the Open is the immediate that mediates the connections between all things, which are constituted thanks to such mediation – and this is made possible in Heidegger's account by the poet who brings beings into unconcealment in the Open through the founding of Being in the word.[36] Blanchot agrees that the term has this meaning for Hölderlin, but adds that in his poetry the word also retains the everyday meaning of 'open air, to go out into the open air [*air libre*]' (WF 113). Here there is evidence of the disagreement between Blanchot and Heidegger: the everyday meaning of the term stresses the limitlessness of this region which the poet is required to integrate and include within a totality that poetry itself initiates and so necessarily extends beyond, thus challenging the limits of any such totality and the existence of the poet himself. 'To question Hölderlin is to question a poetic existence so strong that, its essence unveiled, it was able to make itself proof of its own impossibility and extend out into nothingness and emptiness, without ceasing to accomplish itself' (WF 114). In the slippage between these two definitions, there is evidence of the fundamental aporia revealed by Blanchot to be the site of Hölderlin's poem, which refuses reconciliation between Being and *Dichtung*. With only itself as object, the poetic language of Hölderlin reveals its abyssal foundations and the poet experiences absence and rupture, rather than the presence and unity of Being, which is pertinently related by Blanchot to the Open taken in its simple poetic meaning: 'Ruin, contestation, pure division, really *jedem offen*, [Hölderlin] writes, open to all, because it is now no more than absence and tearing' (WF 129).

'Why Poets?'

Heidegger's essays of the 1930s focused on the foundational and redemptive nature of Hölderlin's poetry; these ideas are developed in relation to broader views on writing and technology in 'Why Poets?' (1946). 'Why Poets?' was ostensibly written to mark the twentieth anniversary of Rilke's death, and the essay addresses modernity or the age of the fulfilment of metaphysics which had repeatedly been the focus of hostility in Heidegger's essays since the mid-1930s. Underlying the overt reasons for this essay is, however, its date of publication: 1946. The recent defeat and destruction of Germany at the hands of the Allies and the powerful sense that something went wrong for National Socialism provide the backdrop for a discussion which develops an understanding of dwelling to counteract the rootlessness and nihilism of technology.

Hölderlin remains the figure around whom Heidegger constructs his view of poetry – the essay opens with a question posed in the elegy 'Bread and Wine' ('... and why poets in a desolate time?') – and a subsequent reading of Hölderlin prefaces an inquiry into the work of Rainer Maria Rilke.[37] In this desolate or needy time, the ground for world ceases to be grounding and the abyss opens up. Heidegger's *Abgrund* is to be understood as an abyss without [*Ab-*] bottom; it is the absence of any ground whatsoever:

> Abyss [*Abgrund*] originally means the soil and ground toward which, as the lowest level, something hangs down a declivity. In what follows, however, let us understand the '*Ab-*' as the total absence [*völlige Abwesen*] of ground. Ground is the soil for taking root and standing. The age for which ground fails to appear hangs in the abyss.[38]

There is an urgent need to address the abyss because, without grounding, beings are revealed in their totality, all presencing is reduced to mere resource, and the rootlessness characteristic of modern technology takes hold. Without grounding there is no shelter or dwelling for Being. In order to prompt the turn, the poet must abandon himself to this groundless place and encounter the salutary trace of what has been lost: an indication of the gods' departure. Heidegger quotes Hölderlin on this point: 'Mortals first reach into the abyss. For so it turns | with them.'[39] The abyss is the mark of the desolate time which offers redemption; Hölderlin's poetry dwells most intimately here, opening up a place, dwelling, or homeland where there was previously total absence of ground.[40]

Decidedly inferior and anterior ('in its course within the history of Being') to Hölderlin's poetry, the work of Rilke has more in common with Nietzsche, the last metaphysician who exhausts the possibilities of Western metaphysics, than the poet who offers salvation in Heidegger's estimation. Rilke is accused of a fatal error: mistaking beings in their entirety for Being. His poetry lacks the mystery – the earthliness that shelters Being and forges a dwelling in the abyss – of Hölderlin's poetry and remains firmly trapped within a metaphysical view in which objectivity reigns and from which Being has withdrawn. Heidegger will endeavour to prove this by looking at a 'few basic words [*Grundworte*]' of Rilke's poetry.[41] Much turns here on divergent interpretations of one of these words: the Open.

Rilke thinks the Open as the unobstructed whole of all that is present or absent; in so doing he seeks an expanded awareness that no longer opposes life and death and aims to move beyond the limitations of subjectivity and objectivity. In the eighth *Elegy*, he writes that only animals have access to this region because they see without looking; they live in a pure space without concepts, expectations and projections: 'With all its eyes the creature-world [*die Kreatur*] beholds | the OPEN. But our eyes, as though reversed, | encircle it on every side, like traps | set round its unobstructed path to freedom.' Unconstrained by subjectivity, animals are dispossessed of their self, projected outwards and absorbed into the limitless Open: 'its own Being for it | is infinite, inapprehensible, | unintrospective, pure, like its outgazing.' Humans, on the other hand, are turned away at a very young age from this unseparated region by our sense of self and awareness of our mortality; we consequently see everything as if in reverse from this final knowable limit: 'We face always World | and never Nowhere without the No [*Immer ist es Welt | und niemals Nirgends ohne Nicht*].'[42] Rilke thus reverses the traditional hierarchy between humans and animals, privileging the figure of the animal and unreflective perception over human subjectivity, a reversal that Heidegger staunchly contests in the *Parmenides* lectures delivered between 1942 and 1943.[43]

Heidegger objects to Rilke's limitless and unobstructed region, arguing that the representation of the 'sphericality of the globe of Being' in non-objective terms is mere wordplay and that the Open must be thought in terms of *aletheia*: 'The sphericality must be thought in terms of the essence of original Being in the sense of unconcealing presencing.'[44] To see the Open as non-objective is simply to invert the metaphysical view and so to remain within it. What Rilke calls the unobstructedness or completeness of vision, from which humans are excluded, is nothing other than beings in their entirety; this, along with the danger that is the animalisation of humans, is a view inherited from Nietzsche.[45] In this false Open there is no earthly figure to shelter Being and thus no binding rift between earth and world; all beings are drawn together in undifferentiated uniformity by the play of forces which form the 'unheard midst'. In this sense, Rilke does not think the Open as the clearing that allows beings to stand revealed in the structure of time, but totalises the realm of manifestation by thinking the Open as completeness.[46]

Rilke's false, limitless and undifferentiated Open is the final consequence of the forgetting of Being and the reign of spatiality characteristic of metaphysics. Heidegger defines the Open onto-historically as the rift caused in the conflict between earth and world which forms as a result of the event that is the creation of the work of art and the happening of truth; the Open is therefore the result of techne in the sense of *Dichtung*. The abyss characteristic of modernity, rendered ever more pressing in 1946 by the recent destruction of Germany, can be transformed into the Open through the mythological moment that is Hölderlin's saying, which creates a dwelling for Being where there previously was none. It is man, not the figure of the animal, who, through language, can find his own stance within the Open and understand Being.

The distinguishing feature of these two conceptions of the Open is the mode of techne from which they emerge: Heidegger's Open, understood in terms of *aletheia* as the clearing formed in the conflict between earth and world, is the abyss transformed through techne as *Dichtung*; Rilke's Open is the consequence of techne as *Technik*. According to Heidegger, will has been masquerading as the Being of beings in the age of metaphysics: this will is specifically human and has the character of an unconditional command, ensuring humanity's domination over the earth; it demands that everything, earth and all of its beings, including man, is transformed into material to be exploited and derives from techne as *Technik*. By excluding man from the Open and placing this region, the entirety of beings, before man as material to be exploited, Rilke is working within the framework of Nietzschean will to power in Heidegger's view:

> If Rilke experiences the Open as the unobjectiveness of full Nature, by contrast the world of willing men must stand out for him as correspondingly objective. Conversely, to look out for the integral entirety of beings is to take a hint from the phenomena of advancing technology [*heraufkommenden Technik*], a hint in the direction of those regions from where, perhaps, an originary, constructive overcoming of the technical [*bildende Überwindung des Technischen*] could come.[47]

Heidegger's critique of the Open in Rilke is closely associated with his critique of modern technology (and totalitarian political organisation). This sets this essay apart from his previous work: 'Why Poets?' is probably one of the most explicit early denunciations of the deleterious effects of technological progress – 'The Question Concerning Technology' was published seven years later in 1953.[48] At the midway point of the essay, Heidegger states that technical domination threatens man in his essence. He argues that the mastery which is a consequence of the essence of technology threatens to dehumanise the human in a world which is increasingly becoming a calculable resource to be exploited, and so man is exposed to the growing danger of becoming mere material.[49] Nonetheless, suggested in the above extract is also the possibility that Rilke's poetry, from its metaphysical viewpoint, might begin to show us the way back from the objectification of technical domination and help us to come to a way of thinking that moves beyond the self-accomplishment of metaphysics.

Rilke proposes that by turning inwards, towards the worldly inner space of the heart which he calls *Weltinnenraum*, we can experience a fusion between the inner world of feeling and the outer world of animals and overcome the objectification which prevents humans from accessing the Open. This inner space is nonetheless, in Heidegger's estimation, the sphere of subjectivity which continues to think Being as worldly presence; it does not move beyond metaphysics because it 'remains attracted to representation in consciousness'.[50] The poet's saying needs to be spoken from the very limit of consciousness, where the poet no longer wills but allows language to speak through them:

> Making statements [*Das Aussagen*] remains a way and a means. In contrast, there is a saying [*Sagen*] that is specially engaged with what is said [*das sich eigens in die Sage einläßt*] without, however, reflecting on language and thereby turning it too into an object. To enter into what is said characterises a saying that pursues what is to be said solely in order to say it. What is to be said would then be that which, in accordance with its essence, belongs in the precinct of language.[51]

It is the mythic saying of Hölderlin's poetry that offers the possibility of a redemptive turn back from representation and from the fulfilment of Western metaphysics. This is a poetic language that articulates itself at the limits of the sayable, eschewing objectivity and self-reflexivity. From out of the groundless abyss thus surges the Open; this binding difference between earth and world allows beings to stand revealed in time while sheltering Being, providing a dwelling for man and nation.

Heidegger states that the more venturesome ones dare the saying.[52] The poets are more daring because they risk an encounter with their own mortality, otherwise distanced in modernity by technology: 'The self-assertion of technological objectification is the constant negation of death. Through this negation, death itself becomes something negative; it becomes the archetype of the inconstant and the void.'[53] Authentic existence, in Heidegger's account, involves facing up to our own mortality, and mythic saying is the opportunity to do just that in this destitute time, taking the poet to the limit of consciousness, to the limit of the human, and enabling them to reappropriate Being. The possibility of dying and the possibility of language constitute human existence and ensure that we, and not animals, who do not 'die' in the true sense of the word, are the beings who may understand Being: 'To die [*sterben*] means to be capable of death as death. Only man dies [*stirbt*]. The animal drops dead [*verendet*].'[54]

Véronique Fóti comments that Heidegger should have stopped his criticism of Rilke at the moment he identified that the poet is trapped within metaphysical representation. From there Fóti argues that Heidegger's attempt to explore *Sage* as the possibility of a redemptive turn from representation is flawed: 'Heidegger seeks to voice his own insights and his response to the destitution of the age in the poetic language he has exhaustively criticised, while also affirming the insurpassability of Hölderlin's poetic thought which reaches across and beyond destitution into the futurity of the pure advent.'[55] The saying as Heidegger observes it in Hölderlin's poetry remains beyond metaphysical representation, so that language does not become an object. However, as Fotí maintains, Heidegger constructs this argument from within the language that he so vehemently criticises, and positions the coming of this redemption in the future, so that it remains to be seen whether there is a language that can evade objectification. *Sage* in this sense remains a mythic idea of myth.

This evasive form of poetic expression is the event that is yet to arrive. It hinges on the idea of authenticity: without an authentic relation to his or her death, without confronting his or her mortality, the poet does not speak from the limits of consciousness where language escapes all metaphysical representation and it becomes possible once again to appropriate Being. Any saving power in the desolate time relies on this authentic relationship to death, which is, for Heidegger, rendered problematic in modernity by the development of modern technology. The atomic bomb is not dangerous as a deadly machine with the capacity to kill thousands, but as a manifestation of the totalising will which demands that everything is transformed into raw material to be exploited. Death withdraws itself in the face of technological objectification; the event that is the arrival of the poet's saying is therefore perpetually delayed.

On the question of death in modernity, Rilke might seem close to Heidegger in his only work of prose, *The Notebooks of Malte Laurids Brigge*, which was based on the writer's time in Paris after arriving there in 1902 and published twelve years before the *Duino Elegies* in 1910. The narration of events in Paris gives way to childhood memories and broader literary and historical reflections as the narrator tries to make sense of his experiences in this foreign city. In a passage from the opening section of the book, more like a diary than the later sections, the narrator likens death in modernity to a form of anonymous production:

> This excellent hôtel is very ancient. Even in King Clovis' time people died in it in a number of beds. Now they are dying there in 559 beds. Factory-like, of course. Where production is so enormous an individual death is not so nicely carried out; but then that doesn't matter. It is quantity that counts. Who cares today for a finely finished death? No one.[56]

Unlike the hundreds dying anonymously in the death factory that is the modern hospital, Rilke's protagonist wishes to confront his own death in the virile and authentic manner that he believes to have witnessed in the passing of the Chamberlain, who is said to have died 'his own hard death', a 'wicked, princely death', one which he had 'carried within him and nourished on himself his whole life long'.[57] The narrator of the *Notebooks* suggests that language and death are intertwined and that writing is the way out of this impersonal impasse: 'this third person who pervades all lives and literatures, this ghost of a third person who never was, has no significance and must be disavowed [. . .] He is the noise at the threshold of the voiceless silence of a real conflict.'[58] Malte seeks to overcome this anonymous humming that drowns out a personal and authentic experience in language and dying, but repeatedly fails to do so. Blanchot challenges the very notion of authenticity in his essay on Rilke: the anonymous hum, the noise of the impersonal third person resented by Malte, is the only possible-impossible experience of dying.

Death: The Impossibility of Possibility

Blanchot makes three explicit references to Heidegger in a section of *The Space of Literature* entitled 'The Work and Death's Space' in which his essay on Rilke is collected.[59] The first concerns the possibility of a personal – authentic – relation to one's death (a key bone of contention with the Heidegger of *Being and Time* since 'Literature and the Right to Death'):

> The decision to be without being is this very possibility of death. The three systems of thought – Hegel's, Nietzsche's, Heidegger's – which attempt to account for this decision and therefore seem to shed most light on the destiny of modern man are all, however much they may be set in opposition, attempts at making death possible. (SL 96)

For all three names cited in this extract, death represents an extreme possibility. Hegel's death is productive; it is a moment in the progression of Spirit through different forms of consciousness to absolute knowing. Nietzsche's death is reserved for the *Übermensch*, the one who maintains the pure essence of the will and moves beyond nihilism. And finally the possibility of an authentic relation to death in Heidegger's philosophy would complete the existential analysis of *Dasein*; death must be confronted in a virile and authentic manner, resisting the anonymous relation to death pervasive in modernity.

The two later references to Heidegger in this section concern authenticity. The first considers the ambiguity of the German word *eigen* as it is employed by Rilke and Heidegger, meaning both personal and authentic.[60] Blanchot comments that Heidegger seems to dwell on the ambiguity of this word when he considers death as both the most extreme and the most personal event (SL 149–50). Blanchot would return to this point some years later in *The Writing of the Disaster* to stress that the word 'authentic' is anything but authentic:

> ♦ There is no doubt that we weaken Heidegger's thought when we interpret 'being-for-death' as the search for authenticity through death. Vision of a persevering humanism. For a start the term 'authenticity' does not correspond to *Eigentlichkeit* where the ambiguities of the word *eigen* – as they later appear in *Ereignis* which cannot be thought in relation to 'being' – become apparent. Nevertheless, even if we abandon the illusion of Rilke's 'proper death', dying [*le mourir*] in this account still cannot be separated from the 'personal', thus neglecting what is 'impersonal' in death, in relation to which it must be said not that 'I die' but that *one* dies, dying always other [*mourant toujours autre*]. (WD 117–18)

Any thought of death must respect what is foreign to me in that death, which is therefore constituted at once by authenticity and inauthenticity. The final reference to Heidegger in this section of *The Space of Literature* concerns the origin of the Heideggerian term *Entschlossenheit* in the language of Rilke's poetry. 'Decision' [*Entschluss/résolution*], pointedly connected by Blanchot to 'disclosure' [*erschließen/s'ouvrir*], is the origin of Heidegger's 'resoluteness' [*Entschlossenheit/acceptation résolue*], defined in *Being and Time* as 'authentic Being-one's-Self', the recognition of the possibility unique to oneself that cannot be shared by any other, which is to say the possibility of having no more possibilities, or death.[61] This move through language, from disclosure to decision, reveals the historical task of the artist according to Heidegger; it underscores the work as disclosure, or an opening, and associates this origin with an authentic death: 'the point of departure is the approach to the point where nothing begins, it is "the tension of an infinite beginning" – art itself as origin or the experience of the Open, the search for a true dying [*un mourir véritable*]' (SL 153). Blanchot is folding Heidegger back to the fundamental ontology of *Being and Time*, because the historicising of Being endlessly holds open the possibility that we can understand Being and have an authentic relation to death, but this possibility never materialises: Hölderlin's mythic saying remains the 'pure advent' to come. Blanchot demonstrates that death as the essential possibility is simultaneously impossible, undermining the hierarchy between an authentic and an inauthentic relation to death. The impossibility of this possibility is played out in Rilke's work.

The essay on Rilke opens with a reference to Nietzsche, the last metaphysician, in whose work, according to Heidegger, Being is reduced to a series of metaphysical representations. Blanchot notes that Nietzsche sought to overcome the human and to die a death unique to him, two aims which are entwined. Rilke shares a similar ambition: in *The Notebooks of Malte Laurids Brigge* he seeks to overcome death by articulating an authentic relation to death, which is to say by portraying the death unique to Malte, an aim that goes unfulfilled because his writing is premised on impossibility. The experience of writer and narrator overlap in Blanchot's account, where both are described as coming face to face with the horror of an impersonal neutral death from which they continually turn.

> Mass-produced death, ready-made in bulk for all and in which each disappears hastily; death as an anonymous product, an object without value, like the things of the modern world from which Rilke always turned away: from these comparisons we can already see how he slips from death's essential neutrality to the idea that this neutrality is but an historical and temporary form, the sterile death of big cities. (SL 123)

Rilke attributes his failure to the brutality of the modern world and the anonymity of large cities. Blanchot does not overlook modernity and the modern city as a feature of Rilke's writing, but presents this as a distraction from what is really at stake. Rilke ought to confront the banality of death, which is not an historical condition. Blanchot writes elsewhere in this section of *The Space of Literature*: 'to think death is to introduce into thought the supremely doubtful, the disintegration of the unsure, as if, in order to think authentically the certainty of death, we had to let thought sink [*s'abîmer*] into doubt and inauthenticity' (SL 95). Rilke and Malte repeatedly return to the impossible attempt to capture what evades all consciousness because dying is constituted by both authenticity and inauthenticity.

Repetition is therefore the mark of the impossible task of dying and writing. The first of three subsections in this essay ends by noting Rilke's comment that what made the existence of Malte impossible becomes the condition of possibility for life once again in the *Duino Elegies*, completed twelve years after the publication of *The Notebooks* in 1922. The following section opens with an extract from a letter to his Polish translator, Witold von Hulewicz, where

Rilke explains his view of death in the *Elegies* as the side of life that is turned away from us: death forms part of 'the great unity' which is the 'true form of life' (SL 133). Blanchot's first move in this section is to criticise the desire evident in this letter to substitute the clarity of ideas for the obscurity of the poetic movement. Here we see, once again, Blanchot as writer and critic seeking to address what philosophy neglects, forgets or represses: we should seek not the clarity and understanding of an absolute in literature, but the obscurity of the poetic movement which has ambiguity at its very core. The movement of Blanchot's own critical thought in the remaining two sections of 'Rilke and Death's Demand' further reinforces this view.

Blanchot repeatedly returns to Rilke's 'failure' to attain an authentic relationship to death in order to demonstrate that such failure is the condition of the possibility of dying. In the *Duino Elegies*, we are turned away from death because we are limited beings who perceive things as objects; consciousness and representation ensure that we remain trapped within the everyday realm of doing, acting and possessing. In order to access life and death as 'the great unity', we must turn away from objectified worldly reality towards the imaginary space of literature. The conversion proposed by Rilke towards a more interior consciousness is described as the transformation of the visible into the invisible, a movement of dispossession by which objects are no longer the tools of the everyday. For both Blanchot and Rilke, this is the task of dying and the task of writing, but Blanchot undermines the view that this task is achievable. A few lines later, 'transformation' is placed in quotation marks and 'transformed' is repeated twice in italics (SL 141). These stylistic devices suspend the process of becoming or dying; they place its completion in doubt and tease out the uncertainty and ambiguity inherent to death and literature. The movement of Blanchot's criticism echoes what he sees in play in the literary experience: 'little by little in the course of the experience, [Rilke] dissolved the substance and reality of death' (SL 142).

Throughout this essay Blanchot sets up the conditions for the possibility of dying, only to then demonstrate the impossible basis of such conditions. In the subsection 'Death's Transmutation', for instance, his argument shifts over the course of one paragraph from the recognition that the task of attaining an authentic relationship to death must begin with things, saving things by rendering them invisible, to the admission that things are only available to us as such when we are free of all limits: 'It is necessary, then, no longer to start from things in order to make possible the approach to true death, but to start from the depths of death in order to turn myself toward the inner space [*intimité*] of things' (SL 154). If Rilke thinks he has in some way grasped death, he has been fooled. Death as the unattainable certainty, the elusive inevitable, gives us the impression of dying but only ever errs around its hidden and ambiguous centre: 'it is its own imposture; it is disintegration, empty destruction – not the term but the interminable, not particular death [*la mort propre*] but featureless death [*la mort quelconque*], not true death but, as Kafka says, "the sneer of its capital error"' (SL 155). The failure of Rilke is inevitable, because the poem is premised on a ruinous impossibility that cannot be overcome.

Heidegger and Blanchot therefore agree that Rilke is thinking within the framework of the Nietzschean individual: restricted by the limitations of will and subjectivity, Rilke's more interior consciousness is simply a more conscious consciousness (SL 139). This failure is avoidable for the Heidegger of *Being and Time* because death is the possibility of impossibility:

> *The closest closeness which one may have in Being towards death as possibility, is as far as possible from anything actual.* The more unveiledly this possibility gets understood, the more purely does the understanding penetrate into it *as the possibility of the impossibility of any existence at all.* Death, as possibility, gives Dasein nothing to be 'actualized', nothing which Dasein, as actual, could itself *be*. It is the possibility of the impossibility of every way of comporting oneself towards anything, of every way of existing.[62]

In contrast, the failure of Rilke is necessary for Blanchot, who some years later would challenge the statement 'death is the possibility of the impossibility' by asking what difference, if any, there is between suicide and death by any other cause:

> he who has seen the desire for death through to the end, invoking his right to death and exerting the power of death on himself – opening, as Heidegger said, *the possibility of impossibility* – or, believing he makes himself master of non-mastery, lets himself get caught in a sort of trap and halts eternally – for a moment, obviously – at the point where, ceasing to be a subject, losing his stubborn liberty and other than himself, he comes up against death as what does not happen or as what turns into (betraying, as though demented [*démentant, à la façon d'une démence*], the dialectic by bringing it to its conclusion) the *impossibility of all possibility*. (WD 70)

This is not a simple refusal or negation of Heidegger's thought, but a radicalisation of his thinking which deconstructs the notion of authenticity by teasing out the paradox at the heart of this understanding of death. Blanchot focuses on the moment this thought turns on itself. Heidegger assumes a power or control over death that lures him into a trap: death can never be experienced as one's own; it is only ever the death of an other ('other than himself, he comes up against death as what does not happen'). Derrida echoes this point in his analysis of the aporia of dying in Heidegger: 'nothing is more substitutable and yet nothing is less so than the syntagm "my death"'.[63]

Derrida stresses that Heidegger's existential analysis requires limits: a hierarchical order between *Dasein* and other entities is structured by impassable edges, most notably the limit separating the dropping dead of animals from the properly dying of *Dasein*. Death, as the most proper possibility of *Dasein*, is the limit that determines all subsequent distinctions drawn between human, animal, plant and stone:

> What, then, is it to cross the ultimate border? What is it to pass the term of one's life (*terma tou biou*)? Is it possible? Who has ever done it and who can testify to it? The 'I enter', crossing the threshold, this 'I pass' (*peraō*) puts us on the path, if I may say, of the *aporos* or of the *aporia*: the difficult or the impracticable, here the impossible passage, the refused, denied or prohibited passage, indeed the nonpassage, which can in fact be something else, the event of a coming or of a future advent [*événement de venue ou d'avenir*], which no longer has the form of the movement that consists in passing, traversing, or transiting. It would be the 'coming to pass' of an event that would no longer have the form or the appearance of a *pas*: in sum, a coming without *pas*.[64]

The aporia is the interminable experience of the limit, an impossible and necessary passage signalled by the word *pas* in French, meaning both 'step' and 'not', on which Derrida writes elsewhere in relation to Blanchot.[65] To experience the aporia is not necessarily a failure or simple paralysis, Derrida writes; neither is it a stopping at or an overcoming of the limit; it touches on an event that is always arriving and so never arrives. The *arrivant* is new and unexpected; it makes possible everything to which it cannot be reduced, simultaneously marking a limit and crossing that limit.[66] The same logic of presupposition evident in Heidegger's discussion of the reliability of equipment is here revealed to be at work in this thinking of death, where Derrida categorically states that Heidegger takes for granted how to recognise death 'properly speaking' when he speaks of the modes of passage and lived experience of the living thing which passes out of life.[67] Possibility refers both to what is most proper to *Dasein* and to what I am capable of doing, and the implication is that I can lay my hands on *Dasein* (as Blanchot also suggests in the extract quoted above). Derrida shows that the only way to avoid confusion between *Dasein* and what is *Vorhandensein* or *Zuhandensein* is to come back to the ontological determination of the limit, which he challenges, by doubling it, in his analysis.[68]

Death in Heidegger is non-access to a non-border. Death in Blanchot is a relentless turning on or around the threshold which undoes that very threshold. Derrida is reluctant to draw an opposition between Heidegger and Blanchot, and recognises the way in which the refrain of the impossibility of dying in Blanchot says at once the same thing and something very different to Heidegger: 'It is just a question of knowing in which sense (in the sense of direction and trajectory) one reads the expression "possibility of impossibility".'[69] Blanchot does indeed read this expression in reverse, but he avoids directly opposing Heidegger because his writing, like the laces lacing those shoes in the painting by Van Gogh, is the experience of the endlessly repeated turning which complicates any distinction between inside and outside; this experience contests the ultimate limit of dying, with consequences, as we will see, for any claim to the purely natural or any attempt to establish a hierarchy between human, animal and stone.

The poetic work in Blanchot's account is therefore not a disclosure of time spoken from the limit of consciousness, as Heidegger would have us understand it, but an encounter with that which exceeds all consciousness and complicates all limits: 'Malte's is the discovery of that force too great for us, *impersonal* death [. . .] He cannot master this discovery, he cannot make it the basis of his art' (SL 131). The neutral, anonymous, impersonal death encountered by Malte forms the lack of foundation above which the work hangs. Blanchot teases Heidegger's thinking out to its paradoxical conclusion: the *Abgrund* from 'Why Poets?', a bottomless pit where the poet can forge a dwelling, becomes the *abîme* that is truly bottomless rather than mere absence of ground. Death is synonymous with this abyss as an endless void in which notions of foundation do not belong: 'death as abyss, not that which founds but the absence and the loss of all foundation' (SL 154).

The association between death and the abyss is closely related to Blanchot's reading of the Open as it is explored in the *Duino Elegies*. For Heidegger, the non-objective nature of Rilke's Open is simply an inversion of the traditional metaphysical view. Blanchot agrees that subject and object persist in the Open, and so Rilke remains trapped within representation, but he also argues that there is something radical about Rilke's Open which Heidegger overlooks: the Open as a mystical moment of confrontation with the outside. 'He names it *Weltinnenraum*, the world's inner space, which is no less the intimacy of things than our own intimacy and the free communication from one to the other – a powerful and unchecked freedom in which the pure force of the indeterminate is affirmed' (SL 136). The Open is a fusion between the inner world of feeling and the outer world of animals; in this moment of confrontation subject and object merge, and there is absolute uncertainty. Where Heidegger sees an inversion of the hierarchy between human and animal and persistent subjectification, Blanchot sees an extreme limit-experience, one that leaves us teetering on the edge of the abyss.

The affirmative endorsement of experience is evident throughout the chapter, where the term features in the opening paragraphs of all three essays, and is particularly relevant to Blanchot's reading of Rilke: 'What is, moreover, very striking in Rilke's itinerary [*le mouvement de Rilke*] is the way the force of the poetic experience led him, and almost without his knowing it, from the search for a personal death [. . .] to a completely different demand [*une tout autre exigence*]' (SL 155). The poetic experience is the movement, evident in Blanchot's essay and Rilke's work, which undermines the possibility of an authentic death; it is the experience of the limitless affirmation of the limit – *I cannot die so I am dying interminably*. In a footnote, Blanchot notes Rilke's comparison of existence to a vase which would be full of water if we were to have an authentic relationship to death, but which culminates in the void:

> The desire to die may be considered the expression of [. . .] a certain need for plenitude, the pursuit of the extreme edge, the liquid urge to fill the vase. But is reaching the edge enough? 'Overflowing' is the secret liquid passion that knows no bounds. And overflowing does not signify plenitude but emptiness, the excess by comparison to which fullness is still lacking [*en défaut*]. (SL 129–30)

The experience of the Open is this exposure to the uncertainty of death, at once limitless excess and void, which is never authentic and can never be overcome. The infinite void beyond this limit displaces Heidegger's view of the abyss as 'total absence' [*völlige Abwesen*] and of the Open as the entirety of beings mistaken for Being. In neglecting Rilke's poetic experience, Heidegger overlooks the conditions that undermine the possibility of foundation in literature.[70] When the poet allows *Sage* to speak through them from the limit of consciousness, when death marks the completeness and authenticity of existence, when the vase is full of water, the poet experiences the limitless affirmation of the limit: the emptiness into which existence overflows, the absence of all foundation, the abyss as truly bottomless. Any attempt to grasp and understand the Open, evident in Rilke's letter to Hulewicz, risks transforming the boundless demand of the limit into an ordinary and mundane region. Blanchot shows that only the poetic peripheral experience of the Open maintains the movement which is the transformation of the visible into the invisible, the interminable task of dying and writing.

A Turning

The Open, the rift caused in the conflict between earth and world, is the happening of truth in the work of art according to Heidegger. The Open is defined onto-historically because it offers the West the chance to found the inception of another history through the mediation of Being. In the turn to the Open, the poet – Hölderlin – founds the inception of another history. What sets Hölderlin apart is his ability, in the desolate time, to reach into the abyss and prepare the ground for the turning; he is the intermediary between the absent gods and the human in modernity.

Blanchot cites Hölderlin in his essay on Rilke as the first to have expressed and celebrated the task of the poet, which is one of mediation; he notes that this task involves giving form to, rendering more exact and decisive, the ambiguity of being [*l'indécis de l'être*]. In the reference to what is indistinct or undecided about being, there is again the acknowledgement that this task is impossible: it is within our power to say finite things in an accomplished manner that excludes the infinite, Blanchot paraphrases Rilke, but in doing so we transform the Open into something graspable and worldly, and we do so in a language that fixes things and denies their transmutability. In the turning towards the worldly inner space of the heart in Blanchot's account – and here he is challenging Rilke while at the same time developing this understanding of a turning – there is an experience not of singular redemptive reversal but of metamorphosis, which is the 'happy destruction of being' – not an entrance to the eternal, as Rilke conceives it, but a space where death is the promise of living on (SL 143–5). The reference to Hölderlin and metamorphosis is significant because it points beyond Heidegger's singular and redemptive turn and his limited reading of Rilke's Open.

An essay focused on Hölderlin and originally published as 'The Turning' (1955) is the last to be included in the appendix to *The Space of Literature*. The essay is in part a response to Beda Allemann's reading of the turning or reversal undertaken by Hölderlin between earlier commentaries on *Empedocles* and *Hyperion* – in which Hölderlin expresses the desire for reconciliation with the divine which is formulated as the desire to unite with the fiery element, to pass into another world, the desire for immediacy, for death – and later writing where the task of the poet is one of mediation between mortals and the gods.[71] Here Blanchot references 'As When on a Holiday' as a well-known example thanks to Heidegger's commentary, which itself became known in France thanks to his 1946 review 'The "Sacred" Speech of Hölderlin'. This turning is deemed necessary for the poet to save himself from the dangerous experience of fire which threatens to consume him; Blanchot notes that it has also been interpreted by critics as a glorification of the earthly fatherland and as a patriotic return to the duties of this world. Blanchot challenges the interpretation of the turning offered by Allemann – and Heidegger, although he is not named – by focusing on a reversal which is never 'one easy metamorphosis' (SL 276).

Allemann understands the idea of reversal in Hölderlin as a response to the experience of fire which threatened to consume the poet at the time he was writing *Hyperion* and *Empedocles*. Blanchot writes that Hölderlin denounces this experience as not only dangerous but, more significantly, false, 'insofar at least as it claims to be immediate communication with the immediate'. Blanchot cites Hölderlin's commentary on a fragment by Pindar on the law, where Hölderlin writes that both the gods and man must distinguish between worlds to maintain celestial pureness (the gods) and the opposition of contraries that alone allows knowledge (man) (SL 273). The immediate is impossible for both men and gods alike, and the poet is not intermediary between these two worlds but the one tasked with safeguarding this absence; Blanchot reminds us that when Hölderlin writes of 'the categorical reversal', he is commenting on his translation of the tragedy of Oedipus, who was condemned to live apart from both gods and men and to maintain the empty place opened up by this double infidelity (SL 272).[72] In the absence of the gods our relationship to them is not purely negative, and this is what makes it terrible; it has been replaced by a relation with what is higher than the gods – the 'Sacred', the law, or what Hölderlin names 'the Most High' – and it is this relation without relation that threatens to tear and disorientate us (SL 275).

The reversal is an indication of the impossibility of the mediation of the immediate at the edge of this abyss; it is man's heart that must become 'the intimacy where the echo of the empty deep becomes language, but not through one easy metamorphosis' (SL 275–6). Blanchot cites the hymn *Germania* as an example of the richer conception of inspiration which results from the reversal understood not as singular and redemptive but as repeated and reversed: with Allemann, he notes that the focus of earlier hymns (when the poet felt the necessity of not giving himself over to the experience of the fire) becomes appeased power in *Germania*; Allemann argues that this is because Hölderlin has accomplished the reversal and opened that pure region of mediation between sky and earth; but Blanchot sees the poet as turned aside from both heavens and earth as the one tasked with maintaining this rupture. The closing lines of the essay cite Hölderlin at a time when 'madness had completely obscured [his] mind':

> And when we read these words gleaming with madness: 'Would I like to be a comet? Yes. For they have the speed of birds, they flourish in fire and are as children in purity', we sense how the desire to be united with the fire, with the day, may have been realised for the poet in the purity guaranteed by his exceptional integrity. And we are not surprised by this metamorphosis which, with the silent speed of a bird's flight, bears him henceforth through the sky, flower of light, star that burns but unfurls innocently into a flower. (SL 276)

Hölderlin suggests that the turn to the divine, the immediate, the Open, is achievable; perhaps his madness is evidence of this indifference.[73] Blanchot's rewriting of this quotation in the lines that follow, however, does not bear witness to the incineration of this comet but to its light, which at once destroys and unveils. Figurative language becomes more literal in this rewriting as the comet transforms into blossoming flower, signalling not reconciliation between the human and the gods but multiple metamorphoses which result from this endless confrontation with the void.[74]

The poetic experience is sketched as a hedgehog curled up on a road by Derrida when asked, by the Italian journal *Poesia* in November 1988, 'Che cos'è la poesia?' What is poetry? 'Not the phoenix, not the eagle, but the *hérisson*, very lowly, low down, close to earth. Neither sublime, nor incorporeal, angelic, perhaps, and for a time.'[75] This is not a meeting between the otherwise absent gods and the human, but a lowly nocturnal affair concerning the possibility of grounding. Derrida's response echoes Blanchot's rewriting of Hölderlin through the sober selection of the hedgehog; the lack of any verb, any designation of existence, similarly stresses the suspension of world in this poetic experience. We may here be reminded of Schlegel's hedgehog, that animal turned in on itself and detached from the surrounding world, like the fragment which represents organic individuality and the work, but the hedgehog of Derrida's response is very different.[76]

In rolling itself up into a ball the hedgehog is not protected from the elements but all the more fragile and vulnerable, exposed to the mechanical dangers of the road; it anticipates death in a way that Heidegger refuses to the animal, but remains open to the outside because, Derrida explains fifteen months later in an exchange with Maurizio Ferraris, the aporia of dying, death as the most proper possibility of *Dasein*, is never closed in *Being and Time*.[77] In crossing and curling up on the road, the hedgehog is the *arrivant*, the new and unexpected, which signals the coming of the event that never arrives (the poem); it simultaneously marks and crosses a limit, making possible everything to which it cannot be reduced.

Central to the history of Being for Heidegger is our ability to recollect a primal relationship with Being through the poetic saying of Hölderlin. The opening lines of Derrida's response underscore the aporia of forgetting which prevents the completion of this turning and the inception of another history. Derrida writes that a response to the question 'What is poetry?' requires that we forget in order to remember, but we can never renounce all knowledge: 'demobilize culture, but never forget in your learned ignorance what you sacrifice on the road, in crossing the road'.[78] You would like, Derrida writes, to retain by heart a singular event; you desire absolute inseparation; but it is precisely this 'by heart' which is problematic, because confided 'to a certain exteriority of the automaton, to the laws of mnemotechnics, to that liturgy that mimes mechanics on the surface, to the automobile that surprises your passion and bears down on you as if from an outside: *auswendig*, "by heart" in German'.[79] The 'by heart' means automaticity or technicity, at the very least animality (and here there is an echo of Rilke, who turns towards the worldly inner space of the heart to access the Open, which is otherwise reserved for animals). In crossing the road, we sacrifice the poetic to the automation of artificial memory which is precisely what Heidegger wants to maintain outside poeticising and thinking. 'By heart' therefore reaches beyond organic bodily limits and signals an originary contamination by the inorganic: 'it erases the borders, slips through the hands, you can barely hear it, but it teaches us the heart'.[80]

The critique of modern technology in Heidegger is closely associated with this turning: in the age of metaphysics, the essence of technology threatens to transform everything into a calculable resource to be exploited, and the turn back towards the Open offered by *Sage* is the event that marks the beginning of a new era. Blanchot borrows much from Heidegger's 'Why Poets?' but remains carefully guarded in relation to Heidegger's history of Being and omits any discussion of technology from his essay. The emphasis placed on experience and the movement of his own critical thought throughout 'Rilke and Death's Demand' indicates why Blanchot does not follow Heidegger down this route. Blanchot is attentive to the mobility of syntax, whereas Heidegger focuses on static words. A footnote to an essay published later that decade accuses Heidegger of abusing etymology:

> The extremely insistent attention which Heidegger pays to language treats words as discrete units, concentrated in themselves, and torments those words deemed fundamental until the history of Being is heard in the history of their formation – but this is never attention to the connections between words, and even less to the anterior space implied by these connections whose originary movement alone makes possible language as unfolding. (BC 265)

This note goes some way to explaining why Blanchot was not convinced by the history of Being. Heidegger presupposes finding in words the evidence of truth; in his philosophical desire for the unity and totality of truth, he tortures words, lifting them out of their context and considering them in isolation. In 'Why Poets?', for instance, the term *das Offene* is extracted and translated into numerous 'synonyms' which seem disjointed from the original context of the *Duino Elegies*: 'The gravity of the pure forces, the unheard centre, the pure *Bezug*, the whole *Bezug*, full Nature, life, the risk are all the same. All the names just offered name beings as such in their entirety.'[81] Rather than focusing on single immobile words, Blanchot seeks to capture the incessant movement of Rilke's syntax, which signals the radical non-foundation of the neuter – that indeterminate element felt in death, the abyss, and once too hastily attributed by Rilke to the modern city.

The possibility of an authentic death is repeatedly implied, only to be crossed out by its impossible premise; the transformation of the visible into the invisible is implied and then suspended in quotation marks and italics; the turn to death and the Open plays a significant role throughout the essay but is annulled by the errant movement of the discussion. Blanchot substitutes the experience of the limitless affirmation of the limit for Heidegger's founding event by focusing on the mobility of language, which implies a turning only to leave that turning hanging above an abyss, simultaneously marking a change and suspending it. He employs a similar tactic in a fragment in *The Writing of the Disaster* where the question of the event [*Ereignis*] as it is discussed by Heidegger is raised in the context of the following terms listed at the beginning of the fragment: 'Last witness, end of history, epoch, turning point, crisis – or end of (metaphysical) philosophy.' Blanchot asks why writing, understood as a change of epoch or (non-)experience of disaster, implies the terms listed above only to revoke them, 'even if what they announce is announced as something new which has always already taken place, a *radical change* from which all present is excluded' (WD 102). He argues that it would be naive to think that the requirement to withdraw, which makes this event possible, ceases from the moment a decisive historical change is announced, and names *Gestell* – the enframing that is the mode of revealing that holds sway in the essence of technology – as the modern version of the ways in which Being gives by withholding itself. To put this another way, as Blanchot does at the beginning of the following fragment in the context of the postulates of etymology, the demand of the infinite (those connections between words overlooked by Heidegger) is necessary in order to grasp the finite. Blanchot reminds Heidegger that there is something facile and peremptory in translating *aletheia* as truth because errancy comes first. The claim that everything is historical is based on a state of being which is anything but historical and so disproves itself; the idea that there might be an end to metaphysics is itself a metaphysical view: 'To write in ignorance and without regard for the philosophical horizon, as punctuated, gathered, or dispersed by the words that delimit that horizon, is necessarily to write with self-satisfied ease' (WD 103). Blanchot names Hölderlin and Mallarmé as two writers, among others, who do allow such complacency. In this fragment writing bears the fluid traits that imply a turning only to leave it hanging above an abyss, simultaneously marking a change and suspending it. The movement of language here and in 'Rilke and Death's Demand' challenges the identification of metaphysics with technology. Blanchot moves beyond the historicising of death and technology alike, relating the inhuman, the mechanical, repetition, the impersonal, to the non-experience of dying.

The technical, which plays a significant role in 'Why Poets?', is therefore omitted from 'Rilke and Death's Demand' not because Blanchot has in some way misinterpreted Heidegger's claims: the technical resonates from that unknowable outside in which all that is inhuman is located. Again there is a significant divergence between these two readings of Rilke: where Heidegger disregards the notion that animals have access to the Open, Blanchot accepts that there is an inhuman aspect to this space of confrontation and merger; he notes that Rilke too had to admit that the literary experience had an inhuman aspect which he labelled the void (SL 151). Indeed, Blanchot's account of the flies in Malte's bedroom seems to contain within it all of the complexities of his view of death as the impossibility of possibility, of the Open as the experience of the limitlessness of the limit, of the turn as mobile and yet suspended, as well as his rejection of the historicising of an authentic relation to death:

> Sometimes, when fear seizes [Malte], he cannot avoid hearing the anonymous hum of 'dying' which is by no means a consequence of the times or of people's negligence: in all times we all die like the flies that autumn forces indoors, into rooms where they spin blindly in an immobile dizziness, all of a sudden dotting the walls with their mindless death. (SL 123–4)

Human beings 'die' just as these flies 'die' (the quotation marks suspending this process in the extract above). The extent to which Blanchot excludes any discussion of the animal in this essay is perhaps surprising, given that animals play a large role in the formulation of the Open in the eighth *Elegy*; however, contained within the above reference to flies in Rilke is Blanchot's entire conception of the possible-impossible experience of dying, which is not reserved for the human. The experience of dying is a confrontation with an outside in which all that is inhuman errs – this is not outside thought in opposition to inside, but an outside which, like the other night, is irreducible to any such binary.

Animals and Automation

Animals, in their ignorance of their own mortality, gaze into the boundless Rilkean Open; humans, constrained by the knowledge of their approaching death, can only look backwards.

> What *is* really out there we only know
> by looking at the countenance of creatures.
> For we take a young child and force it
> to turn around, to see shapes and forms,
> and not the Open that is so deep in the face
> of an animal. Free from death.[82]

Heidegger inverts the hierarchy constructed by Rilke; the human stands at the top of the clear and stable order which composes *Dasein*: 'The stone is worldless, the animal is poor in world, the human forms a world [*der Stein ist weltlos, das Tier ist weltarm, der Mensch ist weltbildend*].'[83] The animal is poor in world because it does not perceive being as Being; beings only appear to the animal as elements of its environment; consequently the animal is surrounded by a circle of its urges rather than things. Only man sees being in the light of Being. The difference between man and animals is underscored by the animal's lack of language; the animal is deprived of speech because it does not have access to the world as the struggle between concealment and disclosure. This account of the negativity of the animal's worldly or spiritual poverty, from a lecture course from 1929 to 1930, led Derrida to argue that Heidegger's characterisation of animal life perpetuates the humanistic and anthropocentric prejudices that have long dominated Western philosophy. There is no animal *Dasein*, nor is the animal *Vorhandensein* or *Zuhandensein*; Heidegger thinks the animal only as a median between stone and human being, and so his thesis remains 'fundamentally teleological and traditional, not to say dialectical'.[84]

References to animals by Blanchot might be easily overlooked because there are only ever fleeting glimpses or passing comparisons; the creatures that do appear are not majestic beasts, household pets or farmyard animals, but almost always what we might consider unexceptional, perhaps even base or dirty, and alien: several rodents, numerous flies, a butterfly, a caterpillar, dragonflies, cuckoos, a magpie, a nightingale, a skylark, a stag beetle, a squirrel, woodlice, toads, fish, a lizard, a wolf. These creatures, from fictional and critical work, tell us something significant about the experience of writing and dying when they appear.

Blanchot had tentatively proposed a comparison between writer and animal in the opening essay written for *Faux pas* in 1943, remarking that both live a lonely existence, only to then reinscribe some sort of Heideggerian hierarchy: 'These images, natural as they may be, are not convincing. It is to the intelligent witness that the silent animal [*bête*] seems prey to solitude' (FP 2). The implication is that this witness is a human and it is only down to their presence that the animal can be deemed solitary, because the mute beast lacks language and therefore a sense of otherness. Furthermore, the writer has privileged access to this solitude or sense of anguish: Blanchot writes that it does not occur to us to consider the anguish of the cobbler in the same way (FP 3). The solitude reserved for the writer is not a solipsistic refuge but an exposure to the outside; the anguish experienced by the solitary writer deprives them of the relation with another, estranges them from human reality, and likens them (perhaps surprisingly following the previous quotation) to something inhuman, in this instance vermin: 'Thus stripped bare [*dépouillé*], and ready to plunge into his monstrous particularity, [anguish] casts him outside himself and [. . .] confuses him with what he is not' (FP 12). From an early point in his career as a novelist and critic, then, the difference between animals and humans proves to be extraordinarily fragile for Blanchot, as he recognises the otherness reserved for the writer as the figure who experiences the frailty of world. The elaboration of the inhuman in Blanchot's writing demonstrates the extent to which he moves beyond an understanding of language as the sheltering 'house of Being', solely accessed by the human, towards a view of literature as the medium that dismantles the sovereign subject through exposure to the alterity of the outside.

An inhuman interruption occurs at the midway point of *Death Sentence*, the first in a series of shorter narratives published by Blanchot between the late 1940s and late 1950s, in a scene in which one of the female protagonists, Nathalie, enters the narrator's hotel room early one morning. She stands in the middle of the room like a statue, but is paralysed with fear rather than made of stone. The narrator remarks that something irremediable had happened before recounting the time he witnessed a squirrel become trapped in a cage hanging from a tree:

> I once saw a squirrel get caught in a cage that hung from a tree: it leaped across the threshold with all the energy of its very happy life, but hardly had it touched the planks inside when the light trigger clapped the door shut, and even though it had not been hurt, even though it was still free, since the cage was enormous, with a little pile of shells inside, its leap broke off abruptly and it remained paralysed, struck in the back by the certainty that now the trap had caught it. (DS 38–9)

The vastness of the cage means that the squirrel remains free even once the trap has closed, and the small pile of nuts inside ensures its survival: this is both a death sentence and the suspension of death, transforming the squirrel and Nathalie alike into living statues. Neither are sovereign subjects in this debilitating experience which shakes the human–animal hierarchy to the core. The irremediable is therefore a realisation that something other is in control, something beyond the limits of the cage which has always already preceded any account of being. This anonymous force is what Levinas calls the *there is* [*il y a*], a sort of impersonal field that presents being and cannot itself be negated, since the necessity of affirmation always precedes the possibility of negation. The *there is* constitutes a radical challenge to dialectical thought and renders any origin or event, beginning or ending, impossible.[85]

In an earlier review of *The Notebooks of Malte Laurids Brigge* from 1943, Blanchot writes: 'Anguish reveals to man that in every particle of air there exists something terrible, and this existence of the terrible is the very proof of existence' (FP 49). The *there is* is so terrible for Malte because he staunchly tries to remain faithful to himself, refusing to embrace what terrifies him in his death: its impossibility. He clings on to the hope that he will die an authentic death; however, as his childhood fear, referred to in one episode as 'the Big Thing', reminds him, death brings with it a radical transformation into something completely other:

> Now it was there. Now it grew out of me like a tumour, like a second head, and was a part of me, though it could not belong to me at all, because it was so big. It was there like a huge, dead beast, that had once, when it was still alive, been my hand or my arm.[86]

Limbs, distanced from any bodily identity, morph into strange animals in this anonymising experience. What emerges is nothing familiar, comforting or natural, but an unrecognisable inhuman. Rilke maintains in the *Duino Elegies* in 1923 that animals are ignorant of their mortality. Significantly for Blanchot by the time of writing *Death Sentence*, this anguished revelation is not reserved for the human; Blanchot is therefore far from the philosophical position attributed to him by Ulrich Baer, who names him alongside Heidegger and Agamben as thinkers who interpreted the eighth *Elegy* as 'a treatise about the ontological difference between human and animal'.[87] Blanchot's concern is what precedes or gives ontology, which itself has no origin and exceeds the distinction between human and animal.

To return to the ensnared squirrel of *Death Sentence*: within this cage it is free to move and to survive, but this is a limited freedom normally reserved for people. Here the squirrel is exposed to the experience of death and so, like Nathalie, it is irreversibly altered, transformed into a moribund figure. One page later, Nathalie, her hair longer than usual, makes a bid for freedom when reminded of the room's limitations after she knocks into a table:

> She reacted to the noise with a frightened laugh, and fled like an arrow. Then everything becomes confused. I think that after she cried out I grew wild [*J'imagine qu'à partir de ce cri j'étais hors de moi*]. I saw her lunge toward the open air [*air libre*], and the instinct of the hunter seized me. I caught up with her near the stairway, grabbed her around the waist, and brought her back, dragging her along the floor as far as the bed, where she collapsed. My fit of rage was one of the few I have had since my very angry childhood, and it was uncontrollable [*n'avait plus de borne*]. I do not know where this violence

came from; I could have done anything at a time like that: broken her arm, crushed her skull, or even driven my own forehead into the wall, since I do not think this furious energy was directed at her in particular. Like the blast of an earthquake, it was an aimless force which shook beings and knocked them over. I have been shaken by this blast too, and so have become a tempest which opens mountains and maddens the sea. (DS 40)

Both characters are overcome by their instincts in this passage. Assuming the roles of predator and prey, they behave like animals: Nathalie bounds for freedom sniggering fearfully; the narrator chases after her, dragging his prey along the floor in an uncontrollable and limitless rage, comparable to a natural disaster powerful enough to tear the ground from beneath them. Neither the narrator nor Nathalie can be described as human in this brief moment; like the squirrel, both assume a disturbing otherness. The possibility of an authentic death and language constitute human existence for Heidegger and ensure that we, and not animals, understand Being as such. When the conditions of authenticity are shown to be impossible for human and animal alike, the distinction between the two is suspended and the response to this 'completely different demand [*tout autre exigence*]' is a non-linguistic mode of expression bearing some resemblance to animalistic cries and gestures, rather than any redemptive poetic language.

The fragility of the difference between human and animal in this narrative has consequences beyond their responses to death and dying. As beings that are partly inhuman, bearing animalistic or feral traits, the narrator, Nathalie and the other female protagonist J. experience the solitude that occurs in the presence of an estranged and unhearing other. Linguistic communication is consequently often ineffective and replaced by other forms of expression: touch conjures thoughts where words fail ('Slowly I put my hand on hers; this contact was like a bitter memory, an idea, a cold, implacable truth [. . .] At one moment I saw her lips move and was aware that she was talking, but now I, in turn, no longer made an effort to grasp those words'); facial expressions communicate strong emotions and demands ('I noticed that her mood had changed: a sort of cold respectability was mounting in her face'); and the silent gaze has the power to transform the listener ('A gaze is very different from what one might think, it has neither light nor expression nor force nor movement, it is silent, but from the heart of strangeness its silence crosses worlds and the person who hears that silence is changed [*devient autre*]') (DS 77, 35, 68). Michel Haar has criticised Heidegger's view of the animal, arguing that he overlooks other forms of expression beyond language: 'one could object that

Heidegger's phenomenology has taken into account neither the cries, moaning, nor the grimaces, mimicry, gestures, and postures which are irrefutably modes of expression among, for example, mammals'.[88] Haar's criticism cannot be directed at Blanchot. Dialogues in this narrative are brief and often unsuccessful, generally failing to communicate any decisive message:

> For the first time, I decided to telephone her. It was around noon. [J.] was alone. I could hardly hear her, because after the first word or two she was overwhelmed by a violent fit of coughing and choking. For a few seconds I listened to this ragged, suffocated breathing; then she managed to say to me, 'Hang up,' and I hung up. (DS 13)

The ability to reach out to the being that witnesses one's solitude is what is at stake in this failed communication and in the indeterminate nature of the various cries, howls, splutters and sneers that feature throughout the narrative: 'a sort of breath came out of her compressed mouth, a sigh which little by little became a light, weak cry'; 'her voice was naturally surprising – fairly harsh, lightly veiled, clouded by disease and yet always very gay or very lively'; 'This was said in the most tempestuous tone of voice; it was a sort of frenzied cry which would not have seemed natural to me even coming from the most violent sort of person' (DS 20, 21, 59). The narrator endeavours to make himself understood, but this moment of comprehension never takes place in the here and now.

The question of an inhuman transformation in the face of impossible death again arises in a lengthy study of Lautréamont's *The Songs of Maldoror*, first published one year after *Death Sentence* in 1949. Blanchot remarks that the creatures who populate the definitive edition of the first song – the octopus with the silken gaze, the horseshoe bat, the toad, the itch bite that causes scabies – have taken the place of the name Dazet, which appears in the first edition of the song published one year earlier (LS 79). Georges Dazet is an old classmate, a relic from the author Isidore Ducasse's past. This is not some mere literary artifice, writes Blanchot; we have not caught Lautréamont in the act of replacing one name for another. This interruption signals something far more radical: that the author has been transformed by the experience of writing this text (LS 80–1). Dazet ceases to be Dazet and the inhuman emerges from the depths to take his place. How does this happen? Surely Ducasse is not complicit in his own transformation? Blanchot has a theory: 'The truth is that at this moment Dazet effectively dies, and dies so completely that the hand which casts him into nothingness will later return to the past to erase every trace of his existence' (LS 82). A second hand returns to the text to haunt the first: in doubling the hand in this way Blanchot contests the limit between nature and technology, because this second hand cannot be described as organic.

The experience of Lautréamont, or Isidore Ducasse, when writing *The Songs of Maldoror* is an exposure to what Blanchot in the opening essay of *The Space of Literature* calls the solitude of the work. This is the first essay Blanchot wrote for his new monthly column in the *Nouvelle Nouvelle Revue française* in 1953; he was living in Èze at the time, a Provençal hilltop village where he would remain until his return to Paris in 1958, and so the essay may be read as a reflection on Blanchot's own experience as writer and critic. Here Blanchot distinguishes between the meditative solitude discussed by Rilke – 'For weeks, except for two short interruptions, I have not pronounced a single word; my solitude has encircled me and I am inside my efforts just as the core is in the fruit' (SL 21) – and the radical solitude of the work. He maps this on to the distinction between the book which is unreliable or insufficient action in the world, and the work which suspends the familiar world (SL 23). In the background is an engagement with Levinas, whose stated aim in a series of lectures given in 1947 was to go beyond the definition of solitude by sociality and to repudiate the Heideggerian view of solitude in the midst of a prior relation with the other.[89]

Levinas understands solitude as the unity between an existent and its existing where the existent possesses such mastery over its existing that all objects in the world are encountered as if they emanated from the subject.[90] The approach of death challenges this solitude because it marks the end of the subject's virility when something unknowable and absolutely other appears and reveals that existence is pluralist.[91] The *there is* is this state prior to solitude, encountered in the approach of death and suffering, which Levinas defines in direct response to Heidegger as an existing which is not an 'in-itself' but the absence of all self, 'being without nothingness which leaves no hole and permits no escape'.[92] Blanchot is similarly concerned with the *there is* as the undercurrent that precedes or gives ontology, but his is a more radical insurmountable solitude that nonetheless allows an exposure to alterity and belongs to the work. What Blanchot and Levinas both take from Heidegger in dissident fashion is that essential solitude precedes the familiarity of world and is in that sense an exposure to alterity and the outside. The difference between them at this stage is that Levinas is thinking as a philosopher – one who has to account for subjectivity – and therefore seeking to defend the primacy of what he calls ethics over ontology, while Blanchot as a writer is more interested in the 'experience' of the outside through the work.

Blanchot asks what it means for the writer that something like the work exists, and exists in a strange way – without proof, use, marker of completion or incompletion – as an impersonal and anonymous affirmation: it is and nothing more. To write is to withdraw language from the world, and so words become images and appearances that indicate the shadow of events, rather than signs and values that are bound to reality. The solitude experienced by the writer stems from belonging to a work that offers no shelter from the *there is*: writing is an exposure, in language and through language, to 'the opaque, empty opening onto that which is when there is no more world, when there is no world yet' (SL 33). The impulse felt by some writers, often the most literary, to keep a diary or journal is evidence of this experience because it reveals a desire to maintain the self, to attach writing to daily reality, and to root the movement of writing in time (SL 29). This rupture in world exposes them to alterity: 'The third person is myself become no one, others become the other [*autrui devenu l'autre*]' (SL 28). Here we might recognise the experience of Isidore Ducasse or Lautréamont, whose childhood friend is replaced by a mass of writhing creatures, or the experience of Oedipus who is tasked with maintaining the rupture between gods and humans. The solitude of the work allows a thinking of relation in Blanchot which only occurs in the absence of all mediation.

The difference between Blanchot and Levinas is further underscored by their treatment of hands. Levinas considers how we work with our hands in the 'concreteness of need' to suppress the distance between ourselves and objects, noting that what is interesting about the modern tool, more so than its instrumental function as analysed by Heidegger, is its function to suppress work and thus the pain and suffering of the subject. Hands in Blanchot do not always reach out to the world: there are always at least two hands involved in writing, one which deals in the possible and looks to assert itself as master by bringing the writer's task to an end and releasing the pencil, another which continues to write even when asked to stop by the first hand. 'The mastery of the writer is not in the hand that writes, this "sick" hand which never lets the pencil go, which can't let it go, because what it holds it doesn't really hold' (SL 25). The quotation marks suspending 'sick' highlight the uncertain status of this other hand as it hovers over the page, neither grasping nor letting go of the pencil; it is impossible to tell whether it is dead or alive, singular or plural, animal or human. This other hand deals with something beyond the world in a time that is 'barely human'. The writer belongs to the work but only ever achieves the book; torn between action in the world and the worklessness of the outside, they are unable to put an end to this task. This more radical solitude of the work reveals a fissure between writing and world: 'To write is [. . .] to withdraw language from the course of the world, to detach it from what makes it a power through which, when I speak, the world is spoken and the day is built through work [*travail*], action and time' (SL 26). The writer is exposed to the radical solitude of the work by the hand that withdraws language from world.

Blanchot's consideration of hands in this subsection bears some resemblance to a passage from *The Notebooks of Malte Laurids Brigge* which, given the reference to Rilke in the opening paragraphs, he may have had in mind. In this passage a young Malte drops a crayon while drawing a picture of a solitary knight on horseback. He kneels down under the table, his left hand supporting him, and gropes around in the dark with his right hand looking for the crayon. He watches as this hand becomes distanced from him to the extent that it resembles 'an aquatic animal, examining the ground'. A ghostly disembodied hand suddenly emerges from the wall – a fur rug stretches between Malte and this wall – and Malte comments that he felt that one of the hands belonged to him and was committing itself to 'something irreparable': 'With all the authority I had over it, I checked it and drew it back flat and slowly, without taking my eyes off the other, which went on groping. I realized that it would not leave off.'[93]

Malte's left hand is engaged in work in the world. Malte's right hand reaches out, pulls away from bodily identity and transforms into an indeterminate animal. The hand that reaches out to him is described as 'a larger, extraordinarily thin hand, such as I had never seen before'. This hand is also not necessarily human; it does not bear any human characteristics and it seems at least noteworthy that a fur rug marks the region where this encounter takes place. It is unclear whether this hand is a reflection of Malte's own hand, the hand of another human, the hand of another animal, dead or alive. It reaches out to grasp Malte's hand but it is refused. Could it have grasped or touched him in the first place? If it were like the hand that writes in 'The Essential Solitude' it would have been able neither to grasp nor to release. Nevertheless, one thing is certain: what Malte has embarked upon cannot be undone. This encounter with the other forever exposes him to the alterity of the outside and to the impossible and irreversible experience of dying and writing.

Thinking is described by Heidegger as a craft [*Hand-werk*].[94] The hand serves a purpose beyond its everyday use as a bodily organ because it is the means by which the human stretches out and receives itself in the other. Heidegger restricts the hand to the human (paw, fin and claw are excluded) and denies the hand as first instrument, arguing that the essence of the hand does not let it be determined as an organic part of the body for grasping – apes have organs that can grasp – but as a thought that gives and is given. Derrida reveals an aporetic logic governing this thinking of the hand ('*Dasein* is neither *vorhanden* nor *zuhanden*. Its mode of presence is otherwise, but it must indeed have the hand in order to relate itself to other modes of presence')[95] and shows that a critique of modern technology is evident in the privileging of the singular hand of thinking and craftsmanship which is threatened by industrial automation and modern mechanisation.

Blanchot welcomes the view that the hand is the organ by which we might reach out to the other; however, in stark contrast to Heidegger, hands in his work are always plural, possibly animal, and disperse rather than gather. Hands surface in *Death Sentence* as characters perform mundane tasks ('She had the telephone to hand and she could call the concierge without dialling'), as they try to communicate ('I received a few words in J.'s hand, in her hand rather than her handwriting'), and as they reach out to others ('I took her hand gently, by the wrist (she was sleeping), and scarcely had I touched it when she sat up with her eyes open, looked at me furiously and pushed me away, saying, "Never touch me again."') These hands have a transformative, even destructive, effect on those they touch: 'I was no longer at all afraid for myself, but for her I was extremely afraid, of alarming her, of transforming her, through fear, into a wild thing which would break in my hands' (DS 8, 12, 25, 68). The plaster casts of the hands of J. and Nathalie have an uncertain status in the eyes of the narrator; the survival of J.'s hands beyond her death in plaster form and the disunity that characterises the lines spreading across the palms incite wonder in the narrator towards the beginning of the text (DS 10–11), while the infinite mortality of the cast produced from Nathalie's hands horrifies the narrator in the closing pages: 'And now that thing is over there, you have uncovered it, you have looked at it, and you have looked into the face of something that will be alive for all eternity, for your eternity and for mine!' (DS 79). The hand is at once what is most human and most inhuman; the two versions of the plaster casts reveal that hands transgress the presumed border between nature and technology.

The sight of these inhuman hands, the acknowledgement of their finitude which traps the narrator and Nathalie, provokes the irreversible realisation that something other that cannot be negated, that precedes any account of being, is in control. The writing hand always intervenes and suspends this world. A further passage from *The Notebooks of Malte Laurids Brigge* echoes the experience of

Blanchot's protagonists. Rilke's narrator speaks, in the second person, of exceeding your own boundaries: like a beetle that is trodden on you gush out of yourself, beyond your limits; your hands cannot contain your 'infinitely ramified being [*deines zahlloszweigigen Daseins*]'.[96] The role of hands in both texts is not to gather existence into one unified and finite bodily identity which would represent some philosophical truth, but to reach beyond existence towards the outside, death, the inhuman, and a dispersion that precedes all gathering.

A hand haunting the suppressed third section of *Death Sentence* stresses the significance of this motif to the text. At the end of the first edition of this text, Blanchot's narrator, commenting that there is 'no end for a man who wants to end alone', asks us to imagine the hand that once wrote and is still writing these pages: 'let [anyone who might read these pages] try to imagine the hand that is writing them: if he saw it, then perhaps reading would become a serious task for him' (DS 81). The brief third section containing this plea would be deleted in the 1971 French edition, along with the subtitle 'story' [*récit*], and the second edition of this text bears no acknowledgement of the fact that it is a later edition.[97] The continued non-presence of the other hand ensures that the work never achieves completion and can always be copied, edited, rewritten – evidenced by the silent modifications to this text some twenty-three years after its initial publication. Rilke's Malte similarly recognises the power of the hand to continue in his absence: 'For a while yet I can write all of this down and express it. But there will come a day when my hand will be far from me, and when I bid it write, it will write words I do not mean.'[98] Blanchot and Rilke are in many ways anticipating Derrida's understanding of iterability as already a kind of technology: 'To write is to produce a mark that will constitute a kind of machine that is in its turn productive, that my future disappearance in principle will not prevent from functioning and from yielding, and yielding itself to, reading and rewriting.'[99] Iterability is that paradoxical doubling, not reliant on the authority of any author, which means that a text or a word can be repeated; as the condition of possibility of writing it simultaneously undermines the possibility of any 'original' copy. Iterability is the logic linking repetition to alterity. There is a connection, for Blanchot as well as Derrida, between the mechanical and the inhuman.

Nowhere is this clearer in Blanchot's work than in the essay on Lautréamont. 'Analysis is a machine that is not easily stopped', writes Blanchot in a section entitled 'The Perpetual Movement of Analysis' (LS 66). Analysis is not easily stopped because any definitive interpretation of the work is shown to be illegitimate or insufficient, and so analysis is compelled to continue its 'underailable' mechanical movement, producing differing interpretations of the work with each turn of the faulty wheel. One such interpretation of *The Songs of Maldoror* is that this text recounts the struggle between God and man; this is the view of H. R. Linder who published *Lautréamont: sein Werk und sein Weltbild* in 1947. Blanchot cites Linder in his essay and continues:

> what then becomes significant is that, during this struggle, the work allows itself to be invaded incrementally by an obscure confusion of metamorphosed beings, it gives way to marshy phantoms, a pile of octopuses, toads, crabs, humming spiders, bloodsucking leeches, countless snakes. Lautréamont's poetry perhaps reveals nothing to someone who naively questions it about God and about evil, but it reveals itself through its tendency to be able to speak about God only by means of fantastic animal figures – and not to speak to us about him, but to forget to speak to us about him, by condensing around thick living substances which are at once excessively active and limply inert. (LS 68)

'God' appears in this work not as one figure but as shifting animal forms. The work is constructed around these marshy phantoms which reveal the absence of any creator beyond its limits, or iterability as its condition of possibility. Blanchot is not here replacing faith in God with the faith in progress characteristic of modernity, because analysis is a faulty machine which never delivers any definitive interpretation or truth. These strange animals are ominous, perhaps even terrifying (bloodsucking leeches, humming spiders, countless snakes), because they signal danger as the work turns on itself and confronts its own impossibility, that enigmatic outside that can never be conceptualised, and when it is, by critics such as Linder, is only ever 'a rudimentary framework, clumsily reconstructed from the outside [*maladroitement reconstruite du dehors*]' (LS 69). The work as a result is as fluid and unstable as the amorphous creatures that Linder seeks to solidify by imposing a concrete meaning on the text. Repetition, for Blanchot in 1949 as much as Derrida in 1971, and this includes critical interpretations of the literary work, is bound to alterity because it interrupts the self-identity of the same. Iterability is the condition of possibility of all language, but its effect is heightened in the literary work by the work's ability to point to itself; such outward self-reflection is the reason why these haunting beasts flood *The Songs of Maldoror*.

The closing chapter of the new version of *Thomas the Obscure* (1950), in which Thomas takes a springtime walk through the countryside, is perhaps the most sustained engagement with the 'natural' world in Blanchot's entire oeuvre, but this is not nature as we know it. This chapter demonstrates the extent to which Blanchot seeks to draw a parallel between the human and the animal as creatures inhabiting a world traversed by the outside. The animals described in this chapter are deprived of world: there are dragonflies without wings, blind toads and deaf cuckoos. Like the animals of the Rilkean Open, they live in ignorance of their mortality: the toads look to the future, the notion of perishing compels the pupa to become a butterfly, mayflies give the defiant impression that life will last forever. The backdrop is no richer: the sky is transparent and empty, trees bear no fruit, birds fly through nothingness, and an immense sea stretches out beneath Thomas's feet. On first inspection, this scene could appear gloomy, but there is something overwhelmingly positive about Thomas's walk through the countryside where he exists harmoniously with these strange creatures: 'The spring enveloped Thomas like a sparkling night and he felt himself called softly by this nature overflowing with joy' (TO 113). Even the stone, the inanimate object that Heidegger once sentenced to worldlessness, gains a world of its own in this joyous scene: 'A stone rolled, and it slipped through an infinity of metamorphoses the unity of which was that of the world in its splendour. In the midst of these tremblings, solitude burst forth' (TO 114).[100] The weird and wonderful transformations of the stone and the animals mentioned above indicate the suspension of the familiar world and an exposure to something completely alien. They affirm the impossibility of dying for both human and animal, neither of whom are able to address death as a personal or individual experience. The concept of the subject, at least any sovereign subject, is here dismantled by Blanchot.

The mood of the chapter shifts as Thomas enters the town and encounters the humans who have raised themselves to the top of the hierarchy of beings: 'They rose up as stars, ravaging the universal order with their random course. With their blind hands, they touched invisible worlds to destroy them' (TO 115). These hands are concerned with action in the world: they reach out, touch and destroy from within their finite world. The hand that writes, conversely, never touches or grasps; it responds to the demand of the outside, reaches out to the other and suspends the world, opening up the abyss above which the poem hangs and creating a non-hierarchical society which favours no people or being. Thomas leads these 'star-men' to the sea, in a literary experience comparable to his own in the first chapter, where they encounter the impossibility of dying: 'leaning over the crypt, [they] remained there in a profound inertia, waiting mysteriously for the tongue [*langue*] whose birth every prophet has felt deep in his throat to come forth from the sea and force the impossible words into their mouths' (TO 116–17). Unlike the animals compelled to transform when confronted with the impossibility of dying, these people await the arrival of a redemptive poetic language which will save them from their forlorn state. This redemption never occurs; the impossible words never fill their mouths; and they do not die an authentic death. Instead, they are called back to the sea where this narrative began, lured there by the promise of an ending which Thomas recognises will never arrive. The difference between animal and human is fragile in this closing chapter: both are condemned to interminably transform, to affirm the abyss above which they all hang when world is suspended.

The opposition between techne and technology upheld by Heidegger thus gives way in Blanchot's fiction and criticism to a very different experience of language: the mechanical. The experience of writing *Thomas the Obscure*, his first novel, prompted the evolution which sees Blanchot move away from a nationalist agenda and a Heideggerian understanding of literature as foundation and truth as revealing. For Heidegger the possibility of a new historic dwelling on earth for the German people is revealed through Hölderlin's mythic saying; Blanchot shifts from such a foundational view of literature through his engagement with Mallarmé, the poet of the abyss, and the recognition that literary language can take itself as object. Literature is founded on a ruinous impossibility – the bottomless abyss, the outside, the neuter, the *there is* – which cannot be overcome, and so writing is condemned to repeat what it cannot articulate: the experience of dying. There is no redemptive turn or event, only incessant exposure to the outside. The appearance of hands and animals in Blanchot signals the suspension of world, exposing its frailty, shaking the hierarchy holding such an isolated system in place to its very core, and creating non-hierarchical differences as opposed to a single hierarchical distinction between writer and man, man and animal. This mechanical, repetitive, impersonal, inhuman experience is therefore inseparable from the possibility of literature, which does not reside in *aletheia*, but in radical errance. Such nomadism explains why Thomas is depicted as shepherd at the end of *Thomas the Obscure*, guiding the lost beings back to the sea to start again at the beginning (or the end).

In Blanchot's writing we encounter a strange environment beyond human control or understanding into which we may reach and meet, at the limits of the human, an inhuman resistance that can only be affirmed. Unlike Rilke, and subsequently Heidegger, Blanchot privileges neither animal nor human, but indicates a region where difference is maintained but released from an anthropocentric teleology. For Blanchot, writing cannot be enclosed within anthropological or anthropocentric mastery, which it challenges in the name of the other to which it gives voice. Perhaps at first, because of the urban climates that dominate his fiction, Blanchot's thought seems irreconcilable with ecological thinking. His writing is almost bereft of references to landscapes of any sort: in his fictional work we occasionally glimpse the sea, a beach, a distant mountain range, but on the whole his characters are located within anonymous urban surroundings. On his green credentials, Timothy Clark writes: 'Ultimately, Blanchot's work may adumbrate a thinking that meets one of the most urgent demands of post-enlightenment thought, that is, resources towards a re-enchantment of the natural world that would not at the same time be a kind of mystification, evasion or deception.'[101] While Clark rightly highlights a thinking of world that destabilises our traditional view of the environment, the description of this work as a 're-enchantment of the natural world' suggests a residual romanticism. This is not a work that seeks to captivate in its presentation of the natural world but to expose the impossibility of any such 'nature', which is always already contaminated by the technical. Earlier we saw that Heidegger was accused of presiding over the naturalisation of technology, where the tool or instrument exists simply for *Dasein* who alone discloses the world. In Blanchot, hands transgress the presumed border between nature and technology, they are simultaneously what is most human and most inhuman. These hands are evidence of an unruly technology that is not subordinate to pre-technological ontological questioning, because it precedes and exceeds the human subject.

Notes

1. Hill, *Blanchot: Extreme Contemporary*, p. 79.
2. Richard Polt, *Heidegger: An Introduction* (London: UCL Press, 1999), p. 54. See Heidegger, *Being and Time,* trans. John Macquarrie and Edward Robinson (Oxford: Blackwell, [1962] 1988), pp. 91–107. For an overview of Heideggerian world, see Michael Inwood, *A Heidegger Dictionary* (Oxford: Blackwell, 1999), pp. 245–8; and Polt, *Heidegger: An Introduction*, pp. 49–55, 136–40.
3. See Bradley, *Originary Technicity*, p. 75.
4. Polt, *Heidegger: An Introduction*, pp. 137–8.
5. For a discussion of equipmentality in *Being and Time* that summarises charges of anthropocentrism, the idealisation of technology, and technophobia, see Bradley, *Originary Technicity*, pp. 68–93. Derrida argues

that Heidegger privileges the human and presupposes a thought free from technics; see, for instance, Jacques Derrida, *Of Spirit*, trans. Geoffrey Bennington and Rachel Bowlby (Chicago: University of Chicago Press, 1989). Stiegler argues that the account of the tool given by Heidegger reduces technics to a supplemental role; see Stiegler, *Technics and Time*, I, pp. 243–5, 274.
6. Keith Hoeller, 'Translator's Introduction', in Heidegger, *Elucidations of Hölderlin's Poetry*, pp. 7–19 (p. 11).
7. Heidegger, 'Hölderlin and the Essence of Poetry', in *Elucidations of Hölderlin's Poetry*, p. 59.
8. Martin Heidegger, 'The Origin of the Work of Art', in *Off the Beaten Track*, ed. and trans. Julian Young and Kenneth Haynes (Cambridge: Cambridge University Press, 2002), pp. 1–56 (p. 19).
9. Ibid., p. 23.
10. Polt, *Heidegger: An Introduction*, p. 137.
11. Heidegger, *What is Called Thinking?*, trans. J. Glenn Grey (New York: Perennial Library, [1976] 2004), p. 16. Derrida notes that an implicit but nonetheless clear hierarchy is evident in Heidegger's thinking of *Hand-werk* [the work of the hand, handiwork, handling]. The true or authentic joiner, for instance, 'accords himself with the hidden plenitude of the wood's essence, and not with the tool and the use value'. 'The meditation on the authentic *Hand-werk* also has the sense of an artisanalist protest against the hand's effacement or debasement in the industrial automation of modern mechanization.' Jacques Derrida, '*Geschlecht II*: Heidegger's Hand', trans. John P. Leavey, in *Martin Heidegger*, ed. Stephen Mulhall (London: Routledge, 2006), pp. 431–66 (pp. 440, 442). The final section of this chapter considers unruly hands in Blanchot as examples of such automaticity.
12. Heidegger, 'The Origin of the Work of Art', in *Off the Beaten Track*, p. 14.
13. Ibid., p. 24.
14. Meyer Schapiro, 'Still Life as Personal Object: A Note on Heidegger and Van Gogh', in *Theory and Philosophy of Art: Style, Artist and Society: Selected Papers* (New York: George Braziller, 1994), pp. 135–42.
15. Jacques Derrida, 'Restitutions of the Truth in Pointing [*pointure*]', in *The Truth in Painting*, trans. Geoffrey Bennington and Ian McLeod (Chicago: University of Chicago Press, 1987), pp. 255–382 (p. 333).
16. Ibid., p. 283.
17. Ibid., p. 339.
18. Ibid., p. 349.
19. Heidegger, 'The Origin of the Work of Art', in *Off the Beaten Track*, pp. 46–7.
20. Ibid., p. 46.
21. Martin Heidegger, 'Letter on "Humanism"', trans. Frank A. Capuzzi, in *Pathmarks*, ed. William McNeill (Cambridge: Cambridge University Press, 1998), pp. 239–76 (p. 239). This essay was originally a response

to a letter from Jean Beaufret written in 1946, revised and first published in 1947.
22. The last quotation is a reference to a poem by Hölderlin quoted by Heidegger: 'Since we have become a discourse [*Seit ein Gespräch wir sind*]'. See Hölderlin, 'Conciliator, you that no longer believed in . . .', in *Poems and Fragments*, pp. 422–31 (pp. 428–9).
23. Heidegger's is a controversial reading of Hölderlin. Paul de Man argues that Heidegger distorts the meaning of 'As When on a Holiday . . .', making Hölderlin say that reconciliation between the Sacred and the poetic is possible when his is in fact a 'philosophy of separation'. Paul de Man, 'Heidegger's Exegeses of Hölderlin', in *Blindness and Insight: Essays in the Rhetoric of Contemporary Criticism*, 2nd edn (London: Routledge, 1983), pp. 246–66.
24. For an overview of the significance of Hölderlin for Heidegger as 'The Poet of the Germans', see Miguel de Beistegui, *Heidegger and the Political: Dystopias* (London: Routledge, 1998), pp. 94–113.
25. Robert Savage, *Hölderlin after the Catastrophe: Heidegger, Adorno, Brecht* (Rochester, NY: Camden House, 2008), pp. 5–7.
26. Authorship of this fragment is uncertain, but it is known to originate from a conversation between Hegel, Schelling and Hölderlin and dates from 1796/7. See Philippe Lacoue-Labarthe, *Heidegger and the Politics of Poetry*, trans. Jeff Fort (Urbana, IL: University of Illinois Press, 2007), pp. 28–9.
27. Ibid., p. 14.
28. Ibid., pp. 17–37.
29. See Heidegger, 'The Question Concerning Technology', in *Basic Writings*, pp. 311–41.
30. Lacoue-Labarthe, *Heidegger*, pp. 83–92.
31. For Hölderlin's post-war reception in Germany by those on the left and the right, see Savage, *Hölderlin after the Catastrophe*. For Mallarmé's reception in France and how those on the right struggled to accept him as the 'national poet', see David Carroll, *French Literary Fascism: Nationalism, Anti-Semitism and the Ideology of Culture* (Princeton, NJ: Princeton University Press, 1998), pp. 80–1, 107–9.
32. Blanchot's close friend Levinas writes in 1947: 'If at the beginning our reflections are in large measure inspired by the philosophy of Martin Heidegger, where we find the concept of ontology and of the relationship which man sustains with Being, they are also governed by a profound need to leave the climate of that philosophy, and by the conviction that we cannot leave it for a philosophy that would be pre-Heideggerian' (*Existence and Existents*, p. 19).
33. Blanchot, *Thomas l'Obscur* (1941), p. 33 (my translation).
34. Ibid., p. 27 (my translation).
35. Blanchot's neuter, which will be discussed in the following chapter, ensures that his work resists classification and speaks from a place free of oppositions; it is neither inside nor outside philosophy. Derrida argues with reference to Blanchot that philosophy constitutes itself by

determining its own outside; it is therefore difficult to hold on to the opposition between what is inside and what is outside philosophy: 'The neuter and not neutrality, the neuter beyond dialectical contradiction and all opposition: such would be the possibility of a "narrative" [*récit*] that would no longer be simply a form, a genre or a mode of literature, and that is carried beyond the system of philosophical oppositions. The neuter cannot be governed by any of the terms involved in an opposition within philosophical language or natural language.' Jacques Derrida, 'Living On', trans. James Hulbert, in *Parages*, pp. 103–91 (p. 132) (translation modified).

36. Heidegger, '"As When on a Holiday . . ."', in *Elucidations of Hölderlin's Poetry*, pp. 67–99 (p. 83).
37. Hölderlin provides a partial answer to this question in 'Bread and Wine': 'They are, you say, like the wine-god's sacred priests, | Who roamed from land to land during the sacred night.' The response ties together religion, myth, the sacred and poetry, conforming neatly to Heidegger's description of *Sage* which will play a significant role in the essay to come. Hölderlin quoted in Heidegger, 'Why Poets?', in *Off the Beaten Track*, pp. 200–41 (p. 202).
38. Heidegger, 'Why Poets?', in *Off the Beaten Track*, p. 200.
39. Extract from Hölderlin's 'Bread and Wine' quoted in Heidegger, 'Why Poets?', in *Off the Beaten Track*, p. 201.
40. Heidegger, 'Why Poets?', in *Off the Beaten Track*, p. 203.
41. Ibid., pp. 205–6.
42. Rainer Maria Rilke, *Duino Elegies*, trans. Martyn Crucefix (London: Enitharmon, 2006), pp. 62–3.
43. For the opposition to Rilke's inversion of the human–animal hierarchy, see Martin Heidegger, 'Significance of Dis-Closure', in *Parmenides*, trans. André Schuwer and Richard Rojcewicz (Bloomington, IN: Indiana University Press, 1992), pp. 131–60.
44. Heidegger, 'Why Poets?', in *Off the Beaten Track*, p. 226.
45. Ibid., p. 214.
46. For an overview of Heidegger's criticism of Rilke in 'Why Poets?, see Véronique M. Fóti, *Heidegger and the Poets: Poiēsis, Sophia, Technē* (Atlantic Highlands, NJ: Humanities Press, 1992), pp. 30–43.
47. Heidegger, 'Why Poets?', in *Off the Beaten Track*, pp. 216–17.
48. The basis for 'The Question Concerning Technology' was therefore underway a few years before the paper was first given as a lecture on 18 November 1953. Another key text in the development of Heidegger's thinking on technology, although not published until much later, is 'Das Ge-Stell' (1949), which is a preliminary version of the later essay according to the *Gesamtausgabe*. See Martin Heidegger, 'Das Ge-Stell', in *Gesamtausgabe* (Frankfurt am Main: Vittorio Klostermann, 1975–), LXXIX: *Bremer und Freiburger Vorträge* (1994), pp. 24–45.
49. Heidegger, 'Why Poets?', in *Off the Beaten Track*, pp. 217–21.
50. Ibid., p. 233.
51. Ibid., p. 237.

52. Ibid.
53. Ibid., p. 227.
54. Heidegger, 'Das Ding', in *Gesamtausgabe*, VII: *Vorträge und Aufsätze* (2000), pp. 165–87 (p. 180) (my translation). On the difference between perishing and properly dying according to Heidegger and how to translate these terms, see Jacques Derrida, *Aporias*, trans. Thomas Dutoit (Stanford, CA: Stanford University Press, 1993), pp. 30–2.
55. Fóti, *Heidegger and the Poets*, p. 35.
56. Rainer Maria Rilke, *The Notebooks of Malte Laurids Brigge*, trans. M. D. Herter Norton (New York: W. W. Norton, 1992), p. 17.
57. Ibid., pp. 22–3.
58. Ibid., p. 27.
59. Maurice Blanchot, 'Death as Possibility' (1952), 'The *Igitur* Experience' (1953), 'Rilke and Death's Demand' (1953), in *The Space of Literature*, trans. Ann Smock (Lincoln, NE: University of Nebraska Press, 1982), pp. 85–159.
60. Blanchot was not alone in querying the translation of *eigentlich* as 'authentic': Levinas notes that the connection to *eigen* was overlooked when *eigentlich* was translated into French as 'authentique' in the 1930s. See Emmanuel Levinas, *God, Death and Time*, trans. Bettina Bergo (Stanford, CA: Stanford University Press, 2000), p. 26.
61. For these terms as they are used by Heidegger, see *Being and Time*, pp. 343–4.
62. Ibid., pp. 306–7.
63. Derrida, *Aporias*, p. 22.
64. Ibid., p. 8.
65. 'Every transgression operates from then on against or beyond transgression to the extent that it would be the fact of a (non)pace [*pas*]; transgression transgresses the (non)pace itself, steps across a pace beyond the pace, across a not beyond the not [*franchit un pas au-delà du pas*]; and what we might call the digression of distance diverts, from *Thomas the Obscure* on, every logic of the limit, of opposition, of identity, of contradiction, but as well sets free, under the apparent normality of his language (vocabulary and syntax), the contamination of noun (*pas*, pace) and adverb (*pas*, not, no).' Jacques Derrida, 'Pace Not(s)', trans. John P. Leavey, in *Parages*, pp. 11–101 (p. 36).
66. Derrida, *Aporias*, pp. 33–5.
67. Ibid., p. 44–5.
68. Ibid., pp. 76–8. See also Derrida, '*Geschlecht II*: Heidegger's Hand'.
69. Derrida, *Aporias*, p. 76 (translation modified).
70. Paul de Man similarly argues that Rilke's language puts into question what it seems to promise ('a form of existential salvation that would take place in and by means of poetry'): 'The promise contained in Rilke's poetry, which the commentators, in the eagerness of their belief, have described in all its severe complexity, is thus placed, by Rilke himself, within the dissolving perspective of the lie. Rilke can only be understood if one realizes the urgency of this promise together

with the equally urgent, and equally poetic, need of retracting it at the very instant he seems to be on the point of offering it to us.' Paul de Man, 'Tropes (Rilke)', in *Allegories of Reading: Figural Language in Rousseau, Nietzsche, Rilke, and Proust* (New Haven, CT: Yale University Press, 1979), pp. 20–56 (pp. 23, 56).

71. See Beda Allemann, *Hölderlin et Heidegger*, trans. François Fédier, 2nd edn (Paris: PUF, 1987). The text was published in German in 1954 and first appeared in French translation five years later in 1959; Blanchot's article appeared in January 1955 and is one of the last to be included in *The Space of Literature*. Paul de Man is critical of Allemann, who proposes a homogeneity between Heidegger and Hölderlin that rests on the movement of reversal that occurs in both: 'There is not to be found in Hölderlin a singular ontological reversal, but a lived philosophy of repeated reversal, that is nothing more than the notion of becoming. Since there is always reversal, there is never any effective reconciliation, not even in the early works' (*Blindness and Insight*, p. 265).

72. 'At the frontier Man forgets himself because he is wholly in the moment; and the God forgets himself because he is nothing but time; and both are unfaithful, time because in such a moment it is a categorical turning-point in which beginning and end cannot at all be made to fit; and Man because at the moment of categorical turning he must follow but in what follows he cannot at all match what was there in the beginning.' Friedrich Hölderlin, *Hölderlin's Sophocles*, trans. David Constantine (Highgreen: Bloodaxe, 2001), p. 68.

73. Blanchot will later write of madness in terms of indifference in 'Forgetting, Unreason' (1961), in *The Infinite Conversation*, trans. Susan Hanson (Minneapolis, MN: University of Minnesota Press, 1993), pp. 194–201. He equates madness in *The Madness of the Day* to being blinded by light. See Chapter 4 for a discussion of both texts.

74. Lacoue-Labarthe, breaking with the Romantic Hölderlin of Heidegger, points to the sober literalness of the poet when he writes that Adorno is correct to contradict Heidegger's 'emphatic and pious commentary' on the poem 'Remembrance', 'which lends itself so poorly to the diction proper to this poem, concerned as it is with "sobriety"'. Lacoue-Labarthe argues that Heidegger reads Hölderlin in bad faith and with very precise intentions (*Heidegger*, pp. 41–2).

75. Jacques Derrida, 'Che cos'è la poesia?', in *Points . . .: Interviews, 1974–1994*, trans. Peggy Kamuf and others (Stanford, CA: Stanford University Press, 1995), pp. 288–99 (p. 297).

76. Schlegel writes of the fragment: 'A fragment, like a work of art, has to be entirely isolated from the surrounding world and complete in itself like a hedgehog.' See 'Athenaeum Fragments', trans. P. Firchow, in *Classic and Romantic German Aesthetics*, ed. J. M. Bernstein (Cambridge: Cambridge University Press, 2003), p. 251. See Chapter 4 for a discussion of how the Blanchotian fragment differs from that described here.

77. Derrida, 'Istrice 2: Ick bünn all hier', in *Points . . .*, pp. 300–26.

78. Derrida, 'Che cos'è la poesia?', in *Points* . . ., p. 289. Blanchot writes elsewhere: 'You will not find the limits of forgetting, however far you may be able to forget' (AO 34). See Chapter 4 for a discussion of forgetting and exteriority in Blanchot.
79. Derrida, 'Che cos'è la poesia?', in *Points* . . ., p. 295.
80. Ibid., p. 299. Leslie Hill writes that, in refusing any explicit or implicit appeal to an ontology of the artwork and any reliance on the metaphysical category of the aesthetic or the supposed autonomy of poetic language or discourse, Derrida's modest yet radical purpose in this response 'was to reconsider the minimal conditions of possibility of what in the Western tradition has come to be known as literature'. If there was something distinctive about literature in general for Derrida, it derived 'from the remarkable diligence with which a literary work, radicalising a feature inherent in all inscription as such, could always point to itself, among others, as a so-called literary text'. Leslie Hill, 'On the Persistence of Hedgehogs', in *Philosophy and Poetry: Continental Perspectives*, ed. Ranjan Ghosh (New York: Columbia University Press, 2019), pp. 235–47.
81. Heidegger, 'Why Poets?', in *Off the Beaten Track*, p. 212.
82. Rilke, *Duino Elegies*, pp. 62–3.
83. Martin Heidegger, *The Fundamental Concepts of Metaphysics*, trans. William McNeill and Nicholas Walker (Bloomington, IN: Indiana University Press, 1995), p. 176. It is unlikely that Blanchot read this particular essay given the publication date of this lecture course, but we have seen that similar statements were made by Heidegger in earlier works such as *Being and Time* and 'The Origin of the Work of Art'.
84. Derrida, *Of Spirit*, p. 57.
85. See Levinas, *Existence and Existents*, pp. 57–64.
86. Rilke, *The Notebooks of Malte Laurids Brigge*, p. 59.
87. Ulrich Baer, *The Rilke Alphabet*, trans. Andrew Hamilton (New York: Fordham University Press, 2014), p. 126.
88. Michel Haar, *The Song of the Earth: Heidegger and the Grounds of the History of Being*, trans. Reginald Lily (Bloomington, IN: Indiana University Press, 1993), p. 29.
89. Emmanuel Levinas, *Time and the Other*, trans. Richard A. Cohen (Pittsburgh, PA: Duquesne University Press, 1987), pp. 39–40.
90. Ibid., pp. 44–5, 65.
91. Ibid., pp. 74–5.
92. Ibid., pp. 49–50.
93. Rilke, *The Notebooks of Malte Laurids Brigge*, pp. 84–5.
94. Heidegger, *What is Called Thinking?*, pp. 16–17.
95. Derrida, '*Geschlecht II*: Heidegger's Hand', p. 446.
96. Rilke, *The Notebooks of Malte Laurids Brigge*, p. 69.
97. Derrida considers the unacknowledged changes to *Death Sentence* in 'Living On', in *Parages*, pp. 127–9.
98. Rilke, *The Notebooks of Malte Laurids Brigge*, p. 52.
99. Derrida, 'Signature Event Context', in *Margins of Philosophy*, pp. 307–29 (p. 316).

100. I am here referring to the abridged 1950 edition of the text with the subtitle 'new version' in French; in this passage, a few words from the first version published in 1941 have been removed: 'and although [the stone] was still stonelike' (*Thomas l'Obscur* (1941), p. 318 (my translation)). This omission in the later version signals a shift towards a much more fragile world. In an earlier draft of this novel, written during the 1930s, the narrator explicitly refers to 'nature' several times in a much longer description of the trees, plants, insects and animals inhabiting a timeless imaginary universe (*Thomas le Solitaire*, pp. 258–66).
101. Timothy Clark, 'A Green Blanchot: Impossible?', in *Blanchot's Epoch*, ed. Hill and Holland, pp. 121–40 (p. 123). See also Timothy Clark, 'Maurice Blanchot and the End of Nature', *Parallax* 16, no. 2 (2010): 20–30.

Chapter 3

The Neuter and Modern Technology

The fluid animal forms in the fiction and criticism of the late 1940s, the recurring motif of hands, the impersonal and mechanical experience of language, the eternal repetition played out in his writing through the impossibility of dying, the silent reproduction of his texts: while Blanchot might not explicitly discuss modes of *technique* in his essay on Rilke, where Heidegger's condemnation of technology looms in the background, or in other essays of this period, the traits listed above and explored in the previous chapter render his view of literature indissociable from an understanding of the complex relationship between the artwork and technology. Almost twenty years earlier, in 1936, Walter Benjamin had suggested that technological innovations could create a new experience of art past, present and future. Claiming that the 'production' of a unique work is but a special case in the reproducibility of works of art – imitation should not necessarily be considered in terms of an original and its replicas – Benjamin points to a new technological structure of experience:

> It might be stated as a general formula that the technology of reproduction detaches the reproduced object from the sphere of tradition. By replicating the work many times over, it substitutes a mass existence for a unique existence. And in permitting the reproduction to reach the recipient in his or her own situation, it actualizes that which is reproduced. These two processes lead to a massive upheaval in the domain of objects handed down from the past – a shattering of tradition which is the reverse side of the present crisis and renewal of humanity.[1]

Technology offers the potential for constant innovation through infinite transformation: if the borders of the work of art are permeable and open, then technology enables this constant becoming other of the work.[2] Technology may thus be considered an art of repetition. Much of what Benjamin says in this essay resonates with the view of the work of art offered in Blanchot's writing of the 1940s and early 1950s, yet Blanchot does not discuss in detail the technological, modes of technique, techne – however the rather ambiguous French term *technique* should be translated or understood.[3]

Significant appearances of the term *technique* in essays first published in the 1950s will be traced in this chapter, before a consideration of essays from the early to mid-1960s in which there is an explicit discussion of modern technologies such as the atomic bomb, space travel and the printing press. The neuter as a quasi-concept emerges in Blanchot's writing in 1958, and it is no coincidence that this is also when a discussion of technique, the technical, or the technological takes precedence in several essays.[4] The neuter is a mode of techne (different from, but always implicated in, technologies of the modern kind) that makes art possible:

> If art is defined and constituted by its distance in relation to the world, by the *absence* of world, it is natural that everything that puts the world in doubt – what one calls in one word, which has come to be used so imprecisely, transcendence –, everything that exceeds, negates, destroys, threatens the whole of relations that are stable, comfortable, reasonably established and keen to remain [*durer*], all of these powers, be they pure or impure, proposed for the 'salvation' of man or for his destruction, insofar as they shatter the validity of the common world, work for art and open the way for it, call it forth. (F 23)

The call is the seductive form that these powers take here and in other fictional and critical works by Blanchot from this period. The origin and the destination of this call are the concern of Derrida in an analysis of the apocalyptic tone that has dominated Western philosophy since the time of Kant. Noting that apocalypse in the Hebrew Bible says discovery, disclosure, uncovering and unveiling, Derrida observes that any attempt to shed light on the apocalypse leads only to a further, brighter apocalypse which blinds; the apocalypse does not just destroy, it also unveils: 'every apocalyptic eschatology is promised in the name of light, of seeing and vision, and of a light of light, of a light brighter than all the lights it makes possible'.[5] A deconstruction of such discourse (Derrida names, among others, Heidegger on the history of metaphysics, the essence of science or technology) must fold to [*se plier à*] (in the sense of giving in to and doubling over) the finest diversity of apocalyptic ruses.[6] Any discourse on the apocalyptic risks becoming apocalyptic, but there is the suggestion that through such a folding, or doubling, it might be possible to derail the apocalyptic tone – to interrupt the unity of the destination, the self-identity of the addressee or sender – and to hear the other tone, or the tone of the other: 'If one wanted to unmask [. . .] all the interests of the apocalyptic tone today, it would be necessary to begin by respecting this differentially proliferating division [*démultiplication*] of voices and tones that perhaps takes them beyond a distinct and calculable plurality.'⁷ This chapter will listen to the various apocalyptic tones in fiction and criticism of the 1950s and early 1960s to reveal a continuity between the experience of the technological and the imaginary for Blanchot.

The technical aspect of narrative in Blanchot's account is revealed by the selection of a particular moment from Franz Kafka's *The Castle* to show how, between everyday language and the simple prose of a narrative, there is an important change in the 'nature' of language: 'The head clerk called' (WF 74).⁸ The quotation provided in Blanchot's essay is not a precise citation from *The Castle* but a paraphrase of a moment in the opening chapter; it assumes the origin of the phone call to be the head of the department, whereas in Kafka's narrative the words of this figure are reported indirectly. In the opening chapter K. arrives in the village at the foot of the Castle and arranges to spend the night at the inn; the landlord rings the Castle (K. notes with some surprise that they have a telephone) and is told by an assistant that no Land Surveyor is expected; the landlord accuses K. of deception before the telephone rings again: 'A mistake, is it? I'm sorry to hear that. The head of the department himself said so? Very queer, very queer. How am I to explain it all to the Land Surveyor?'⁹ Blanchot does not dwell on the significance of the telephone, but one must question why he selects and adapts this particular phrase. He explains that Kafka's narrative is symbolic, and not allegorical or mythical, because in revealing our ignorance of this other world of *The Castle* and of the Castle, which is to say in signifying nothing, it lays bare the void as the milieu of all imagined form; it is the reversal of the world in its totality through the imagination (WF 78–80).¹⁰ Blanchot here echoes the account of the telephone call given by the Superintendent in *The Castle*: 'You [K.] haven't once up till now come into contact with our authorities. All those contacts of yours have been illusory, but owing to your ignorance of the circumstances you take them to be real.'¹¹ The account of *The Castle* given by Blanchot is apocalyptic because it is related to everything that puts the world and human existence in its totality in question, but it also disrupts our perspective by refusing knowledge.

La technique

In a series of essays published in the 1950s on topics ranging from Ulysses' encounter with the Sirens in the *Odyssey* to André Malraux's imaginary museum and Claude Lévi-Strauss's anthropological project, Blanchot uses *la technique* to refer to a broad and ambiguous category ranging from artistic techniques to technological developments of the twentieth century. The term appears relatively infrequently in his writing in the 1940s, and never to refer to technology in the sense of tools and machines, so its appearance across these essays signals a shift in Blanchot's engagement with technology and its relationship to nature, history, culture.

The first essay in this period to mark a new, albeit still tentative, engagement with the question of modern technology is a review of André Malraux's *The Psychology of Art*. Malraux was a novelist, thinker and leading intellectual, who had been a communist and strong defender of the Spanish Republic in the 1930s but lost faith in communism during the Occupation and later became De Gaulle's Minister for Culture in 1958. In this three-volume work from the end of the 1940s, he considers how photography has made various art forms from across the world – notably sculpture but increasingly, following recent advances in colour reproduction, frescoes and stained-glass windows – easily available to a wide public. Not only has photographic reproduction multiplied the number of known masterpieces, it has also invented new styles thanks to the techniques of lighting, perspective and scaling (Malraux argues that fragments of ancient works enlarged and presented in isolation appear distinctly modern). A new domain of art is being opened up which is vaster than any previously known: each person can now assemble their ideal collection of works in what Malraux calls the imaginary museum, also translated into English as the museum without walls. 'This domain – which is growing more and more intellectualised as our stock-taking and its diffusion proceeds and methods of reproduction come nearer to fidelity – is for the first time the common heritage of all mankind.'[12]

Blanchot does not engage in any detail with photography or technologies of reproduction in his 1951 review, which is perhaps surprising given that the ability to reproduce and broadly disseminate works of art is of some importance to Malraux's imaginary museum. Where the word *technique* is used by Blanchot it is to refer to the means by which Malraux appears to set art in opposition to nature ('Does the painting of a landscape reduce that landscape, does it transform the landscape through its application of technique, and thus turn it over to the disinterestedness of art?'); when reproduction is mentioned it is done in passing as Blanchot indicates a more pressing aspect of Malraux's argument ('thanks to the advancement of our knowledge, as a result of our means of reproduction as well – but also for more profound reasons –, each and every artist has universal art at their disposal for the first time') (F 19–20, 13). Malraux argues that in the age of mechanical reproduction, art is revealed for the first time as an autonomous whole in an eternal present. But the very condition on which this eternal 'presence' is based, Blanchot responds, is the absence of the everyday world of work and action which means that nothing is realised, achieved, attained, but rather infinitely repeated. This is the time not of eternity but of eternal recurrence, 'this time-space that takes hold of us when the world moves away' (F 35). Radically outside history, not simply to be thought of as eternity or timelessness, this time of absence renders the realisation of the work impossible:

> At the heart of this absence, works are in perpetual dissolution and perpetual motion, each one being but a marker of time, a moment of the whole, a moment that would like desperately to be, all on its own, this whole in which absence alone rests without rest. And because this wish is impossible, the work itself, as it becomes more and more aware of this impossibility, always reaches further to assert itself as a poignant sign, a fascinating arrow, pointed in the direction of the impossible. (F 38)

The possibility to reproduce precedes all reproduction, and repetition is a characteristic of the work of art not because of the technological developments of the nineteenth and twentieth centuries but because the work of art is premised on a ruinous absence.[13] It seems likely that Blanchot does not discuss technology or methods of reproduction in this essay because to do so would be to suggest that there is something unique about the age of mechanical reproduction, to agree with Malraux that the imaginary museum emerges 'for the first time' in this age, when in fact, in Blanchot's account, the museum is this nowhere beyond world which is always already there, which precedes and traverses the whole of history, work, world.

When art is understood as nothing historical, when its essence is perceived as radically outside time, Malraux's understanding of the artist as master comes undone. Malraux regards artistic development and mastery as a highly technical process, involving imitation and reproduction of existing artistic styles over a period, by which the artist seeks the power to transform art through their own style or technique. Blanchot challenges the view that the artist becomes master of their craft through the imitation of previous forms, because the repetition identified by Malraux is not the consequence of artistic endeavour or mastery but of the abyssal non-foundation of art.

In Blanchot's account, the child who is ignorant of the world and the madman who has almost lost the world are 'naturally' (Blanchot's own scare quotes) artists (F 33); and the imaginary museum reveals the essence of artistic creation through the painter who transforms disordered colours on the palette into a great work, but also through the fortuitous sketch drawn by the hand of an unintentional artist (F 39). Blanchot refuses the association of art with mastery and conquest; he does this by highlighting a withdrawal from world in the artistic experience:

> The absence of time denoted by art only alludes to our ability [*pouvoir*] to put an end to the world, to stand before or after the world – that space of practical life but also of truth as it is expressed, of culture and meaning – a power that is perhaps a sovereignty but that also asserts itself in all situations in which man renounces, and accepts that he will not recover, his self-control. This is why art is tied to everything that puts man in danger, to everything that places him violently outside the world, outside the security and intelligence of the world to which the future alone belongs. (F 33)

The power of man to end the world is affirmed in those moments when man is powerless; it is affirmed in the imaginary museum when man has conquered the world through art but equally when the individual artist now relinquishes all power to this impersonal museum standing outside of the relationship between conquest and the work.

It might seem unusual that a figure such as Malraux, the first and only Minister for Culture during De Gaulle's presidency, should appear in a book entitled *Friendship* published years after Blanchot's transition from right-wing nationalist to left-wing radical. The political paths of Blanchot and Malraux crossed and diverged as they headed in different directions following the war: Malraux moved from his pre-war pro-communist stance towards a nationalism that would see him become a key figure in De Gaulle's government, as Blanchot moved in the opposite direction, the latter's shift being most clearly signalled in a 1946 article on Malraux's Spanish Civil War novel *Days of Hope* (1937), in which he praises the Republican Popular Front forces he had once criticised.[14] While there are radical differences between the two writers, what they share and what explains the presence of Malraux's name here and at the end of *The Instant of My Death* is an experience of the imminence but impossibility of death: both narrowly escaped execution during the war, as recounted by Blanchot in the aforementioned text and by Malraux in *Anti-Memoirs*.[15]

What emerges from this 'staged execution' for Malraux is the notion of the imaginary museum (around this time, just as Blanchot had a manuscript confiscated in 1944, Malraux lost the beginnings of what would later become *The Voices of Silence*), that domain of artistic immortality in which the work overcomes death and time. The end of art for Malraux is myth and its purpose is the salvation of humankind, civilisation and history. Malraux's imaginary museum, tied up as it is with his near-death experience, appeals in some respects to Blanchot, who nonetheless diverges from the view that death and time can ever be overcome: the impossibility of dying means that the imaginary museum can never be present or subject to any teleology.[16] Blanchot and Malraux therefore share an encounter with death, but head in different directions as a result, both literarily and politically.

Leslie Hill explores how the divergence between these two writers is used by Godard at the end of *Histoire(s) du cinéma* – who quotes, with some alterations, from 'The Museum, Art, and Time' – to explore the relationship between cinema and death: 'Like death, [the image] makes clear; but like death it also brings the human world to a realisation of its endless, unmasterable impotence.'[17] The darkness that precedes the image renders the completion of the imaginary museum and the history of cinema impossible because it affirms the excess of textuality, image or sound that makes the repetition or reproduction of artworks, and so these two projects, possible in the first place. The impersonal force felt through Malraux's imaginary museum is therefore impossible death, enabling reproduction but denying any finality: 'in [the image] this dark powerlessness, with no master, advances; it is the powerlessness of death as a beginning-again' (F 40).

Two years later in 'The Disappearance of Literature' (1953), Blanchot summarises the view of art in the technological world in the following terms: 'Apparently, art is nothing if it is not sovereign' (BC 195–6). Blanchot notes that it was around 1850 that the work of art was seen to have assumed this autonomy. Perhaps this date marks the beginning of the technological era – it roughly coincides with Baudelaire's essay 'Modernity' in *The Painter of Modern Life* (1863), which was so important for Benjamin, and it is the moment too when photography is invented – but Blanchot does not say as much. He notes that there were writers and artists who fought against the perceived autonomy of the artwork in an attempt to ensure their own status as creators. Mallarmé and Cézanne, on the other hand, understood that art precedes history and did not react to historical tasks and goals in an attempt to save art from some technological onslaught: 'art does not negate the modern world, or the technological world [*le monde de la technique*], or the effort toward liberation and transformation that relies on this technology [*technique*], but it expresses and perhaps achieves connections that *precede* all objective and technological accomplishment [*tout accomplissement objectif et technique*]' (BC 197). The result is not the complete disappearance of the artist in exchange for a sovereign art: the artwork stands radically outside history but is not aesthetically autonomous because, rather than giving itself its own rule, it challenges the rule. Art – literature – becomes a question and the artist is the powerless conqueror whose task it is to respond to the impossible.

The relationship between Ulysses and the Sirens in the essay selected to open *The Book to Come*, 'Encountering the Imaginary' (1954), provides an oblique insight into the power relationship between the technical and the work of art for Blanchot. Of Homer's narration of this encounter – in which Ulysses orders his men to tie him to the ship's mast and not to release him under any circumstance so that he may hear the Sirens without succumbing to their call – Blanchot writes: 'After the Sirens had been defeated by the technical power [*pouvoir*] that always tries to play safely with unreal (inspired) powers [*puissances*], Ulysses was still not in the clear' (BC 5). Ulysses and his tools might foretell the dominion of modern technology,[18] but worldly technical power does not overcome the otherworldly call in this encounter, as the struggle endures beyond the Sirens' disappearance. The Sirens' call reaches beyond the limits of the *Odyssey* as they continue to call to Ulysses and others: Blanchot states that the novel is born from this struggle between the story [*récit*] and the encounter with the Sirens (BC 5).

The novel mediates what was once immediate, although this is itself misleading because the encounter with the Sirens never takes place in the here and now.[19] The story is the event that never arrives because always arriving, simultaneously marking and crossing a limit. A similar failed experience is recounted in Herman Melville's *Moby-Dick* – Blanchot writes that both encounters represent a metaphysical struggle – but this is a different sort of failure, one that does not deny the impossibility of the limit. Ahab was described by Blanchot in 1941 as bearing witness to an invisible order (myth), but by 1954 what matters is the endless confrontation between the real and the imaginary: the story is possible only as an impossible effort. Ulysses coldly and calculatedly seeks what remains possible when faced with this other force by giving the impression that he has restricted his power: 'He will be everything, if he maintains a limit and this gap between the real and the imaginary, which is precisely what the Song of the Sirens invites him to cross.' Stamping his technical authority on the narrative and keeping his distance from this 'other force', Ulysses makes the world firmer, surer, but poorer; he is comparable to those nineteenth-century writers and artists discussed in 'The Disappearance of Literature' who struggled against the perceived autonomy of the artwork to ensure their own status as creator. Ahab, in contrast, the captain of the ship dragged into the depths by the lure of the whale at the end of *Moby-Dick*, is lost in the image of this encounter: 'Ahab does not return and, for Melville himself, the world endlessly threatens to sink into this worldless space toward which he is drawn by the fascination of one single image' (BC 8). *Moby-Dick*, once described by Blanchot in 1941 in mythical terms as the written equivalent of the universe, a description which now evokes Malraux's imaginary museum, is seen thirteen years later as a space of confrontation and merger between the real and the imaginary.[20] The contestation of this limit is felt by Melville, for whom the world ceaselessly threatens to sink into this worldless space. The difference between these two experiences may be attributed to the role of the technical: 'But it is clear that if the novel lacks this role today, it is because technology has transformed the time of men and their ways of being diverted from it' (BC 6).

It is thanks to his technical capabilities that Ulysses is deprived of the rich possibilities of Melville's *Moby-Dick* and Homer remains entrenched in the world where the artist is master. Is Blanchot setting art and technology in opposition to one another in this essay? The two descriptions of the Sirens' song indicate that art and technology are mutually implicated:

> What was the nature of the Sirens' song? Where did its fault lie? Why did this fault make it so powerful? Some have always answered: It was an inhuman song – a natural noise no doubt (are there any other kinds?), but on the fringes of nature, foreign in every possible way to man, very low, and introducing him to the thrill of the descent which he does not experience in everyday life. But, say others, the enchantment was stranger than that: it did nothing but reproduce the regular song of men, and because the Sirens, who were only beasts, and very beautiful because of the reflection of feminine beauty, could sing as men sing, they made the song so unusual that whoever heard it began to suspect the inhumanity of all human song. (BC 3)

The difference between these two interpretations is fragile. The point is that the song is both natural and technical, a reproduction of an always forgotten original, and simultaneously what is most human and most inhuman. Blanchot is perhaps reflecting on Heidegger's famous claim that the essence of technology is nothing technological, made at the beginning of 'The Question Concerning Technology' (1953) and repeated in *What is Called Thinking?* (1954), where Heidegger adds that nor is this essence anything human:

> For the essence of technology is not anything human. The essence of technology is above all not anything technological. The essence of technology lies in what from the beginning and before all else gives food for thought. It might then be advisable, at least for the time being, to talk and write less about technology, and give more thought to where its essence lies, so that we might find a way to it. The essence of technology pervades our existence [*unser Dasein*] in a way which we have barely noticed so far. This is why in the preceding lecture, precisely at a juncture which almost demanded a reference to the technological world, we kept silent about technology.[21]

Blanchot, also writing in 1954, may be suggesting something similar: the essence of technology, which enables the repetition or the reproduction of the artwork and the retelling of this story, is located in the abyss from which the call of the Sirens and the whale emanates. To listen carefully to this call is to hear a tone that differs from the usual apocalyptic foretelling of technology. The technical as writing, the technical thought in its relation to writing, is no longer monotonal; in it we hear a shifting multiplicity.

There is a shift to a more explicit discussion of technology two years later in a review of Claude Lévi-Strauss's self-consciously literary and autobiographical text *Tristes tropiques*, which considers the para-philosophical status of anthropology and ethnography as a key 'human science'. It is the status of Lévi-Strauss's writing as a self-reflexive questioning of human knowledge, straddling the scientific and the non-scientific, that appeals to Blanchot in 'Man at Point Zero' (1956), where he argues that the ethnographer's project is more interesting than the scientific technicity of Einstein and Oppenheimer (F 73–5).

The precarious status of technology is evident throughout *Tristes tropiques*, as Lévi-Strauss recognises that the tools and technological advancements that have enabled ethnographers to access their objects of study have simultaneously wiped out these people. This is a condition he sees repeated throughout civilisation: '[the human] appears as a machine, perhaps more effective than any other, working towards the disintegration of the original order of things and hurrying on powerfully organized matter towards ever greater inertia, an inertia which one day will be final'.[22] The paradoxical position of the ethnographer and the uncertain status of technology is stressed early in Blanchot's discussion as he notes that the successes of the modern world carry the ethnographer to the edge of the earth, where the object of study is promptly transformed or destroyed: 'The ethnographer is the uneasy companion of imperialism, which with one hand gives and with the other takes his science and the object of his science' (F 75). The hands of the ethnographer are comparable to the hands of the writer: one hand accepts the gift of imperialism and reaches worldly limitations thanks to technological prowess – like those human hands at the end of *Thomas the Obscure*, it destroys invisible worlds. The other hand can never grasp the object of study – like the hand hanging over the suppressed third section of *Death Sentence*, unable to either hold or put down the pen, it is assigned an impossible task.[23] The ethnography of Lévi-Strauss undoubtedly bears literary traits for Blanchot as his work leads to the imaginary in its search for the impossible origin; but implied here is also a technicity which Blanchot recognises and cautiously praises, noting that Lévi-Strauss's ambition to return to the source of the human is not merely a nostalgia for a more natural and simple humanity that would avoid 'the denaturation that technological power [*la puissance technique*] tirelessly pursues' (F 80).

There is a universal human logic found everywhere according to Lévi-Strauss, what might be thought of as a technology of sorts running through all societies, a point clearly argued in the conclusion quoted above and evidenced specifically in his discussion of the art of so-called 'primitive' societies. The face-paintings of the Caduveo, for instance, ensure the transition from nature to culture or from beast to civilised human, and they have a sociological function because variations in style and pattern express different social statuses.[24] These face-paintings have a meaning and function as a form of writing. When Blanchot comments that a nostalgic view of these peoples is to some extent avoided in *Tristes tropiques*, it is because Lévi-Strauss recognises that technology is not something belated or reserved for the modern world but is already there in 'primitive' societies as a form of writing. Blanchot concludes on this point:

> The truth of the technological world therefore lies to a certain extent in its poverty, and its great – intellectual – virtue is not to enrich us but to denude us. A barbarous world, without respect, without humanity. It cruelly empties us of everything we love and love to be, drives us from the happiness of our shelters, from the pretence of our truths, destroys that to which we belong and sometimes destroys itself. A fearsome test. But this contestation, precisely because it leaves us destitute of everything except power [*puissance*], perhaps

also gives us the chance that accompanies any rupture: when one is forced to abandon oneself [*renoncer à soi*], one must either perish or begin, perish in order to begin again. This is perhaps the meaning of the task represented by the myth of the man without myth: the hope, anguish and illusion of man at point zero. (F 82)

When led beyond our shelter and exposed to an inhuman and barbaric new place by technology, it becomes evident that the human subject is universally constituted by a different mode of technique ('it leaves us destitute of everything except power'), expressed here as an aimless and impersonal power which succeeds only in reproduction: writing. The achievement of *Tristes tropiques* is the laying bare of techne as art.

The engagement with the question of technology therefore becomes more explicit over the course of the 1950s in Blanchot's critical work, and a second essay on Malraux, 'Museum Sickness' (1957), now stresses that the imaginary museum continues to be enriched by improvements in technologies of reproduction (F 41). The names of other writers, critics, thinkers figure prominently in the opening pages of this essay: the famous German literary scholar Ernst Robert Curtius, the art historian Georges Duthuit, Plato, Heidegger and Socrates. Each of these names represents a desire to link writing or art to presence, either in the 'eternal present' of Malraux, in the wholly accessible and reproducible literature of Curtius, in the reality of a past conceived by Duthuit, or as the spoken language with its living and breathing source extolled by Plato, Socrates and Heidegger.[25] Blanchot builds a rebuttal to all of these views over the course of this essay through an understanding of art as techne. 'It is no accident that what poses as "pure presence" is immediately frozen and stabilized in a lifeless permanence and in the rotting eternity of a solemn and indifferent void.' This sentence, quoted above as it appeared in *Friendship* in 1971, originally read in 1957: 'It is no accident that what is pure presence, severe light, is immediately frozen [. . .]' The words 'pure presence' are withdrawn as Blanchot suggests that art was never present in the first place in the amended version of the essay. There are two further notable changes made to the later version of the essay: 'Are the works of the Museum deprived of world? Are they left to the insecurity of a pure absence without certainty?' had previously read 'Are they left to the insecurity of a pure presence?'; and the description of a world 'far from the questioning of art' (F 49) had previously read 'far from the truth of art'.[26] Presence becomes absence and the status of art is obscured as truth becomes questioning. At work here is the neuter as a neutralising and displacing technique; while more pronounced in 1971, its effect is still palpable in the original version of the essay, as Blanchot recognises that photography and other technologies of reproduction have indeed enriched the imaginary museum, but only in a way that serves to create an ungraspable, unachievable, uncontrollable excess that is never present – the possibility of reproduction precedes all world and the machine functions 'as if outside duration' (F 43).

The precarious status of technology as both destructive and enabling power is central to Blanchot's 1957 critique of the imaginary museum: 'Technology gives us art, just as it gives us the earth; it gives us possession of everything and access to everything through a power of domination that scares some and motivates others but can be stopped by no one' (F 41). What technology gives with one hand it withdraws with the other: we do not experience works in the time or setting in which they were produced or for which they were intended, and the imaginary museum therefore achieves only the illusion of presence or the experience of the 'non-present presence' of art. For the first time, Blanchot writes, all works become available to us, and they are no longer sheltered within our world, but without shelter and as if without world (F 48). A subtle shift has occurred in Blanchot's thinking since he first wrote about the imaginary museum in 1951: the impact of technology is greater by 1957 and closely related to the work of art. Technology as a power belonging to the human becomes disobedient techne beyond our control, which allows the possibility of art, literature, language. Blanchot, unusually, refers to one of his earlier essays in a footnote: 'The Beast of Lascaux' (1953).

This essay is a pre-Derridean attempt, against Plato, to link the disobedience of writing to the possibility of the artwork.[27] 'The impersonal knowledge of the book', Blanchot writes, '[. . .] is bound to the development of technology in all its forms, and it treats speech, and writing, as technology' (BL 9). This impersonal knowledge linking all technologies is impossible death: that force enabling reproduction but denying any finality. All technologies reveal an end void of significance, but writing harnesses this side of power beyond human control:

> Any word that begins, though it be the gentlest and most secret of movements, because it is infinitely ahead of us, is what moves and demands of us the most: just like the sweetest of daybreaks in which all the violence of an inaugural light makes itself apparent, or like the oracular word that dictates nothing, obliges nothing, that does not speak, but turns the silence into a finger pointing imperiously in the direction of the unknown. (BL 14)

Blanchot glosses Heraclitus in this extract to argue that this language does not reveal and conceal, it is not bound to the visible and the invisible, and therefore is not subject to Heideggerian *aletheia*. This language does not dictate future events, nor does it rely on any truth, pre-existent language, or indeed anything which already is: 'It *points* toward the future, because it does not yet speak [. . .] it is like a future language which is always ahead of itself, having its meaning and legitimacy only before it, which is to say that it is fundamentally without justification' (BL 12). Suggested here is the possibility that by listening to the silence that accompanies the violence of the first speech we may hear a radical otherness announced in this forever-deferred beginning. The next section of this chapter will consider what writing as techne might have to say to technology of the modern kind.

Writing as techne and Modern Technology

The 1950s was a tumultuous decade for France: the Cold War was building beyond its borders, driving France to make the decision to arm itself with nuclear weapons in 1954, with the first French tests taking place in 1961; and the Algerian War was also intensifying, leading to the collapse of the Fourth Republic in 1958 and De Gaulle's controversial return to power. Blanchot did not distance himself from such events: in 1958 he moved to Paris from Èze, a small hilltop village overlooking the Mediterranean where he had spent most of the last nine years, and resumed an active interest in politics as a member of the radical non-communist left. He openly contested De Gaulle's government in publications such as *Le 14 Juillet* and fiercely opposed the Algerian War, not least as one of the principal authors and signatories of what became known as the 'The Manifesto of the 121'.[28] Beyond such political upheaval, the 1950s also saw great social change in France with the growth of mass culture, as documented by Roland Barthes in a series of short articles later collected in *Mythologies*. The impact of technology on the work of art had already been scrutinised by Walter Benjamin in 'The Work of Art in the Age of Mechanical Reproduction' (1936); but the publication of Barthes' *Mythologies* (1957) and the appearance and subsequent translation into French of Heidegger's 'The Question Concerning Technology' (1958), *What is Called Thinking?* (1959) and *Off the Beaten Track* (1962), containing 'The Origin of the Work of Art' and 'Why Poets?', ensured that technological developments remained a concern of philosophical and literary circles of the period.

The launch of the Livre de poche collection in 1953 by the Librairie Générale Française, which made popular novels available at a low cost by reproducing them in small paperback format, was one of the significant social changes in France in this period made possible by technological developments. The subsequent success of this format, which resulted in similar collections being launched by Gallimard and Plon and the move to the publication of more intellectual material, sparked a lively debate in the early 1960s which centred on the contribution of the art historian Hubert Damisch, who argued that rather than offering cultural democratisation, the format transformed the book into an everyday consumer commodity and neutralised its revolutionary potential.[29] The inclusion in his original article of an epigraph from Heidegger's 'The Question Concerning Technology' left Damisch open to the accusation that he was simply taking a traditional stance against the dangers of technology.[30] In the midst of the wide-ranging debate that ensued, and citing Damisch's article in his own essay, Blanchot explicitly welcomed the new paperback format ('Of course, we must celebrate such a success. How could we not want something that expands the distribution of major (and minor) works?'), while recognising that the potential for the wider diffusion of works and the cultural change that this implied was not in fact realised: those who bought paperbacks were often the relatively well-off middle classes, not all texts were available in paperback form, and the driving motivation for the publishing industry was profit (F 68–70). According to Blanchot, the ideology of progress seemingly represented by the affordable paperback and advancing technology masks a capitalist ideology which seeks the appeasement of the people; the mass production and diffusion of the scandalous works of Trotsky and Sade helps to normalise and institutionalise what was revolutionary about their writing while giving the general public the false impression that access to culture is universal and unlimited.

> There is nothing to say against technology. But what is striking is how its use masks the ideology that provides the paperback with its basic meaning, its morality: technology regulates all problems, the problem of culture and its diffusion, so as with everything else there is no need for political upheaval and even less need for changes in social structures. It is enough to reproduce works – make them look appealing at what seems like an affordable price – for them to have free rein (albeit within the well-defined limits of the capitalist market) and for everyone to be able to assimilate them, to appropriate whatever it is that makes them unique. (F 70)

Modern technology is not going to solve any problems; it is not the enabler of progress but the servant of capitalist ideology. In stark contrast, literature is contestatory power: 'contestation of the established power, contestation of what is (and of the fact of being), contestation of language and of the forms of literary language, finally contestation of itself as power' (F 67). While cultural forces might attempt to pacify turbulent works by incorporating them into the whole, transforming them into mere entertaining morsels through the printing press and the television, a structure of exclusion always persists, and it is the changeable outside ensured by this structure that we experience through literature.

The contrast between technology and literature that emerges in this essay is not, however, as unambiguous as it might first appear. Blanchot does not condemn the paperback or indeed the technology which has driven this so-called revolution ('There is nothing to say against technology'). His argument is that rather than limiting the power behind cultural assimilation, we should push it to the extreme, to the point of explosion where the system cannot maintain the limits it has imposed (F 68). There is a convergence of technology at the very limits of its power and literature as contestation, although the relation is not wholly elucidated in this essay. Writing laid bare as techne reveals that side of technology which is not about capitalist progress; to this other side of technology beyond human control Blanchot gives the name the neuter. The remainder of this chapter will explore how the relationship between these two modes of technique, stemming from the same abyssal source, is played out in Blanchot's writing.

The global tremors which had prompted Blanchot's return to Paris and politics at the end of the 1950s coincided with the emergence of the neuter as a noun in his writing in 1958 and a sustained rejection of the idea of the artwork as an autonomous whole entirely subject to aesthetic rules and norms. In the first of two essays responding to the development of nuclear weapons written in 1960 – when the United States and the Soviet Union were developing the first intercontinental missiles and France was testing its first weapons in Reggane during the Algerian War of Independence – Blanchot complains that we think the possibility of global devastation in an outdated language, in which the word war ('together with established mythical imagery, the pursuit of prestige, and the traditions and habits associated with borders and heroic politics') continues to be used while traditional notions of war and peace founder (IC 270). The question posed by nuclear weapons is not isolated from the question of language.

Blanchot demonstrates how cultural forces attempt to rein in the significance of modern technology: while some argue that the power of the bomb can be used for peaceful purposes such as nuclear energy, many scientists see this as a mere alibi and are quick to highlight the infinite possibilities awarded to the human through atomic energy and the impending catastrophe that this implies.

> The bomb gives visible notice of the invisible threat that all modern technology poses to man's way of life. The American chemist Stanley, a Nobel Prize winner (as you can well imagine), made this statement: 'The moment draws near when life will no longer be in God's hand but in the hand of the chemist who will modify, build, or destroy every living substance at will.' We read such statements every day, statements made by responsible men, and we read them alongside other items in the newspapers with negligence or with amusement, and without seeing that through the power of modern technology the way is being paved for an attack that makes the explosion of the bombs pale in comparison. (IC 270)

According to Blanchot, Wendell Stanley's statement may once have been terrifying, but today this warning is downplayed; regularly disseminated far and wide by the press, the threat posed by nuclear energy is reduced to a mere diversion. The idea expressed by Stanley that nuclear power represents infinite human possibility, whether exploited for peaceful or belligerent purposes, is nonetheless a mystification. The significance of the bomb for Blanchot lies in the fact that the human is not master of his or her destiny: 'Be there God or the atom, the point is precisely that everything does not depend on man' (IC 270).

Although not foreseeing global catastrophe, Blanchot is hardly optimistic about the unlimited technological possibilities of the age. One interlocutor persistently rejects the romantic faith in technology advocated by writers such as Pierre Teilhard de Chardin and Ernst Jünger. The latter, in *An der Zeitmauer* (1959), argues that in a world threatened by atomic destruction, humanity is able to think its relation to the earth differently and move, via technological means, beyond nihilism into a new age.[31] 'I have heard it said that we are in the process of crossing the time barrier' (IC 266), remarks Blanchot's unconvinced interlocutor. One can perhaps detect the odour of atomic explosion, sense the imminence of this possibility, but one can never be certain of the end of history:

> I wonder whether, on the contrary, your authors do not feel a sort of loathing for the future since they refuse to entertain the incompletion that it necessarily contains. One could say they do everything to turn away from the simple truth of our death which is always premature

and before term. Hence their haste to affirm: the epoch is complete, a time has ended. (IC 268)

By regarding technology as the means by which the human exerts total control over the earth, writers such as Jünger and Teilhard de Chardin overlook the excessive inhuman possibilities of the atomic bomb and seek to make the future concrete and certain. They turn away from the banality of a death that will never be authentic. Responding to the assertion that the decline of the mythic hero and the rise of the cult of the unknown soldier signal the beginning of a new age, the sceptical interlocutor states: 'You prefer the myth of the end of time, this fear of a global catastrophe which day and night unnerves men's imaginations' (IC 269). Fear of a mystified end is more comforting than facing up to the banal uncertainty of the future for Jünger and Teilhard de Chardin. Blanchot, in contrast, is undoubtedly recalling Nietzsche's admission of faith in an unknowable future which he would cite nine years later in the fragmentary additions to the end of this essay when published in *The Infinite Conversation* (1969): 'My thoughts [. . .] should show me where I stand, but they should not betray to me *where I am going*. I love ignorance of the future and do not want to perish of impatience and premature tasting of things promised.'[32]

Nietzsche is an important reference for Blanchot when thinking the impact of technology. In the first of two essays on Nietzsche first published in 1958, 'Nietzsche, Today', having outlined the falsification of his work by his sister and her husband and the subsequent appropriation of his thought for antisemitic and fascist purposes by the Nazi party, Blanchot stresses the paradoxical and decentred nature of Nietzsche's thought, which contests all certainties, and asks that any interpretation of Nietzsche remain faithful to the following principles:

> Remain unsatisfied until one has found that which contradicts what one has asserted about him. Maintain amid the contradictions the demand of the whole that is constantly present, though constantly dissolved by these contradictions. Never see this whole – the non-unitary whole – as a system, but as a question, and as the passionate pursuit of truth which is bound to the criticism of everything learned in this pursuit. (IC 140–1)

Blanchot notes that Karl Jaspers was the first to alert us to this way of reading Nietzsche, but even Jaspers risks betraying Nietzsche by using his work, which is the exception to any rule and contains something non-transferable, to develop an existential philosophy

(IC 140–1). The disjointed totality that emerges through the reading proposed by Blanchot challenges the limits of systematic thought; the volatility of the contested whole echoes the impact of the printing press, pushing culture to the point of explosion. The aside 'the non-unitary whole' is a later addition to the essay for its publication in *The Infinite Conversation*. This and other small edits made to the essay in 1969 highlight that Blanchot was keen to further stress the impossibility of any such totality, which will always be challenged by the work of the neuter.[33]

The essay ends with Blanchot reflecting on Heidegger's claim that what was once a cry in Nietzsche threatens to become chatter [*bavardage*]. Blanchot writes of this cry: 'we did not hear it, we heard it too well; nihilism became the commonplace of thought and literature' (IC 143). At stake is the difference between what we might call philosophical and literary nihilism. Blanchot writes that Heidegger recognises the exceptional nature of Nietzsche's work but only insofar as he declares it to be the final, perhaps unending, phase of the metaphysical tradition, consequently overlooking what is marginal, incommunicable and fragmentary in his writing (IC 141). Nihilism as contested totality offers a way out of this impasse if we listen with greater care to this chatter.

Nihilism is closely associated with modern technology and originates in metaphysical representation according to Heidegger, who argues that Nietzsche attempts to move beyond nihilism (the process of the devaluation of the highest values) but achieves only a more complete nihilism (the revaluation of all values). Heidegger considers how to think other than metaphysical representation: 'If we hear in the name nihilism that other note [*Ton*], in which there sounds the essence of what it names, then we also hear differently into the language of the metaphysical thinking.'[34] This 'other note' signals that Being is nothing: 'Provided that every "is" is the responsibility of Being, then the essence of nihilism consists in the fact that there is nothing going on with Being itself.'[35] By emphasising that 'nothing is going on with Being', Heidegger gestures to a dispensation of Being beyond the positing of values which allows the possibility of thinking more originally (beyond reason or logic).

There is perhaps a clearer sense from Heidegger of how to respond to nihilism in his later exchange with Ernst Jünger, whose contribution to the Festschrift celebrating Heidegger's sixtieth birthday was an essay entitled 'Über die Linie' (1949), in which Jünger asks whether we live in the age of fulfilled nihilism and, if so, whether such nihilism can be overcome. In his response Heidegger, while noting that Jünger's description of the technical era in *Der Arbeiter* influenced

'The Question Concerning Technology', insists on the prior question about the essence of nihilism and focuses on the line itself as opposed to what lies beyond: 'In the title of your essay Über die Linie means as much as: across, trans, μετά. By contrast, the following remarks understand the über only in the sense of *de*, περί. They deal "with" the line itself, with the zone of self-consummating nihilism.'[36] Heidegger argues that a thinking of the essence of nihilism leads to a thinking of Being as the unthought ground of metaphysics. Representational language is the barrier to crossing the line and overcoming nihilism, and so, in an attempt to retrieve a more original sense of Being unsullied by metaphysics, Heidegger crosses out the word in his essay: 'A thoughtful forward glance into the realm of "Being" can only be written in the following way: ~~Being~~.'[37]

The dialogue between Heidegger and Jünger informs Blanchot's second essay on Nietzsche from 1958, 'Crossing the Line'. Here Blanchot remarks that Heidegger's treatment of the line is more rigorous because sensitive to the movement of nihilism which renders any such line indecipherable; like the end of history, there is an unknowable or impossible element to nihilistic achievement (IC 150). While Heidegger is praised for questioning the possibility of this line, the subsequent deferral of a thinking that goes beyond metaphysical representation is criticised. Heidegger's waiting game is irresponsible, even dangerous, according to Blanchot, for whom the writer and critic break with values via the endless detours of abyssal self-reflexive language.

A few months later Blanchot penned his response to the journal *Arguments* on the purpose of criticism, in which he argues that by liberating thought and history from value, criticism prepares the way for a different and unforeseeable affirmation, thus making it 'one of the most difficult but important tasks of our time' (LS 6). Why, Blanchot asks, can the work not speak for itself? Why between the reader and the work, between history and the work, is this strange hybrid figure of the critic imposed? Criticism, having no reality of its own, disappears in the affirmation of what is otherwise silent in the work; the accomplishment of criticism is signalled by its disappearance as the mediated becomes the immediate – here Blanchot seems close to Heidegger who is referenced in the early pages of his response[38] – but any such relation to the immediate is impossible and both criticism and literature are perpetually turned outwards:

> this sort of sudden distance, in which the completed work is reflected and which the critic is called upon to gauge, is only the last metamorphosis of the opening which is the work in its genesis, what one might call its essential non-coincidence with itself, everything that continu-

ously makes it possible-impossible. All that criticism does, then, is represent and follow outside what, from within, as torn affirmation, infinite insecurity [*inquiétude*], conflict (and in all other forms), does not cease to be present as a living reserve of emptiness, of space, of error, or, better yet, as the power that belongs to literature to make itself while always maintaining itself in lack [*en défaut*]. (LS 4–5)

The domain of literature cannot be stabilised because there is no outside point from which to delimit the parameters of the work. The lack that allows the work and criticism to proliferate offers the possibility of moving beyond metaphysical representation towards this torn affirmation, torn because erring between the yes and the no, between the inside and the outside, contesting all limits, including those of literature. Blanchot goes further than Heidegger when he thinks this other affirmation freed from historical constraints.

A critique of such a teleological perspective is the focus of 'L'Attente' [Waiting], which was Blanchot's contribution to the Festschrift in celebration of Heidegger's seventieth birthday in 1959, published only a few months after those two essays on nihilism. 'As soon as one waited for something, one waited a little less [*Dès qu'on attendait quelque chose, on attendait un peu moins*].'[39] This contribution – which can be categorised neither as fiction nor criticism but assumes an ambiguous status between the two, and which is one of the first examples of Blanchot adopting the fragmentary idiom that would dominate his later works – stresses that the move beyond value, the liberation of thought from history, requires an indirect or oblique attention to the unknowable that allows it to remain unknown. The male figure and the female figure of 'L'Attente' repeatedly comment on or adopt such indirectness. The female figure, for instance, is disturbed by the feeling of a mistake or misunderstanding that she cannot pinpoint; she loses the centre of the room and the discussion as everything turns before her eyes; the male character feels linked to her by failure and watches her surreptitiously.[40]

Such oblique attention also characterises the discussion of nihilism in 1958 in 'Crossing the Line'. Nihilism is a trap if confronted because this then becomes merely an attempt to overcome nihilism, which is in itself nihilistic. Eternal Return, on the other hand, is the nihilistic thought *par excellence*: 'the thought by which nihilism surpasses itself absolutely by making itself definitively unsurpassable' (IC 148). Eternal return offers that radical shift in perspective that does not rely on value:

> But the reversal of time is beyond the realm of possibility, and this impossibility here takes on the highest meaning: it signifies the failure

of the overman as will to power [*puissance*]. The overman will never be capable of the extreme. Eternal return is not of the order of power [*pouvoir*]. The experience of eternal return leads to a reversal of all perspectives. The will that wills nothingness becomes the will willing eternity, in which eternity, without will and without aim, returns to itself. Personal and subjective all-powerfulness is transformed into the impersonal necessity of 'being'. Transvaluation does not give us a new scale of values based on the negation of every absolute value, it brings us to an order to which the notion of value ceases to apply. (IC 149)[41]

Eternal Return, for Nietzsche, is an attempt to overcome the transient nature of time. In Heidegger's analysis, Eternal Return is an attempt to abolish time. This is a fairly brutal refutation by Blanchot of Heidegger, for whom the overman, the will to power and Eternal Return say exactly the same: the subjection of Being (or Time) to the subjective (representational) will. Blanchot reads Eternal Return as the detour of all thought which turns with history; it is announced with fear and hesitation by Zarathustra ('Thus was I talking, and ever more softly: for I was afraid of my own thoughts and the motives behind them'), unlike the categorical announcement of the overman ('Behold, I teach to you the Overman!', repeated three times),[42] prompting Blanchot to ask, 'Why this difference in tone?' (IC 148). This thought experiment is a deconstruction of the will that slackens the philosophical tone, enabling us to hear obliquely or indirectly the other note which points to the impersonal necessity of, or the impossibility of being done with, being: 'Until now, we thought nihilism was tied to nothingness. How ill-considered this was: nihilism is tied to being [. . .] [Nihilism] says the powerlessness of nothingness, the false brilliance of its victories; it says that when we think nothingness we are still thinking being' (IC 149).

This nihilistic thought is abyssal and discontinuous; it is founded on this movement of infinite reversal as it encounters the insurmountable which it bears within itself: death. It is the continual association of nihilism with Being (and also with the denunciation of the modern world and nostalgia for a bygone time) that eventually leads Blanchot to argue in 1962 that we should renounce this term because 'it has ceased to resonate in the direction of what it cannot reach' (IC 403). Already in 1958, Blanchot notes that by crossing out only 'Being', Heidegger privileges Being because this is possible with any word. Blanchot crosses out both 'being' and 'nothingness' in the later version of his essay. This simple strikethrough is how the neuter works; constantly intervening in language, it highlights the possibility of displacement within all words. 'Let us therefore be cautious, handle these provocative notions with care, do not allow words to speak with the realist efficacy they have acquired and gently lead them back toward the silence from which they come' (IC 150). The neuter as this technical intervention allows Blanchot to silently respond to the view that Heidegger has been seduced by words and to approach that other tone which, in 'The Beast of Lascaux', is so despised by Socrates: 'a silence that is majestic, but which embodies a speechlessness that in itself is inhuman and communicates to art the tremor that comes from the sacred, from those forces which, filling men with horror and terror, expose them to all that is alien [*ouvrent l'homme à des régions étrangères*]' (BL 10).

Heidegger once famously declared, 'Only another God can save us now.'[43] The experience of modern technology leads Heidegger to conclude that the human no longer has any agency in this hopeless world. Blanchot will reach a similar conclusion but, in his account, there is something to be celebrated about this shift beyond the sovereign subject which does not entail the complete destruction of the human. Blanchot had written some years earlier, this time in relation to the work of Albert Camus, that we enter nihilism by questioning vermin (IC 182). A strange statement perhaps, one that has proved troubling for some,[44] but it communicates the idea that nihilism cannot be overcome and again emphasises an indirect approach to this line or region through exposure to what is alien to the human. A lengthy passage from the original essay was omitted when it was collected fifteen years later in *The Infinite Conversation*:

> As we can see, the question, if not the answer, is focused on the word impossibility, a necessarily ambiguous word because it presents itself to us only in the inflexibility of negation – absence of power, deprivation of possibility, absolute powerlessness – while nonetheless seeking to draw out an affirmation that would elude both being (understood in the ontological sense: not only beings, but the being at work [*à l'œuvre*] in real or possible existences) and the negation of being.[45]

This affirmation precedes ontology, and this is perhaps why the above extract is replaced in *The Infinite Conversation* with the simpler statement: 'Space where what we call man has as if in advance always already disappeared' (IC 183). The power of man in modernity to destroy the world is limited because it goes hand-in-hand with an affirmation of the unknowable region beyond the world. Roger Laporte calls this 'a new dimension, that of the Neuter, which is not [. . .] a third term located between affirmation and negation, but a completely different term because it establishes a relationship with the essentially other'.⁴⁶ The human, although exposed to something completely alien, persists in this response, which is a helpless abandoning of oneself to nihilism rather than some masterful overcoming of nihilism. The neuter is that impossible and silent force, of neither human nor animal origin, which responds to human power, possibility and speech.

Cautious regarding our prospects in the age of modern technology, and aware that these powers are easily and often abused for political or ideological purposes, Blanchot seeks to demystify the apocalypse and to expose its impossibility, banality, insignificance. These essays carry warnings against complacency but do not endorse a fear of technology. Blanchot's position on modern technology is therefore far from that of Heidegger, who in 1966 spoke of the terror induced by the technological world:

> Everything is functioning. This is exactly what is so uncanny, that everything is functioning and that the functioning drives us more and more to even further functioning, and that technology tears men loose from the earth and uproots them. I do not know whether you were frightened, but I at any rate was frightened when I saw pictures coming from the moon to the earth. We do not need any atom bomb. The uprooting of man has already taken place. The only thing we have left is purely technical relationships. This is no longer the earth on which man lives.⁴⁷

The date of this interview suggests that Heidegger could have been referring to the first images transmitted to the earth from the moon by Lunar Orbiter 1. That 'everything is functioning' within technology need not be something to be feared for Blanchot, who sees in this power an appeal beyond the human.⁴⁸ Earlier that decade, Blanchot had already considered the responses of various heads of state – Khrushchev, Kennedy and De Gaulle – to the first cosmonaut and the significance of Yuri Gagarin's experience:

> beneficiaries ready to proclaim the benefits of technology for their own prestige, but incapable of accepting or welcoming its consequence, which is to ruin all belonging and to call place, in all places, into question.
> – That may be the case. But should we not add that the political and mythical outcome of Gagarin's exploit was to allow the Russians to inhabit Russian land more firmly, and that the relation to the Outside does not appear to have been physically modified in any radical way? (PW 71)⁴⁹

The second half of this quotation demonstrates how Gagarin was going to be recuperated by political powers; but the real significance of this space flight, unable to be embraced by the heads of state because it exposes and challenges the limits of culture, is the experience of dislocation and dispersion and the shift in our relationship to the outside that results. The instance of typographical technology, the dash, included in the version of the essay quoted above but omitted from the original publication of the essay in Italian translation in 1964, serves to remind us that there is always something outside of the text enabling it to take place (and to be repeated).[50] This silent inscription is a form of writing that cannot be put into speech: the neuter as a neutralising and displacing technique which challenges the limit of world, history, culture and subtly shifts our perspective.

It is interesting that 'The Conquest of Space' was Blanchot's contribution to the ill-fated *International Review*, the intention of which was to publish anonymous fragments from a community of international writers that would form a contemporary response to radical historical change.[51] The project – reliant on modern technologies of communication, production and distribution – sought to question place and to break more explicitly from the organic form as the expression of a single authorial intent through the collective, fragmented, anonymous and international nature of the pieces published. The selection of an essay that considers the power of technology to overcome international boundaries is therefore perhaps unsurprising.

While trying to establish this ambitious project, Blanchot wrote that the translator was its most important figure, 'the true writer of the review' (PW 62). Other comments made about the significance of the translator are lifted from an earlier 1960 essay on Walter Benjamin: '[The translator] is the secret master of the difference between languages, who aims not to abolish this difference but to use it to awaken in their own language, through the violent or subtle changes they bring to it, a presence of what is different, originally, in the original' (F 59). Blanchot argues in agreement with Benjamin that translation, rather than bringing together languages in harmonious unity, is founded on the difference between languages and accentuates this original difference. The translator brings the otherness of the work to the fore through its reproduction. It is this otherness, this original difference, which enables the repetition of the artwork and is indicated in 'The Conquest of Space' by the insertion of the dash. The *International Review* therefore represented a sort of harnessing of modern technology (the printing press, translation, fragmentation, the questioning of place, the anonymity of texts) for the purposes of the neuter.

The problem for those listening to the garbled speech of Yuri Gagarin and the interlocutors of 'On a Change of Epoch' is how to formulate a response to what lies beyond traditional structures of expression. Blanchot is able to set aside the metaphysical menace of technological dominance, so feared by Heidegger, and move beyond metaphysical representation, the point at which Heidegger faltered, by looking to a more originary sense of techne which harnesses the power of modern technology: the neuter. The change of epoch is considered in terms of a shift in our relationship to the world, a world described by Blanchot in the first essay on nuclear weapons as an edifice preventing us from seeing things otherwise: do not burn the scientists, do not wipe out the contemporary world to which we happily belong, pleads one interlocutor, but burn the structures to expose something other than the regularity of the concept (IC 269–70). Announced in this oscillating dialogue is the neuter as a response to what always surpasses meaning (the worldly, historical, cultural limit demarcating the boundaries of human knowledge), which (as a more originary form of techne) is also essential to the production of this meaning or the demarcation of this limit in the first place.

The neuter is not explicitly discussed in these essays on technology but it is indicated through the motif of the street on two occasions: in 'The Conquest of Space' only the man in the street grasps the significance of Gagarin's experience; and one interlocutor in 'On a Change of Epoch' notes that it is only when walking in the street that we sense the connection between a way of thinking dominated by value and the exhaustion of historical forces, leading the other to reply: 'The street is therefore much wiser than the careful thinkers who wait until they have new categories to think what is happening' (IC 266). The human participates in the anonymous and collective flow, hum, movement of the street, but is not subject in this errant and unrestricted space. Blanchot refers to this hum elsewhere as chatter [*bavardage*]:

> I have always been struck by the widely enthusiastic endorsement of Heidegger when, under the pretext of analysis and with his characteristic sober forcefulness, he condemns inauthentic speech. A scorned speech, which is never that of the resolute, laconic and heroic 'I', but the non-speech of the irresponsible 'One'. One speaks. This means: no one speaks. This means: we live in a world where there is speech without a subject speaking it, a civilization of speakers without speech, aphasic chatterboxes, spokespeople who report and give no opinions, technicians without name and without power of decision. (F 125)

This chatter, rather than being degraded or inauthentic as the German pronoun *man* is for Heidegger, points towards the unknowable future for Blanchot precisely because it belongs to no one. Michael Sheringham argues that the chatter of the street in Blanchot brings us closer to the 'essence of the everyday', which, 'in its radicality, its immunity from all origins, its anarchic destruction of all established order, will always provide a basis for the future'. Sheringham acknowledges the contestatory power of the neuter but does not think it radically enough when he writes that this chatter 'epitomises the ontology of the everyday', because the neuter also contests the limits of being.[52] Blanchot elsewhere had noted Heidegger's concern that the myth surrounding Nietzsche threatens to reduce the cry of his suffering to 'idle chatter' (IC 143). Heidegger associates this cry with an authentic death, comparable to what Malte thought he witnessed in the Chamberlain's dying in Rilke's *Notebooks*. Any cry will inevitably be reduced to mere chatter in Blanchot's account, but this is not something to be deplored. Anonymous and nomadic, these 'technicians' are a vehicle for the neuter, and the street in which they roam is the region of nihilism. Modern technologies – the printing press, the atomic bomb, the spacecraft – provide the conditions for contesting cultural limits and recognising this excessive background force. We are exposed to an outside, to an unknowable future, to a new place and to human impossibility in these essays on modern technology, which subtly shift our perspective and encourage us to abandon ourselves to the nomadic movement without determination heard in the chatter of the street.

'The Apocalypse is Disappointing' (1964) – written in the wake of the Cuban missile crisis and one month after the first French nuclear weapons came into service – brings together in one essay Blanchot's reflections on nihilism, modern technology, the inhuman and the unknown. This essay was a response to *The Future of Mankind* (1958), published in French translation in 1963, in which Karl Jaspers argues that humanity's newly acquired capacity for self-destruction signals the dawning of a new age. As we saw in 'On a Change of Epoch', Blanchot is critical of debates that frame the question of the bomb in terms of the end of history or use the question as an alibi for leading us to long-standing spiritual or political decisions that are nothing to do with the bomb. He criticises Jaspers for arguing that the existence of atomic weapons radically changes the requirements of thought, while nonetheless framing his discussion as a choice between extermination or totalitarianism, or between the 'free world' and communism. This is a sham reflection on the bomb, according to Blanchot, because it shies away from the ambiguity of the event, so that all we manage to utter is the truism that it would be better to prevent this catastrophe (F 104). The theme of Jaspers's work is change but there is nothing new about his language, thought or political formulations:

> If thought falls back on traditional assertions, it is because it does not want to expose itself in the presence of an ambiguous event whose significance it cannot pin down, with its terrible face, with its appearance as absolute – an excessive but excessively empty event, about which thought can say only this commonplace: that it would be better to prevent it. (F 104)

The apocalypse always disappoints; it is that ambiguous and excessive event that does not reveal the truth of the end because it encounters death as the insurmountable impossibility that we are incapable of dominating or wanting: man is not some sort of 'supreme hero of the negative' or 'final Hamlet' (F 106). Our understanding, which takes us to the limits of comprehension, helps us to see that we will never know this universal death and that our ending will never be of any significance (F 107). Blanchot exposes the difference between the future treated as an object by totalising scientific knowledge and the future as what cannot be negated, as what remains unknowable and uncertain. The latter is why the apocalypse always disappoints: apocalyptic foretelling exposes us to the banality of an end that will never have any meaning for us as subjects.

Michael Holland, one of the few to have considered a thinking of technology in Blanchot, argues that in both essays on nuclear weapons the question of the bomb is radically separated from the question of technology: the latter is a question of language with the potential to indicate a new departure for man because it is associated with his being; the former remains engaged in that nihilistic or catastrophic situation. The image of Gagarin in space is the event that marks 'the true turning before which technology places man' for Holland, who sees in this essay a clearer rejection of Heidegger because engaging with the question of rootedness.[53] This distinction between space flight and the atomic bomb overlooks the implication of the neuter in modern technologies: the essays on the bomb engage with the question of our relation to the future in a way that similarly disrupts our worldly perspective; all modes of technique expose the human to a turning because all relate us to the unknowable and expose us to a profound powerlessness.

Noted at the start of this chapter was Derrida's analysis which claimed that any attempt to shed light on the apocalypse leads only to a brighter apocalyptic tone; Derrida suggests that by listening to the multiplicity of apocalyptic tones, by recognising that there is more than one tone, we allow the possibility that the other tone, or the tone of the other, might be heard. Towards the end of 'The Apocalypse is Disappointing', Blanchot is doing just this when he argues that Jaspers '[dismisses] the abstract shadow of this apocalypse as if it were an irritating fly and [perseveres] with the habits of a tradition and a language in which one sees nothing to change' (F 108). The essay concludes by stressing that the choice between all or nothing, between transformation or destruction, is not the one and only truth of our situation. We should note this fly out of the corner of our eye; we should risk a surreptitious glance in its direction.

The Neuter: Kafka and *The Last Man*

At the height of his involvement with the *International Review* in 1964, Blanchot published two essays on Kafka: 'The Narrative Voice (the "it" [*le "il"*], the neuter)' and 'The Wooden Bridge (repetition, the neuter)'. The first begins by quoting from Kafka's *The Castle*: 'The forces of life are only sufficient up to a point' (IC 379). The meaning of life is limited by fatigue, but in order to draw this limit there must be something other than 'the forces of life'. We saw in the essays on modern technologies that the limits of history, world and culture are contested by an impersonal force which the human cannot master: the neuter as a sort of disobedient techne continuing where other modes of technique have left off. For this reason, the neuter is not spoken by one single authoritative voice in Kafka's texts, and Blanchot is naming not the narrator when he refers to the 'narrative voice', but the neuter as the condition of possibility of narration.

As a non-concept that perpetually evades location, working at the limit to destroy all limit, the neuter is experienced as a sort of emptiness within the work. It has profound consequences for how the author and the reader relate to the work as well as the work's relation to the world; consequences that are experienced in Kafka's writing but are elsewhere eroded or clouded by the misuse of the narrative voice. This 'he' or 'it' [*il*] is described as the unlit event that unfolds within the space or distance [*étendue*] of the narration, here referred to as a song: 'It is in song that Orpheus really descends to the underworld, which can be translated by adding that he does so through the power of singing, but this already instrumental song signifies a distortion of the narrative tradition' (IC 381). Blanchot signals the corruption of the narrative voice which is subsequently played out in the novelistic tradition. Rather than experiencing the neuter as a technique beyond the control of Orpheus, creating this melodic distance and so enabling narration, we understand the song as nothing more than an instrument mastered by Orpheus. Consequently, we take the narrative voice to be the expression of an objective reality or of multiple and personalised subjectivities (IC 381). Here we are reminded of Ulysses tied to the ship's mast in Blanchot's essay: through what are described as 'technical' means he maintains a cold and calculated distance from the Sirens in order to hear their call without becoming implicated in this imaginary space. This controlled distance resurfaces in 'The Conquest of Space', where the heavens are transformed merely into another absolute, 'the space of scientists, which is nothing but a calculable possibility' (PW 70). The impersonal narration employed by Flaubert is cited as the modern outcome of such corruption in 'The Narrative Voice (the "it", the neuter)'. Such aesthetic distance treats the artwork as an autonomous whole and ensures a clear division between spectacle and spectator as if this were classical theatre: 'the narrator is there only to raise the curtain; the play is performed down on the stage, for all eternity and as though without him; he does not tell, he shows, and the reader does not read, he watches, witnessing, taking part without participating' (IC 382).[54]

An altogether different sort of distance is in play in Kafka's writing. The contemplative enjoyment of a detached author and reader is no longer possible when the space between spectator and spectacle is restored to its Orphic origins as the very milieu of the narrative. The stability of the measurable, controllable, calculable distance (which was only ever an illusion) between Flaubert or his narrator and the work, between Ulysses and the Sirens, between Gagarin and the earth, is shaken by a volatile distance which cannot be pinned down or controlled because, the limits of the work challenged, there is no external perspective by which to judge the work. The work is decentred by an indeterminate and undetectable distance which subtly alters our perspective and draws us into this space; it is now no longer a distant object upon which we gaze from afar. 'Kafka teaches us [. . .] that narrating brings the neuter into play' (IC 384). The parentheses added to the titles of both of these essays for their publication in *The Infinite Conversation* echo the work of the neuter: there is a difference between the main body of the title and what is marginalised, but this difference is unstable, because while 'named' in parentheses the neuter is also implied in the narrative voice and on the wooden bridge.

The narrative voice is neuter, writes Blanchot; it says nothing but is felt everywhere in the narration and, at the limit, it prevents the work from having a limit (IC 385–6). It precedes and exceeds the omniscient narrator of Flaubert's novels (the narrative voice as it is formulated by Gérard Genette), who is only ever a stand-in, an actor obscuring the stage.[55] It cannot be pinned down to what we traditionally understand by 'place' or attributed to any one subject:

> the [third-person neuter he or it], dispersing itself as a lack into the simultaneous plurality – and repetition – of a place, always shifting but diversely unoccupied, designates 'its' place as somewhere from where it will always be absent (and thus may be thought to remain empty), but also as an excess of place, a place always in excess: a hypertopia. (IC 462)

Blanchot here indicates a new place and new perspective opened up by the neuter; a region that nonetheless resists location or identification, and so it seems fitting that it is discussed in a footnote in the margins of the essay which, via an interruption, refers beyond the limits of this essay to 'The Wooden Bridge (repetition, the neuter)'. K., the main character in Kafka's *The Castle*, bears the traits of a figure exposed to such instability according to Blanchot, because he is foreign to the foreignness of the Castle, foreign to the village, foreign even to himself as he inexplicably breaks with his own familiarity to move towards this new place (IC 462–3). K. is a nomad constantly threatened with homelessness in this new place; moving between inns, the school and the homes of the villagers, he experiences that profound lack of belonging felt by Gagarin at the limits of the earth: '"I can't go away," replied K. "I came here to stay. I'll stay here." And giving utterance to a self-contradiction which he made no effort to explain he added to himself: "What could have enticed me to this desolate country except the wish to stay here?"'[56]

One of the shortcomings identified by Blanchot in the rhetoric surrounding modern technology is the widespread assumption that an individual can say, define, negate or destroy the world; similar difficulties are encountered in those narratives with an omniscient authorial or narrative figure. '[Neutral speech] opens another power in language, one that is alien to the power of illuminating (or obscuring), of comprehension (or misapprehension)' (IC 386). The neuter is that insurmountable power which opens up an unsayable emptiness within the work. Yuri Gagarin, dislocated and exposed as technological man, was momentarily a vehicle for this limitless force: '[Gagarin's chatter] does not stop, it must not stop; the slightest break in the murmuring would already mean the void forever; any lacuna, any interruption, introduces something much more than death, it introduces the nothingness of the outside into discourse.' (PW 71). The anonymous speech of the cosmonaut invites the outside into language; testing worldly limits it incites a fearful reaction in those listening within cultural parameters, but enables a more liberated perspective for the attentive listener.

Marthe Robert is an example of a critic working within the prism of culture to fill similar gaps and inconsistencies in *The Castle*. She argues that *The Castle* is not only the unique work of a solitary writer, but the palimpsest where we can read a thousand years of literature: Kafka's attempt to classify the monstrous archives of Western culture from which he could not exclude his own work.[57] There are similarities between Robert and Gagarin; both are 'scapegoats' sent to the very edge of literary space with an impossible task: to say the world in its totality, to complete the authentic work.[58] In contrast, Blanchot points to the wandering structure of the narrative; he describes K. erring from interpretation to interpretation until the narrative opens out on to the possibility of writing, which invites endless commentary (IC 393). Blanchot suggests that the opening lines of *The Castle* are perhaps where the 'meaning' of the work is to be found: 'K. stood for a long while, gazing into the empty appearance [*l'apparence vide*] above him' (IC 463). The original German reads 'die scheinbare Leere [*apparent emptiness*]'.[59] Blanchot, in his own translation, subtly alters our perception of the text so that K. now observes 'empty appearance', a move that nudges Kafka's writing closer to the neuter. Suggested in the conditional tense and placed in a footnote in the margins of his essay, Blanchot does not propose that this is the definitive meaning of the text because such a concrete interpretation is impossible; his argument is that, the limits of the work challenged by the neuter, 'internal' commentaries on the Castle and 'external' commentaries on *The Castle* are equally justifiable and equally powerless.

The work derives its power from the non-difference between inside and outside: '(ambiguity: the difference of the identical, the non-identity of the same)' (IC 395). The parentheses again signal the trembling of the difference between what can no longer be described as subject and object; they expose the empty relationality that founds the work and is most palpable on the wooden bridge, that crossing between places. The critic of *The Castle* is comparable to the translator of the *International Review* because both projects are founded on the original difference between languages. Criticism accentuates this difference, testing the limits of our cultural perspective. Blanchot later writes in *The Writing of the Disaster*: '◆ In the night, insomnia is dis-cussion, not the work [*travail*] of arguments clashing with other arguments, but the extreme tremor empty of thoughts, the shaking fractured until still (the exegeses that come and go in "The Castle", story of insomnia)' (WD 49). The stress is not on the value of individual interpretations but on the trembling relationality between the work and its commentary, which is the condition of possibility for both. Later in the same text Blanchot writes:

◆ It is strange that K., at the end of *The Castle*, should be consigned by some commentators to madness. From the start, he is beyond the debate between reason and unreason, insofar as everything he does is without relation with the reasonable, and yet absolutely necessary, that is, just or justified. Similarly, it does not seem possible that he should die (whether damned or saved is almost unimportant), not only because his struggle is not in terms of living and dying, but also because he is too weary (his weariness, the one feature to be accentuated as the story progresses) to be able to die: for the advent of his death [*l'avènement de sa mort*] not to change into an interminable non-event [*inavènement interminable*]. (WD 141)

K.'s growing fatigue is the only indication we have of a sense of progression in this narrative; it signals that there is another power beyond the limits of life and the narrative. This is the same power that allows the subtle shift in the title (from 'The Castle' to *The Castle*) between the two fragments quoted here, which ensures that the interpretation of the work can never be stabilised. Labelling K. mad is a strange exercise because he has never worked within the laws determined in the Castle and enforced in the village; he belongs to neither place and his condition mirrors that of the writer.[60]

When external and internal commentary become almost interchangeable, when the non-identical difference of the same is the source of the power of the work (of the neuter), then it becomes impossible to attach a value to the work and to commentary, to the Castle and to the village. The concluding footnote to the second of these essays on Kafka reads: 'One of the essential traits of the neuter is that it does not allow itself to be grasped either in terms of immanence or in terms of transcendence, drawing us into an entirely different sort of relation' (IC 463).The neuter does not command from above, but nor does it exist in itself as something self-identical; it dismantles that age-old philosophical distinction between immanence and transcendence. This is why readings of *The Castle* vary according to whether the Castle is seen as transcendent (divine) or as immanent social entity. The neuter is founded on that shifting relationship and so offers a means of moving beyond metaphysical representation. Ending the narrative would allow the relationship to stabilise and we could draw a meaning or value from this text;

but K., Blanchot argues, will never die a personal and heroic death; it would only ever be general, bureaucratic, and thus an interpretation of death. This neutral death is a liquidation, writes Blanchot in 'The End of the Hero' (1965), referring to the hero of *The Trial* who declares that when we die we do so 'Like a dog' (IC 376).

Suspended between life and death, between subject and object, between human and animal, characters, authors and readers are like the eponymous hero of Kafka's short story *The Hunter Gracchus*. Hunter Gracchus declares that he is forever on the staircase leading to the other world: 'On that infinitely wide and spacious stair I clamber about, sometimes up, sometimes down, sometimes on the right, sometimes on the left, always in motion. The Hunter has been turned into a butterfly. Do not laugh.'[61] The theme of this short story is recognisably Blanchotian: the impossibility of death. Blanchot, however, objects to the parabolic status of this short story, arguing that its completeness and precision contradict the absolute ambiguity of negation demanded by its content (WF 82). In contrast to this neatly packaged story which draws us too close to a definitive meaning, *The Castle*, it was noted at the beginning of this chapter, is symbolic because it places the world in parentheses and exposes us to the void which is the milieu of all imagined form. Blanchot writes later in this essay: 'The passage from yes to no, from no to yes, is the rule here, and any interpretation that avoids this alternation, including those with a role in founding it, contradicts the movement that makes it possible' (WF 83). The rule is one of ambiguity, one that contests everything, including itself, in this movement between affirmation and negation. The pressing question is how we are to begin to respond to a narrative that resists all interpretation. It is a question of how to respond to the call that lies both beyond the boundaries of the text and within the text itself, the narrative as the condition of possibility of all narrative: 'K. was called, and it is quite true that death seems like a call; but it is also true that to answer this call is to betray it, to make something real and true of death' (WF 82).

Kafka wrote his own version of the encounter between Ulysses and the Sirens, which was published posthumously. In this retelling of the episode the Sirens are silent, and it is his own ears, rather those of his crewmen, that Ulysses plugs with wax. Ulysses conjures up their song in his imagination and controls these creatures with his gaze: 'Soon, however, all this faded from his sight as he fixed his gaze on the distance, the Sirens literally vanished before his resolution, and at the very moment when they were nearest to him he knew of them no longer.'[62] Elizabeth Boa describes Ulysses as following 'his own inner visionary journey. Intent on the figures in his mind, he does not see the Sirens.'⁶³ But there is a third twist to this retelling of the encounter: 'Perhaps [Ulysses] had really noticed, although here the human understanding is beyond its depths, that the Sirens were silent, and held up to them and to the gods the aforementioned pretence merely as a sort of shield.'⁶⁴ Without the addition, we might consider this a mythical representation of the Sirens ('By embarking upon the mythic story, we begin to live its meaning, we are immersed in it, we really "think" it in its purity' (WF 78)), but the third and final twist – in which Ulysses, hearing the silence of the Sirens, affirms their unknowable presence – introduces an ambiguity that allows an affirmation which is not of the order of knowing.

This is the unforeseeable affirmation for which Blanchot had called in 1959 in what would become the preface to *Lautréamont and Sade*. Within and beyond the text, it is both the call that makes the text possible and its response: the neuter. When K. puts his ear to the telephone in the inn, in a rare instance locating *The Castle* in the twentieth century, the noise he hears through the receiver is the hum of the neuter:

> The receiver gave out a hum of a kind that K. had never before heard on a telephone. It was like the hum of countless children's voices – but yet not a hum, the echo rather of voices singing at an infinite distance – blended by sheer impossibility into one high but resonant sound which vibrated on the ear as if it were trying to penetrate beyond mere hearing. K. listened without attempting to telephone, leaning his left arm on the telephone shelf.⁶⁵

This is not an original noise from a present and visible source; it is the echo of some already repeated sound, signalling withdrawn presence and the impossibility of knowing this inhuman other – a reworking of the Sirens who, in Blanchot's retelling of the episode, continue to call from their tomb. It is the distant call which lured K. to this place; calling from beyond the confines of the text it is the condition of possibility of the narrative. The distance between unknown sender and receiver is distorted by this technical device. The neuter cannot be located, represented, signified ('to name the neuter is perhaps, is surely to disperse it, but this is necessarily still to the neuter's advantage' (IC 395)), but the telephone allows us to hear its echo.

Later, the Superintendent warns K. that any contact he has had with the Castle has been illusory; his attention turns to the telephone: 'Now this humming and singing transmitted by our telephones is the only real and reliable thing you'll hear, everything else is deceptive. There's no fixed connection with the Castle, no central exchange that transmits our calls further.'⁶⁶ This story, it has already been noted, refuses knowledge, indicates the void and deals in the imaginary. The humming heard down the telephone is, however, different: real and reliable, the implication is that it reaches beyond the limits of the text. The Superintendent goes on to explain that a 'stranger' calling the Castle cannot expect to be put through to a particular person. Any exchange across the telephone is anonymous and meaningless; what matters is this background noise. Derrida writes that anonymity is the mark of the apocalyptic text:

> And there is no certainty that man is the exchange [*le central*] of these telephone lines or the terminal of this endless computer. No longer is one very sure who loans his voice and his tone to the other in the Apocalypse; no longer is one very sure who addresses what to whom. But by a catastrophic overturning here more necessary than ever, one can just as well think this: as soon as one no longer knows who speaks or who writes, the text becomes apocalyptic.⁶⁷

Between the neuter, this anonymous force heard down the telephone, and those modern technologies promising the apocalypse and enabling us to hear this noise, there is undoubtedly an unstable relation. The neuter is not a self-identical concept; it means that there is always a different tone and it allows us to hear this in technology.

First published in 1957, *The Last Man* is a fundamental moment of engagement which gives rise to the neuter as a non-concept and allows Blanchot to return to Kafka, in whose writing he senses the neuter tangibly in play. Set chiefly within the walls of a hospital, the first section of the text tells of the suffering and weakness of the last man in the face of his impending death; it explores the relationships between characters when exposed to this heightened sense of mortality. The first section ends with a moment of transition as the narrator follows in the footsteps of the last man and moves, with the technical assistance of an elevator, into a corridor. This corridor is comparable to the wooden bridge in Kafka's *The Castle*: it is a transitional space suspended between life and death, a void that promises eternity and leads to the intrusion of the inhuman other in the disorientating second section of the text:

> I liked that corridor. I walked down it with a sense of its calm, deep, indifferent life, knowing that for me the future was there, and that I would have no other landscape than that clean and white solitude, that there my trees would grow, there would lie the immense rustling fields, the sea, the changing cloudy sky – there, in that tunnel, the eternity of my encounters and my desires. (LM 62)

This corridor is the extreme limit at which nihilism is turned back on itself in this apocalyptic text; it signals the relinquishing of power and identity to this region and a shift towards an experience where the self is exposed to a more radical contestation. What follows is expressed from a new place where the distinction between the narrator of the first section and the last man has collapsed; they belong to an anonymous and fluctuating chatter which is here exposed to a muffled but insistent inhuman murmuring.

The last man sits in an armchair towards the beginning of the narrative, his large tired hands hanging at the end of his arms (LM 6). Around this weak and suffering man other characters acquire a heightened sense of existence, making them stronger, crueller, more dangerous, and on the brink of a dream of extreme power. This power, the narrator remarks, remains a perverse dream; a will to dominate or a sense of superiority felt at a moment when the future looks bleak (LM 21–2). The excessive force is only felt in relation to this weak figure; it cannot be appropriated by an individual but draws its energy from the relation between them on which the first section of this text focuses. The apocalyptic tone of this narrative is, of course, misleading, because the last man will not be the last; his experience will be repeated in the lives of all the individuals who form the surrounding 'community'. With reference to the atomic bomb in 'The Apocalypse is Disappointing', Blanchot writes of an impossible power set in opposition to human community:

> On the one hand, a power that cannot be, and on the other, an existence – the human community – that can be wiped out but not affirmed or that could be affirmed, in some sense, only after its disappearance and by the void, impossible to grasp, of this disappearance; consequently, something that cannot even be destroyed, because it does not exist. (F 106)

The Last Man is the narration of this nihilistic situation. The last man bears the traits of the human in the technological age; exhausted and powerless now that the possibilities of modern technology are not contained within his large hands, he is the momentary (not the last) vehicle for an impossible power. Around him an impossible community forms, drawn together by the experience of dying which will mark each individual existence but will never be achieved, as separate egos dissolve into the chatter of the second section of the text.

Heidegger wrote in relation to Nietzsche in 1951 that the 'last man – the final and definitive type of man so far – fixes himself, and generally all that is, by a specific way of representing ideas'.[68]

The last man is closely associated with metaphysical representation for Heidegger, who goes on to write that '[t]his well made-up and well-staged manner of forming ideas, of representation, with its constantly more refined mechanism, dissimulates and blocks from view what really *is* [*was eigentlich ist*]'.[69] The last man in Blanchot's text is at points associated with representational thinking: speaking 'in a bookish way', he depicts his hometown, a city whose buildings he describes in such detail it is as if he constructs them before his listeners. The narrator is initially disappointed by this representation – the last man describes a town very similar to 'our' own – but he is then struck by the strange character of this town, crossed by a dried-up river, where huge crowds incessantly flow through the streets. 'More than strange: familiar and deceptive and falsifying – or not exactly falsifying, but taking away their basis, their foundation – the pictures of the world closest to us' (LM 36). This is not the representation of a knowable reality but a symbol as it is defined in the essay on Kafka from 1949, exposing us to the void which is the milieu of the imaginary and rendering the familiar world unreal.

Observations of the last man are occasionally made from across the card table, which provides the only reference point (other than doors and walls) in the building in which this narrative unfolds. We have seen that narrating puts the neuter in play for Blanchot. The game occupying the narrator of *The Last Man* allows an oblique exposure to this figure; observations made across the card table read as if the narrator is peering at this figure out of the corner of his eye: 'I left the two of them alone. While she sunk into her alcove, I played. I hid behind the game, deliberately forgetting what an ordeal this intimate conversation in solitude exposed her to'; 'I was at the games table and he was in his armchair, his large body somewhat hunched over, but in a rather graceful position' (LM 22, 49). Blanchot writes in 1965 that the indirect is the medium of literature: 'Strange imaginary tableaux or, failing this, scenes which are as if suspended [*arrêtées*] in their visible immobility, constitute the essential moments of a plot that obeys a necessary play of multiplication' (F 171). *The Last Man* obeys this game of multiplication: suspended scenes and strange immobile images abound in a work that refuses to allow any single description to be pinned down to straightforward representation.

The effects of this game of multiplication, and a desire to shirk its dizzying effects, are felt by the female character in a scene in which she finds some comfort in a nearby fishpond, which bears some resemblance to Heidegger's analysis (in the same text where he associates the last man with metaphysical representation) of the multiple possible interpretations of Plato and Nietzsche. Heidegger writes:

multiplicity of meanings is the element in which all thought must move in order to be strict thought. To use an image [*Im Bild gesprochen*]: to a fish, the depths and expanses of its waters, the currents and quiet pools, warm and cold layers are the element of its multiple mobility. If the fish is deprived of the fullness of its element, if it is dragged on the dry sand, then it can only wriggle, twitch, and die [*verenden*]. Therefore we must always seek out thinking, and its burden of thought, in the element of its multiple meanings, else everything will remain closed to us.[70]

The narrator of *The Last Man* speaks of 'the spectre of an infinite pain' which the last man perhaps represents. He acknowledges that the female character may once have alluded to this burden. What follows is a scene, impossible to know whether a dream or a memory, in which she requests that they go for a walk one night in the hospital grounds. 'There was already a little snow, but the sky wasn't a snowy sky, and it was here that I saw how dark and confined space could be, as though receding to an infinite distance and yet also coming infinitely close to us. "Look how dark the sky is"' (LM 53). The characters are located in what might at first appear more recognisable surroundings when compared with those scenes that take place within the walls of the disorientating hospital, but there is something strange about this wintry environment. The black sky, disjointed from the scene on the ground, provides a vanishing perspective which is at once vast and infinitesimal. At the sight of this sky, the female character is overcome with dizziness. Its uneven quality, the dissymmetrical distance that she experiences here, exposes her to the emptiness which is both within her and beyond world and creates an excess that overwhelms her. This is an experience of the neuter as both transcendence and immanence. The narrator leads her to the edge of the pond which serves as a breeding pool for the nearby kitchens: 'Everything was quiet and we heard only the noise of the water, a mysterious, living noise in which one sensed the confused agitation of the fish, disturbed by our presence' (LM 54). The fishpond is almost overflowing with life; it neatly contains a world that exists solely for the purposes of nourishing the human. Blanchot is perhaps drawing on Heidegger's image of the fish moving within 'the element of its multiple mobility'. In contrast to the excess or incalculable distance of the sky, this image composed of living material is reassuringly finite and provides the female character with a reference point that positions her within the element of human possibility, values and limits, enabling her to dismiss the abstract shadow of the sky.

In contrast to the female character whose relationship with the inhuman, in its captured and restricted state, is marked by human possibility, the last man undergoes an inhuman metamorphosis: he cries like a wolf on more than one occasion and, while sitting in the armchair struggling for breath, his fur hat casts a moving shadow over his face (LM 3, 19, 50).[71] He grows ever weaker as his death approaches; he joins the other patients to eat (LM 15–17), an act which Blanchot refers to elsewhere, in relation to Robert Antelme's account of life in a concentration camp, as the experience of 'man reduced to the irreducible [. . .] the radical need that no longer relates me to myself or to the satisfaction of myself, but to human existence pure and simple, lived as lack at the level of need' (IC 133). No longer sovereign and barely human in the first section of the text, once the last man is at the threshold and dispersed in the chatter of the second section, along with the narrator (who is perhaps the same non-identical figure), he is surrendered to impossibility:

> A mysterious answer, a strange murmur that disturbs us: the voice is weak, harsh like the squeak of a lizard. Our own has the volume and strength of worlds added onto worlds, but it is also silent. The other has something animal about it, too physical. Imperceptible, it shakes us. Even though it may be a sort of ritual, hearing it is troubling, a sublime surprise. (LM 67–8)

Hailing down on us like the screech of a lizard, this strange murmuring, in spite of its weakness, demands that we pay attention. It marks the arrival of something new and unexpected and indicates something profoundly affirmative in the second section of this text: that with danger also comes chance. 'What issues from the earth is a strange voice, a stifled murmur, a dry, arid cry; this disturbs us, obliges us to hear, and who utters it?' (LM 77). No one and no thing says this strange murmuring. It echoes the song of the Sirens and the irritating fly of 'The Apocalypse is Disappointing', and it also takes the form of the inhuman. It is the trace of the impossible which interrupts all possibility, including the possibility of destruction, at a moment in the text when the narrator and the last man seem close to death.

The choice between disappearance or transformation seemingly posed by modern technologies such as the atomic bomb is not really a choice at all. Man both disappears and transforms in this turning, so that only a residue of the human persists. The limit (the end of history, culture and world) is contested but never wholly erased. Of course, it is possible that the world could be destroyed, Blanchot admits as much, but we would never experience this destruction as subjects. The neuter allows a step, which is not a step, over this line; it allows a disjointed perspective which is other than human, an inhuman transformation in which a residual trace of the human persists. Blanchot is not a humanist, as some have claimed.[72] His writing is open to something other than the human, which takes the shape of an inhuman interruption heard at the end of 'The Apocalypse is Disappointing' and *The Last Man*.

Notes

1. Walter Benjamin, 'The Work of Art in the Age of its Technological Reproducibility', trans. Edmund Jephcott and Harry Zohn, in *Selected Writings*, ed. Howard Eiland and Michael W. Jennings, 4 vols (Cambridge, MA: Belknap Press of Harvard University Press, 2004–2006), III: *1935–1938* (2006), pp. 101–33 (p. 104). This essay was first published in French in a translation by Klossowski in 1936; it is unclear whether Blanchot ever read it, although we do know that he was aware of Benjamin's work from at least 1959 when he reviewed a translation of his selected works by Maurice de Gandillac, later published in *Friendship* as 'Translating' (pp. 57–61). This article was mainly concerned with Benjamin's 'The Task of the Translator', but the essay quoted here was included in the same volume.
2. Howard Caygill provides a useful commentary on Benjamin's essay in *Walter Benjamin: The Colour of Experience* (London: Routledge, 1998), pp. 97–117.
3. Stiegler names Blanchot and Benjamin as two thinkers who understood that the question of repetition is a question of techne, in *Technics and Time*, I, p. 219. For an overview of Stiegler's use of Blanchot, see the Introduction.
4. See Blanchot, L'Étrange et l'étranger' (1958), in *La Condition critique*, pp. 278–88 (p. 287 n. 1). Christophe Bident notes that this is the first use of 'neuter' as a noun in Blanchot's work in 'The Movements of the Neuter', in *After Blanchot: Literature, Philosophy, Criticism*, ed. Leslie Hill, Brian Nelson and Dimitris Vardoulakis (Newark, DE: University of Delaware Press, 2005), pp. 13–34 (p. 33 n. 15).
5. Jacques Derrida, 'Of an Apocalyptic Tone Recently Adopted in Philosophy', trans. John P. Leavey, *Oxford Literary Review* 6, no. 2 (1984): 3–37 (p. 22). In this text Derrida refers, implicitly and explicitly, to several texts by Blanchot (*Death Sentence*, *The Madness of the Day*, *The Last Man* and 'The Apocalypse is Disappointing'), which suggests that Blanchot is of considerable importance to his analysis. Derrida also recognises Blanchot's place in the debates of the 1950s on the end of history, which happened in the context of the end of communism, and provides a commentary on 'Marx's Three Voices' in *Spectres of Marx*, trans. Peggy Kamuf (New York: Routledge, 1994), pp. 16–35. See also Blanchot, 'Marx's Three Voices' (1968), trans. Tom Keenan, in *Friendship*, pp. 98–100.

6. Derrida, 'Of an Apocalyptic Tone', p. 23.
7. Ibid., p. 27.
8. Blanchot here comes close to reinstating the opposition between the literary and the everyday, but the difference is one of degree and not of any essential nature. He writes that the phrase read in an office and read in *The Castle* has the same effect: in both cases language destroys the world by reducing it to abstraction and revealing a void. The difference is that everyday language encloses this absence within a presence (in the office: 'As new as I may be, I am pressed on all sides by reality, and I achieve it and meet it everywhere'), whereas literary language goes one step further by destroying this abstraction (WF 74–5). As we saw in Chapter 1, the literary is a radicalisation of the everyday for Blanchot by 1949, and so there is no solid opposing relationship between the literary and the everyday, and the simplest, most mundane of phrases can be literary.
9. Franz Kafka, *The Castle*, trans. Willa and Edwin Muir, additional material trans. Eithne Wilkins and Ernst Kaiser, definitive edn (London: Secker and Warburg, 1953), p. 15. Blanchot would have been reading early versions of the text edited by Max Brod – the first French translation of *The Castle* was published in 1938 by Alexandre Vialatte – and it is for this reason that I refer to translations of the edited 1926 version of the novel.
10. On the difference for Blanchot between allegory, myth and symbol, see Timothy Clark, *Derrida, Heidegger, Blanchot: Sources of Derrida's Notion and Practice of Literature* (Cambridge: Cambridge University Press, 1992), pp. 74–9.
11. Kafka, *The Castle*, p. 95.
12. This quotation originally appeared in *Le Musée imaginaire* (1947), which is collected in André Malraux, *Œuvres complètes*, 6 vols (Paris: Gallimard, 1989–2010), IV: *Écrits sur l'art I*, ed. Jean Yves Tadié (2004), pp. 201–332 (p. 240). An amended version of the three volumes that make up *The Psychology of Art* (1947–49) is more readily available in English, where this quotation is retained, as André Malraux, *The Voices of Silence*, trans. Stuart Gilbert (St Albans: Paladin, 1974), p. 46.
13. The idea that there is no origin to repetition, that there is never a first time and that everything is therefore always a replica, is already evident in essays first published in the first half of the 1950s such as 'The Essential Solitude': 'The irremediable character of what has no present, of what is not even there as having once been there, says: it never happened, never for a first time, and yet it starts over, again, again, infinitely' (SL 30).
14. Maurice Blanchot, '*Days of Hope* by André Malraux', trans. Michael Holland, in *Blanchot's Epoch*, ed. Hill and Holland, pp. 5–12.
15. See André Malraux, *Anti-Memoirs*, trans. Terence Kilmartin (New York: Holt, Rinehart and Winston, 1968), p. 152. Leslie Hill notes the 'oddly chiastic relationship' between the political paths of Blanchot

and Malraux, in *Bataille, Blanchot, Klossowski: Writing at the Limit* (Oxford: Oxford University Press, 2001), pp. 189–91 n. 17.
16. Philippe Lacoue-Labarthe, while noting the convergence between these two figures, argues that in citing Malraux's name at the end of *The Instant of My Death*, Blanchot is attempting to free himself from the mythical with all of its political associations. Philippe Lacoue-Labarthe, *Ending and Unending Agony: On Maurice Blanchot*, trans. Hannes Opelz (New York: Fordham University Press, 2015), pp. 46–61.
17. Leslie Hill, '"A Form that Thinks": Godard, Blanchot, Citation', in *Forever Godard*, ed. Michael Temple, James S. Williams and Michael Witt (London: Black Dog Publishing, 2004), pp. 396–415 (pp. 410–15).
18. Vivian Liska, comparing accounts of the Sirens in Blanchot and Adorno, argues that Ulysses and his tools foretell the dominion of modern technology in Blanchot, and that the transformation of the song into prose is the triumph of the Sirens, as the *Odyssey* becomes the space in which the world is swallowed up by the narrative that it contains. Liska is reading Blanchot from the perspective of Adorno, for whom literature in modernity was autonomous as a protest against capitalism and a retreat from history. See Vivian Liska, 'Two Sirens Singing: Literature as Contestation in Maurice Blanchot and Theodor W. Adorno', in *The Power of Contestation: Perspectives on Maurice Blanchot*, ed. Kevin Hart and Geoffrey H. Hartman (Baltimore, MD: Johns Hopkins University Press, 2004), pp. 80–100. This chapter shows that the relationship between literature and technology in Blanchot is not one of opposition.
19. Ian Maclachlan presents the encounter with the Sirens in Blanchot as a 'temporal quandary' in *Marking Time: Derrida, Blanchot, Beckett, des Forêts, Klossowski, Laporte* (Amsterdam: Rodopi, 2012), pp. 73–9.
20. See Chapter 1 for a discussion of Blanchot on *Moby-Dick* as myth in 'The Secret of Melville' (1941).
21. Heidegger, *What is Called Thinking?*, pp. 22–3.
22. Claude Lévi-Strauss, *Tristes tropiques*, trans. John Weightman and Doreen Weightman (London: Penguin, 2011), p. 413 (translation modified).
23. The role of hands in *Thomas the Obscure*, *Death Sentence* and *The Space of Literature* was discussed in Chapter 2. In 'Man at Point Zero' Blanchot comments that it is naive to believe that 'technological developments will suffice to put the solution to all the difficulties they create into our hands' (F 82). The hand left wanting, forever waiting for a solution or an end, is the hand that writes.
24. Lévi-Strauss, *Tristes tropiques*, p. 195.
25. George Duthuit's criticism of Malraux's imaginary museum, *Le Musée inimaginable*, was published in 1956, and Ernst Robert Curtius's *European Literature and the Latin Middle Ages* (1946) had also appeared in French translation the same year. Blanchot is therefore responding to a debate in progress in 'Museum Sickness'.

26. Maurice Blanchot, 'Le Mal du Musée', *La Nouvelle Nouvelle Revue française* 52 (1957): 687–96 (pp. 695–6) (my translation).
27. See Jacques Derrida, 'Plato's Pharmacy', in *Dissemination*, trans. Barbara Johnson (London: Athlone, 1981), pp. 61–171.
28. For an overview of Blanchot's response in 1958 to De Gaulle's return to power and his contribution to the 'The Manifesto of the 121', see Bident, *Maurice Blanchot*, pp. 303–11, 315–23.
29. Douglas Smith provides a useful overview of the context of this debate and compares the positions of Blanchot and Damisch in 'The Burning Library: Hubert Damisch, Maurice Blanchot, and the "Paperback Revolution"', *French Studies* 72, no. 4 (2018): 539–56.
30. See Hubert Damisch, 'La Culture de poche' (1964), in *Ruptures/Cultures* (Paris: Minuit, 1976), pp. 57–73. For the original article with the epigraph from Heidegger ('When we regard technology as something neutral, we are delivered over to it in the worst possible way'), see *Mercure de France* 1213 (1964): 482–98.
31. 'On a Change of Epoch' is of some importance to Stiegler, who selects a quotation from this essay as an epigraph to the General Introduction of *Technics and Time*. The Introduction demonstrates that Stiegler wants to specify the way technics constitutes our experience of time differently in different epochs, but Blanchot is sceptical that a new epoch can ever be identified and addressed as such.
32. Friedrich Nietzsche, *The Gay Science*, ed. Bernard Williams, trans. Josefine Nauckhoff (Cambridge: Cambridge University Press, 2001), p. 162.
33. For instance, Blanchot writes in 1958 that something fundamental seeks to be expressed in Nietzsche's work, 'a constant thought which is like the call of a unique centre, of a whole, that is never attained, but endlessly supposed and interrogated, sometimes demanded'. In 1969 this reads, 'a constant thought which is like the call of a non-centred centre, of a whole beyond everything, that is never attained [. . .]'. In 1958 Blanchot writes: 'all that relates to [the whole] seems to converge from all sides in order to resemble it'. Eleven years later this becomes: 'all that relates to [the whole] seems to press in from all sides in order to resemble it, all the while differing from it' (IC 140). For the 1958 version, see Maurice Blanchot, 'Nietzsche aujourd'hui', *La Nouvelle Nouvelle Revue française*, 68 (1958), 284–95 (p. 291) (my translation).
34. Heidegger, 'Nietzsche's Word: "God is Dead"', in *Off the Beaten Track*, pp. 157–99 (p. 167).
35. Ibid., p. 198.
36. Heidegger, 'On the Question of Being', trans. William McNeill, in *Pathmarks*, pp. 291–322 (p. 292).
37. Ibid., p. 310.
38. Blanchot's use of Heidegger in this response is discussed in the Introduction.

39. Maurice Blanchot, 'L'Attente', *Botteghe oscure* 22 (1958): 22–33 (p. 26). Also in Maurice Blanchot, *Awaiting Oblivion*, trans. John Gregg (Lincoln, NE: University of Nebraska Press, 1997), p. 10.
40. Blanchot, 'L'Attente', pp. 22–4.
41. See, for instance, Martin Heidegger, 'Who is Nietzsche's Zarathustra?', in *Nietzsche*, trans. David Farrell Krell, 4 vols (San Francisco: Harper and Row, 1979–87), II: *Eternal Recurrence of the Same* (1984), pp. 211–33 (pp. 227–8). I discuss Blanchot's engagement with Eternal Return in more detail in Chapter 4.
42. See Friedrich Nietzsche, *Thus Spoke Zarathustra*, trans. Graham Parkes (Oxford: Oxford University Press, 2001), pp. 11–13, 134–8.
43. '"Only a God Can Save Us": *Der Spiegel*'s interview with Martin Heidegger', trans. Maria P. Alter and John D. Caputo, in *The Heidegger Controversy: A Critical Reader*, ed. Richard Wolin (Cambridge, MA: MIT Press, 1993), pp. 91–116 (p. 107).
44. See Michael Holland, *Avant dire: essais sur Blanchot* (Paris: Hermann, 2015), p. 271.
45. Maurice Blanchot, 'Tu peux tuer cet homme', *La Nouvelle Nouvelle Revue française* 18 (1954): 1059–69 (p. 1061) (my translation).
46. Roger Laporte, 'Le Oui, le Non, le Neutre', *Critique* 229 (1966): 579–90 (p. 587) (my translation).
47. Heidegger, '"Only a God Can Save Us"', in *The Heidegger Controversy*, ed. Wolin, pp. 105–6.
48. In a study of the shifting patterns of 'linguistic negativism' across Blanchot's work, particularly negative affixes and negative modifiers to words (or 'unwords') such as 'inhumain', 'inquiétude' [*anxiety*] and 'immobile', Shane Weller argues that Blanchot belongs to a late modernism that 'develops such forms of linguistic negativism as what it takes to be the only aesthetically and ethically justifiable response to a modernity increasingly perceived as both socially and politically catastrophic'. See Shane Weller, 'Voidance: Linguistic Negativism in Maurice Blanchot's Fiction', *French Studies* 69, no. 1 (2015): 30–45 (pp. 44–5). Blanchot in fact rarely uses the term modernity and, as these essays on technology demonstrate, there is an affirmative tone in any such catastrophe that precedes and outstrips such negation.
49. Blanchot is in part responding to an essay by Emmanuel Levinas, 'Heidegger, Gagarin and Us' (1961), in *Difficult Freedom: Essays on Judaism*, trans. Seán Hand (London: Athlone, 1990), pp. 231–4.
50. Michael Holland comments on the significance of the insertion of such a dash before the words 'our end' in 'Rilke and Death's Demand' for its publication in *The Space of Literature*. Holland argues that Blanchot interrupts his argument at the point where his analysis is face to face with what defies it utterly. Michael Holland, 'Towards a New Literary Idiom: the Fiction and Criticism of Maurice Blanchot from 1941 to 1955', unpublished doctoral thesis, University of Oxford, 1981, p. 305.

51. Blanchot outlined his plans for the *International Review* in a set of papers published posthumously under the title '[The gravity of the project]', in *Political Writings*, pp. 56–66. See also Christophe Bident's chapter on the *International Review* in *Maurice Blanchot*, pp. 324–35; and Christopher Fynsk, 'Blanchot in *The International Review*', in *Blanchot's Epoch*, ed. Hill and Holland, pp. 104–20.
52. Michael Sheringham, *Everyday Life: Theories and Practices from Surrealism to the Present* (Oxford: Oxford University Press, 2006), p. 21. See also Michael Sheringham, 'Attending to the Everyday: Blanchot, Lefebvre, Certeau, Perec', *French Studies* 54, no. 2 (2000): 187–99. Blanchot will later locate a force for revolutionary change in the street in the aftermath of the events of May 1968 which is also associated with an anonymous speaking: 'Since May, the streets have awakened: they speak. This is one of the decisive changes. They have become alive, powerful, and sovereign once again: the place of all possible freedom. It is against this sovereign word of the streets that the most dangerous apparatus of insidious repression and brutal force has been put into place, threatening everyone' (PW 91). These comments were first published as an anonymous pamphlet, dated 17 July 1968, and were attributed to Blanchot by Dionys Mascolo.
53. Holland, *Avant dire*, pp. 297–306 (p. 302) (my translation).
54. Two essays before 'The Narrative Voice (the "it", the neuter)' as collected in *The Infinite Conversation*, 'The Effect of Strangeness' (1957) considers an altogether different sort of distance in Brechtian theatre: 'Constantly, Brecht seeks to animate this distance between spectacle and spectator, to render it workable and available, to prevent it from freezing and becoming the space across which the words that are addressed to us and the images that reflect us change into being (into the absence of being) so that, rather than speaking to us and representing us, these words absorb us and draw us out of ourselves' (IC 366).
55. See Gérard Genette, 'Voice', in *Narrative Discourse*, trans. Jane E. Lewin (Oxford: Blackwell, 1980), pp. 212–62.
56. Kafka, *The Castle*, p. 172.
57. See Marthe Robert, *The Old and the New: From Don Quixote to Kafka* (1963), trans. Carol Cosman (Berkeley, CA: University of California Press, 1977).
58. Blanchot writes in 'The Wooden Bridge (repetition, the neuter)': '[The critic] is a scape goat, banished to the edge of the literary space and responsible for every inaccurate version of the work so that the work, intact and innocent, may be affirmed in the sole copy deemed authentic – unknown, in fact, and probably non-existent – which is conserved in the cultural archives: the unique work, complete only if it is lacking something, lack which is its infinite relation to itself, plenitude expressed as deficiency' (IC 391).
59. Franz Kafka, *Das Schloss*, ed. Max Brod (Frankfurt am Main: Fischer Taschenbuch, [1963] 1983), p. 7.

60. On Blanchot and Kafka, literature and the law, see Hill, *Maurice Blanchot and Fragmentary Writing*, pp. 374–8.
61. Franz Kafka, 'The Hunter Gracchus', trans. Willa and Edwin Muir, in *The Complete Stories*, ed. Nahum N. Glatzer (New York: Schocken Books, 1983), pp. 226–30 (p. 228).
62. Kafka, 'The Silence of the Sirens', in *The Complete Stories*, pp. 430–2.
63. Elizabeth Boa, 'Revoicing Silenced Sirens: A Changing Motif in Works by Franz Kafka, Frank Wedekind and Barbara Köhler', *German Life and Letters* 57, no. 1 (2004): 8–20 (p. 12).
64. Kafka, 'The Silence of the Sirens', in *The Complete Stories*, p. 432.
65. Kafka, *The Castle*, p. 33.
66. Ibid., p. 95.
67. Derrida, 'Of an Apocalyptic Tone', p. 27.
68. Heidegger, *What is Called Thinking?*, p. 62.
69. Ibid., pp. 72–3.
70. Ibid., p. 71.
71. Christophe Bident has argued that the wolf may be a reference to Hermann Hesse, on whom Blanchot wrote in 1956 (*Maurice Blanchot*, p. 548 n. 5). For the essay by Blanchot, see Maurice Blanchot, 'H.H.' (1956), in *The Book to Come*, trans. Charlotte Mandell (Stanford, CA: Stanford University Press, 2003), pp. 165–82. In any case, this pack animal might not be such an unusual reference for Blanchot when one considers the importance of the anonymous chatter of the street.
72. See, for instance, Giorgio Agamben, *Remnants of Auschwitz*, trans. Daniel Heller-Roazen (New York: Zone Books, 2002). Misquoting Blanchot (Agamben: 'man is the indestructible that can be infinitely destroyed'; Blanchot: 'man is the indestructible that can be destroyed' (IC 130)), Agamben writes: 'The human being can survive the human being, the human being is what remains after the destruction of the human being, not because somewhere there is a human essence to be destroyed or saved, but because the place of the human is divided, because the human exists in the fracture between the living being and the speaking being, the inhuman and the human. That is: *the human being exists in the human being's non-place, in the missing articulation between the living being and logos*. The human being is the being that is lacking to itself and consists solely in this lack and in the errancy it opens' (p. 134). Agamben frames his discussion of the concentration camps in terms of human possibility; but for Blanchot the experience of death is premised on impossibility which is what the indestructible names. The screech of the lizard in *The Last Man* is just such a mark of otherness.

Chapter 4

Inorganic Writing

Following a period of relatively frequent engagement with the question of technology in all its forms, the term *la technique* is suppressed in Blanchot's writing from 1965 onwards. When 'Crossing the Line' was revised for publication in *The Infinite Conversation* in 1969, the following line was omitted, 'the concept of technology regarded as the return of the same in its constant rotation: being as rebeginning', and replaced with 'the absence of being as rebeginning' (IC 148).[1] The association of a thinking of technology with the name Heidegger was likely a factor in this decision. Blanchot writes in 1958 that Being is 'an inferior [*peu honteux*] Neuter' and criticises Heideggerian philosophy for its concern with taking root or grounding, quoting Levinas on this point: 'This is an existence which takes itself to be natural, whose place in the sun, its ground, its *site*, orients all signification – a pagan existing. Being directs its building and cultivating, in the midst of a familiar landscape, on a maternal earth . . .'[2]

The lack of any explicit reference to *la technique* from 1965 suggests a more radical refusal of any such thinking of technology in opposition to nature, which is always already traversed or contaminated by something unnatural. This coincides with the emergence of fragmentary writing and the substitution of non-living, but not necessarily inert, stones for those animals and insects which populate earlier work in a more radical contestation of the limits of the human. Leslie Hill has shown that Blanchot resisted the romantic or modernist temptation 'to subordinate fragmentary writing to a conception of the unified artwork and the dialectic of realisation or unrealisation it implied'. If what is at stake in the fragmentary is, as Hill writes, the affirmation of 'an always other promise of futurity' on which we should draw 'as the world threatens to move into a new and perhaps final epoch' dominated by, among other things, technological uniformity, then the reader is challenged to hear in fragmentary writing what we might call technical pluralities or something other than dominion in technology.[3] Ian James has explored how the philosophy of one of Blanchot's most persistent interlocutors,

Jean-Luc Nancy, unfolds as 'a decision to respond to the demand imposed by the multiple and the fragmentary'.[4] One of the ways this is felt is in Nancy's thinking of the intersection of the human subject and body with technology. This chapter asks what the consequences of fragmentary writing are for the subject in Blanchot; focusing on a selection of fragments from *The Infinite Conversation*, *The Step Not Beyond* and *The Writing of the Disaster*, it demonstrates that technology is everywhere implied once the term disappears from Blanchot's idiom. The fragmentary is a more inclusive writing which offers the possibility of transgression through a wayward 'unnatural' proliferation that extends beyond the subject.

Fragmentary Writing and Technology

In 1953 Blanchot had gone so far as to claim that writing was one, albeit privileged, mode of technique among others, and several essays from the 1950s and early 1960s had explored the dislocation, dispersion, suspension and futural uncertainty which result from encounters with various forms of modern technology. But just as Blanchot proposes that we abandon the term 'nihilism' in 1963, the French word *technique* does not appear at all in *The Step Not Beyond* (1973) and emerges twice in the closing pages of *The Writing of the Disaster* (1980), but only to refer to that side of technology associated with mastery, knowledge, possibility.

> ♦ Laws – their prosaic side – arguably mark a release from the Law by substituting for the invisible majesty of time the multiplied constraint of space; in much the same way, regulation abolishes what the power (which always comes first) of the name of law evokes, along with the rights that go alongside, yet establishes the domain of technology – technology which, as an affirmation of pure knowledge, takes over everything, controls everything, administers its every movement [*soumet tout geste à sa gestion*], such that there is no possibility of liberation because we can no longer speak of oppression. (WD 144)[5]

This sentence ends (the fragment continues, the concluding half is quoted below) with a Foucauldian emphasis: there can be no liberation when there is no oppression. In other words, there is no natural order which one can invoke; nature is just as much a product of techne as technology in the restricted sense. In modern times multiple and dispersed laws have replaced the Law of time. Techniques of 'pure knowledge', spread throughout a network of social institutions, exert a more comprehensive but also more subtle control over the individual than brute sovereign force.[6]

The disciplinary power of which Foucault wrote in 1975 is fragmented and dispersed; unlike the sovereign power which is exercised by one individual over many others, disciplinary power is thought in terms of a complex arrangement of forces in society without reference to sources or agents of power. This is a power built from the bottom up rather than wielded repressively from the top down; it concerns individuals as effects of discipline, moulded or generated by techniques that target the body with the aim of rendering it useful and docile. The language employed by Foucault to describe the traits of this individuality implies the natural – individuals are cellular, organic and genetic – but this is a constructed 'nature' and these individuals combine to form a machine which attains a greater efficiency than the sum of its parts.[7] Foucault's point is that there is no origin or essence; rather, any knowledge of a natural state that we have is a construct of the techniques of disciplinary power: 'The body, required to be docile in its minutest operations, opposes and shows the conditions of functioning proper to an organism. Disciplinary power has as its correlative an individuality that is not only analytical and "cellular", but also natural and "organic".'[8] Disciplinary power is, then, productive rather than oppressive, generating identities, knowledges and discourses by meticulously and extensively distributing, controlling, organising and combining the forces of bodies. The chance of rebellion against this power, which permeates every aspect of our lives and every level of society, seems slim.

There is, nonetheless, room for resistance in Foucault's analysis of disciplinary power, because without resistance there would be no power relation. He clarifies this position in *The History of Sexuality*: 'Where there is power, there is resistance, and yet, or rather consequently, this resistance is never in a position of exteriority in relation to that power.'[9] A tame form of resistance is certainly possible; but Foucault also gestures, via Blanchot, a figure for whom he would express profound admiration,[10] to a more radical uprising in a short tribute to the writer and journalist Maurice Clavel published shortly after his death in 1979. Here Foucault, writing in fragments, tries to integrate Clavel ('impatient, startled by the slightest noise, clamouring in the dark, summoning the storm') and Blanchot ('diaphanous, motionless, on the lookout for a day more transparent than the day, attentive to signs that are only revealed in the movement that erases them'). Two very different men, writes Foucault, both of whom introduced into the world the tension that rends apart the fabric of time.[11] There is no further mention of Blanchot in the following five short fragments, but Foucault surely has him in mind when he writes:

> The moment, the fracture, the fissure, the interruption eludes history. The human equivalent of (and perhaps response to) grace is the act of *uprising*. The revolution is structured according to an economy completely within time: conditions, promises, necessities; it resides within history, makes its bed there and eventually rests there. The uprising, however, interrupting time, allows men to stand tall on their ground and in their humanity.[12]

Foucault's is a genealogical study of power; his concept of power is entrenched within history. The sort of uprising envisaged here, conversely, is something like the change of epoch which for Blanchot both inscribes and suspends world, fracturing the present and positioning itself beyond historical parameters. Blanchot attributes this rebellious possibility to literature; the fragment quoted above on laws and regulation continues:

> Kafka's trial may be interpreted as an interlacing between these three domains (the Law, laws, rules): an inadequate interpretation, however, insofar as to give it credence one would have to assume a fourth domain not attributable to the other three – that of the overhang of literature itself, even though literature refuses this privileged standpoint, not allowing itself to become dependent on some other order or any order at all (pure intelligibility) in the name of which it might be symbolised. (WD 144–5)

One law cannot contain all laws, because it would then have to contain itself in an infinite regress. The Law to which Blanchot refers in the opening sentence of this fragment, quoted earlier, is the Law of time or death, that impossible necessity which incorporates its own transgression – I can die but *I* cannot die. Faced with this intractable thought, the Law is, in modern times, replaced with the sort of laws or disciplinary techniques discussed by Foucault which seek to control or to regulate life. The literary overhang, however, offers the possibility of transgression from within the Law; this is an alternative, non-hierarchical and rootless perspective which hangs beyond the limits of knowledge, representation and history. Blanchot's writing occupies that interval identified by Foucault from which it challenges the ruling powers in the same fragmented and dispersed mode as the technologies of disciplinary power. It seems that there is more to Blanchot's rethinking of *technique* from the mid-1960s onwards than a simple rejection.

This is confirmed by two essays from 1953 (the same year that Blanchot claimed that writing was one technology among others) which, when collected in *The Book to Come* in 1959, open the final section entitled 'Where is Literature Going?': 'The Disappearance of Literature' and 'The Search for Point Zero'. Blanchot considers the status of art in the modern technological world in both essays. In the first he writes: 'art does not negate the modern world, or the technological world, or the effort toward liberation and transformation that relies on this technology, but it expresses and perhaps achieves relationships that *precede* all objective and technological accomplishment' (BC 197). A similar point is made in the second essay: 'long before the inventions of technology, the use of radio waves and the transmission of images, it would have been enough to listen to the words of Hölderlin or Mallarmé to reveal the direction and extent of changes which seem unremarkable today' (BC 202). Literature and technology might belong to the same tradition, but the work of Mallarmé and Hölderlin, whose names appear in both essays alongside others, anticipates and outstrips radio and cinema. The second of these essays, a review of Roland Barthes' *Writing Degree Zero*, culminates in a discussion of that 'impersonal neutrality' – also mentioned in the first essay (BC 200) – experienced through modes of technology but more significantly through literature:

> By guiding us [. . .] toward what he called the zero [degree] of writing, Roland Barthes perhaps also shows us the moment when literature might be grasped. But the fact is that at that point literature would be not only a colourless, absent and neutral writing but the very experience of 'neutrality', which is never heard because when neutrality speaks, only the one who silences it prepares the conditions for it to be heard [*les conditions de l'entente*], and yet what there is to hear is this neutral speech, which has always been said, cannot stop being said and cannot be heard – a torment which we sense drawing closer in the pages of Samuel Beckett. (BC 209)

The repetition and lack of origin readily associated with radio and screen is also captured in this inhuman murmuring; the reference to Beckett calls to mind the rambling voice of *The Unnamable*, and one is also reminded of the strange noise heard down the telephone in Kafka's *The Castle*. The disembodied voice tirelessly repeating words in the above extract does not indicate a grey, undifferentiated and pure neuter – 'colourless, absent and neutral writing' are the words of Barthes[13] – but an infinitely contested and vibrant neutrality which cannot be grasped or set in stone and which is not restricted to a traditional notion of 'literature'. Literature cannot be reduced to a question of language, and it is impossible, Blanchot argues in both of these essays, to define the limits of literature: 'the experience of literature is the test [*épreuve*] of dispersion, it is the approach of what eludes unity, experience of what is without understanding, without agreement, without law – the errant [*erreur*] and the outside, the elusive and the irregular' (BC 205). Already in 1953 the influence of the fragmentary is evident, as 'literature' becomes associated with dispersion and disunity. The impact of modern technology reverberates with this experience, but the relationship is simultaneously underscored by discontinuity and difference as 'literature' exceeds and precedes the historical parameters within which technology functions.

The previous chapter demonstrated that Blanchot's engagement with questions surrounding modern technology peaked in the 1950s and early 1960s. During this time he began to develop the fragmentary idiom which he would employ in *Awaiting Oblivion* (1962), *The Step Not Beyond* (1973), *The Writing of the Disaster* (1980) and in later essays and additions in *The Infinite Conversation* (1969). One of the earliest explicit engagements with this mode of writing is a 1960 review of Clémence Ramnoux's doctoral thesis on Heraclitus, in which Blanchot wonders whether cutting up things and words had a precise technical meaning for Heraclitus at a time when Greek was written without spacing or punctuation (IC 443). This enigmatic comment comes at the end of a footnote without any further deliberation or explanation. The work in question was left by Heraclitus in the temple for his readers, Ramnoux stresses, and it was thanks to the separation of words that it could be read. Translations vary significantly depending on where one chooses to separate the signs that make up these fragments.

Dedicating a chapter to the first fragment, Ramnoux arranges two of the three given translations in tables; her suggested translation is presented in a numbered list, each point indicating where she has chosen to separate the words.[14] The significance of this work for Blanchot is not that there is one definitive translation, but that the separation between words is never established because always mobile, simultaneously placing every translation in doubt while affirming an excess that cannot be contained within any one interpretation (IC 90). The fragmentary form of Heraclitus's writing is crucial because it ensures that the double movement which is this dispersion that gathers is never stabilised. This reading of Heraclitus diverges significantly from that offered by Heidegger, for whom the thought of Heraclitus is associated with truth and gathering.[15] Blanchot, in contrast, emphasises that the play of words ensured by fragmentation exposes the original discontinuity that makes language possible:

> Basically, that which is language, that which speaks in an essential manner for Heraclitus, in things, in words, and in the thwarted or harmonious passage from the one to the other, and finally in all that manifests and all that conceals itself, is none other than Difference itself, which is mysterious because always different from whatever expresses it and such that there is nothing which does not say it and relate itself to it in saying, but such, too, that everything speaks because of it, even as itself remains unsayable. (IC 91)

Ramnoux stresses that we only have access to the thought of Heraclitus in quotation.[16] The problem of the origin is therefore extremely pertinent, and Blanchot is keen to demonstrate that this separation indicates an originary void. What speaks through these fragments is not Heraclitus as supreme thinker of Being, but that original difference that enables us to distinguish between words and things that never appears as or for itself: the neuter.[17]

The disembodied rambling discussed in the essay on Barthes finds an echo in the fragmentary writing of Heraclitus: both indicate this difference that is everywhere present but never presents itself as such. The ontico-ontological difference is privileged by Heidegger as a fundamental event in Being, but Blanchot thinks difference prior to ontology as a writing that precedes being and non-being; this difference is multiple and there is no privilege.[18] The neuter is specifically directed at something in the absence of all origin. The content of these Heraclitean fragments is a discourse on nature which, according to Ramnoux and Blanchot, represented a significant departure in the sixth century from those first interrogations of the origin by Hesiod, which focused on the sacred (IC 85–86).[19] One of the sections of the first fragment translated by Ramnoux reads: 'cutting up each thing in accordance with its nature, and arranging signs to say the thing as it is'.[20] Blanchot may have had this particular fragment in mind when he wondered about the technical meaning of cutting up things and words in the earlier footnote, and he writes later in the essay that each Heraclitean sentence is a carefully calculated cosmos (IC 87). Technical separation has always already contaminated the natural, and fragmentary writing exposes the unstable and reversible difference that occurs between nature and technology.

One year later in 1961, Blanchot, reviewing Foucault's doctoral thesis *Madness and Unreason: A History of Madness in the Classical Age*, considered madness in similar terms to those Heraclitean fragments: an unspeakable difference also defines the experience of madness, which cannot be classified as 'natural'. Foucault sets out a history of madness from the Renaissance through to the beginning of the nineteenth century, and practices that are recognisable in the twentieth century. During the Renaissance, the insane were perceived to be bearers of an otherwise hidden truth able to move beyond the boundaries of the known. This changed with the emergence of houses of confinement in the seventeenth century, which expressed the emerging normative order of modern society; those who did not conform to norms were imprisoned and exposed to the public gaze: paupers, prostitutes, the insane, criminals, orphans, invalids, the old, beggars. It was not until the end of the eighteenth and start of the nineteenth centuries that those considered insane were imprisoned in institutions, and madness came to be seen as something to be separated from various forms of unreason and studied and understood in isolation.[21]

In modern times, madness and unreason are therefore distinguished by reason: if one is mad one cannot tell the difference between things, one does not question on waking whether one is still dreaming. Madness is the call of indifference, but lurking in the depths of unreason is similarly this inability to make distinctions: 'The caesura that establishes the distance between reason and non-reason is the origin; the grip in which reason holds non-reason to extract its truth as madness, fault or sickness derives from that, and much further off.'[22] Blanchot questions how one writes a thesis, a reasoned argument, on unreason when the distinction between the two is always on the brink of collapse:

> to what extent can thought maintain itself in the *difference* between unreason and madness if what is revealed in the depths of unreason is the call of *indifference*: the neuter which is also difference itself, which is differentiated in nothing and not differentiated in anything [*ce qui (ne) se différencie en rien*]? (IC 199)[23]

The neuter differentiates, but the mobile difference that it establishes (prior to identity or opposition) creates indifference as much as difference. Foucault must take care to sustain the reversible mobility between reason and unreason, not to fall into the same trap as those psychoanalysts who cling on to a sort of scientific knowledge, 'which aims to situate madness with increasing precision in an unchanging nature and in a temporal, historical and social framework (in reality, it is not yet a matter of science)' (IC 200–1). Reason tries to locate madness within the confines of an understandable nature, but risks itself in this engagement.

The fragility of the difference established by the neuter between reason and unreason, and between unreason and madness, ensures that something always escapes the System. Madness, situated beyond historical limits and eluding classification, is that uprising discussed by Foucault with reference to Blanchot. In a short story first published in 1949 as 'A Story[?]', and later as *The Madness of the Day* (1973), this excess appears as a sort of inhuman resistance.[24] Largely set in a psychiatric hospital, the narrative is centred on the moment someone crushes glass into the narrator's eyes. Now blinded by light, he cannot return the unremitting studious gaze of the ophthalmologist and psychiatrist to whom, we learn at the end of the text, this narrative has been recounted. But behind these figures of authority embodying the laws of this panoptic society lurks that other Law discussed at the beginning of this chapter: 'Behind their backs, I saw the silhouette of the law. Not the law everyone knows, which is severe and hardly very agreeable; this law was different. Far from falling prey to its menace, I was the one who seemed to terrify it' (MD 14–15). Leslie Hill has written that this is the text's transgressive moment, revealing the double bind and fragility of the Law which is always both inescapable and unanswerable.[25] Madness responds to the demand of this Law in a double movement: the day is mad because its light, which enables sight, blinds us when we look at it. Such reversible mobility ensures that madness cannot be confined to the limits of reason. Consequently, when the narrator as 'madman' is imprisoned and studied in an attempt to render him an object of knowledge, a trace evades the scrutiny of the experts: 'I became a drop of water, a spot of ink. I reduced myself to them, all of me passed before their eyes, and when at last nothing was present but my perfect nothingness and there was nothing more to see, they ceased to see me too' (MD 14).

This unknowable trace is a resistance to the Law and is signalled elsewhere in the text by something like a stag beetle, once the narrator, scuttling around the basement of the library. This alien transformation occurs after the first of two references to a telephone: 'One day, I found myself confined in the city; travelling was now only a fantasy. I could not get through on the telephone [*Le téléphone cessa de répondre*]. My clothes were wearing out. I was suffering from the cold; springtime, quick' (MD 9). There are echoes here of K. in Kafka's *The Castle*: trapped in a town, unable to travel further and sinking into poverty, K. attempts to ring the Castle but hears only a strange background hum likened to the sound of children singing. The second reference to a telephone indicates the otherwise unknown destination of this call: 'They gave me a modest position in the institution. I answered the telephone' (MD 12). The telephone call is an externalised monologue between the two non-identical figures of the narrator: one a 'madman' imprisoned in the psychiatric hospital and working for the System, the other a delinquent roaming the city streets. But this exchange is one-sided, the telephone having refused to respond in the first instance. Christopher Fynsk has written of the closing line of *The Madness of the Day* ('A story? No. No stories, never again') in terms of a refusal that comes from 'a space and time other than that of the incarceration described in the lines that precede it. It speaks to the law and to the sovereignty of reason, to be sure, but it now draws a line in relation to the latter's demand.'[26] This analysis could perhaps be more persuasively applied to the telephone, which similarly refuses an exchange with reason, represented paradoxically by the narrator's non-identical double in the psychiatric hospital.

The telephone establishes and annuls a distance which precedes and enables language. It interrupts oral presence and reveals the intervention of techne in what seems most human. Writing of the telephone in Joyce's *Ulysses*, Derrida argues that in the beginning and before the modern device there must have been a telephone call: 'a mental telephony, which, inscribing remoteness, distance, *différance*, and spacing in the *phonē*, at the same time institutes, forbids, and interferes with the so-called monologue'.[27] There is no consequence for the narrator who answers the telephone in the hospital, committed as he is to an exchange within the limits of reason; but the narrator wandering the city, for whom the telephone refuses to respond, is exposed to this interruption, which triggers an identity crisis as he shelters in a library basement: '[the spirit of reading] saw me for what I was, an insect, a creature with mandibles who had come up from the dark regions of poverty. Who was I? It would have thrown me into great perplexity to answer that question' (MD 9–10). Left waiting on the telephone, the narrator refuses in turn to respond to this question. When refusal ceases to be subjective will, it becomes dehumanised in a positive sense. Nine years later, in the context of De Gaulle's return to power, Blanchot wrote of the political dimension of refusal:

> When we refuse, we refuse in a movement free from contempt and exaltation, one that is as far as possible anonymous, for the power of refusal is accomplished neither by us nor in our name, but from a very poor beginning that belongs first and foremost to those who cannot speak. Today, one might say that it is easy to refuse, that the exercise of this power carries little risk. This is no doubt true for most of us. I think, however, that refusal is never easy, that we must learn how to refuse and to maintain intact, by the rigour of thinking and modesty of expression, this power of refusal that each one of our affirmations must evidence from now on. (PW 7)

Refusal is an act of resistance, not one that pits counter-power against power, but one affirmed through something other than power. The telephone in *The Madness of the Day* is precisely that sort of powerless power that is simultaneously this refusal and what precedes it. In this sense the telephone call is fragmentary because, as Leslie Hill has remarked evoking Moses' broken tablets, it is not dependent on any prior law but is itself that abyssal law of interruption that forcibly interrupts all laws, including itself.[28]

The telephone in *The Madness of the Day* indicates that a thinking of technology is implied in the fragmentary idiom developed by Blanchot in the 1960s. Modern technology furthers the forgetting of Being for Heidegger, who identifies technology with representational calculating reason; Blanchot rejects this deeply nostalgic view through the association of the technical with a different sort of power expressed in fragmentary writing. The introduction to his review of Foucault from 1961 features an early example of the fragmentary idiom that takes precedence in his writing during the 1960s; this introduction – not taking Foucault's text as its object and falling under the category of neither fiction nor essay – is more radical than the main body of the review. Blanchot identifies the double movement of forgetting [*oubli*], which is at once the condition of possibility of memory and the condition of impossibility: '❖ You will not find the limits of forgetting, however far you may be able to forget' (AO 34). At stake here is the exteriority of fragmentary writing, about which Blanchot is able to be more specific in the review itself, where he begins by describing forgetting as what is inscribed beyond memory, forming an outside that is never articulated and whose inarticulation by society consequently interns this dangerous and unknowable region (IC 196).[29] Thinking the exteriority of writing without enclosing it within knowable limits is a difficult task. Foucault asks in relation to Blanchot how language can speak from and welcome the outside while working within the parameters of the Law. What is required is a sort of reflexive language: not reflexive in the sense that it is turned inwards towards an internal confirmation or central certitude, writes Foucault, but towards an extremity where it contests and is contested to the point that it is effaced.[30] Foucault looks to Blanchot's fiction to indicate what this language might look like:

> [The language of fiction] must no longer be a power [*pouvoir*] that tirelessly produces images and makes them shine, but rather a power [*puissance*] that undoes them, that lessens their overload, that infuses them with an inner transparency that illuminates them little by little until they burst and scatter in the lightness of the unimaginable. Blanchot's fictions are, rather than the images themselves, their transformation, displacement, and neutral interstices.[31]

Writing is not a productive power but a force that undoes, lightens words of their burden of meaning and scatters. 'Not reflection, but forgetting', writes Foucault of this outward-facing language.[32] Blanchot had considered forgetting in similar terms five years earlier in the introduction to his review of *History of Madness*: 'When we make use of forgetting as power [*pouvoir*], the ability [*pouvoir*] to forget brings us back to forgetting without power, to the movement of that which slips and steals away [*dérobe et se dérobe*], detour itself' (IC 195). Forgetting is power turned outside-in; it is that affirmative dimension to technology that is implied in the movement of fragmentary writing. This is further confirmed when the term *technique* is subsumed into the neuter from 1965 onwards, as the difference between the fragmentary and technology, like any difference established by the neuter, proves to be extremely fragile.

In 1964 Blanchot turned his attention to the version of the fragment put forward by the Jena Romantics in the *Athenaeum*, the influential journal edited by August Wilhelm and Friedrich Schlegel between 1798 and 1800. The latter wrote of the form chosen for some of the contributions to this journal: 'as yet no genre exists that is fragmentary, both in form and in content, simultaneously completely subjective and individual, and completely objective and like a necessary part in a system of all the sciences'. And also: 'A fragment, like a work of art, has to be entirely isolated from the surrounding world and complete in itself like a hedgehog.'[33] Schlegel thinks the fragment as an ideal inclusive totality which promises the all-inclusive work as a theoretical horizon or end point. Blanchot, while noting the revolutionary action implied in this project, is critical of this shift from the fragment to aphorism:

> This shortfall [*altération*] is perhaps unavoidable; but it means: (1) considering the fragment as a quintessential text, having its centre in itself rather than in the field set up by that fragment together with *other* fragments; (2) neglecting the interval (suspension and pause) that separates the fragments and turns that separation into the rhythmic principle of the work in its very structure; (3) forgetting that the tendency of this manner of writing is not to make a view of the whole more difficult or to loosen any bonds of unity, but to make possible new relations that are no longer part of any unity, in the same way that they exceed any whole. (IC 359)

This third excessive characteristic is underestimated by Jean-Luc Nancy and Philippe Lacoue-Labarthe in their mock dialogue of 1982, where they argue that the fragment in Blanchot's account remains dialectical. They quote the following passage from *The Writing of the Disaster*, omitting what follows 'energy of disappearing':

> ♦ The fragment, as fragment*s*, tends to dissolve the totality which it presupposes and sweeps aside in the direction of the dissolution whence it is not formed (properly speaking), to which it is exposed so that, disappearing, and, along with it, all identity, it maintains itself as the energy of disappearing, as repetitive energy and the limit of mortal infinity – or else work of the absence of work [*œuvre de l'absence d'œuvre*] (to say this again and in repeating it consign it to silence). Whence the fraudulent nature [*imposture*] of the System – the System raised by irony to an absolute absolute [*un absolu d'absolu*] – which is one way for the System still to impose itself by the discredit with which the demand of the fragment credits it. (WD 60–1)

Noting that the Greek origin of 'energy' can be translated as 'work', Nancy and Lacoue-Labarthe argue that Blanchot's fragment has the all-inclusive work as its horizon and is therefore no different from the Romantic aphorism.[34] However, read further and the relationship between fragment and totality becomes more complicated than a simple opposition: 'repetitive energy' suggests worklessness rather than work, and the insertion of a quotation from an earlier essay on the Jena Romantics, 'work of the absence of work', and the subsequent response in parentheses silences and exceeds this aphorism.[35] The 'work of the absence of work' associated with Romanticism is not the worklessness at stake in the fragmentary, which is the effect of an uncontrollable repetition or dissemination. The Romantic irony to which Blanchot refers in this passage, like reflexivity in the conventional sense, is a means of further reinforcing the dialectic: the system pretends to be unsystematic only to have a better grip on itself, to include its own opposite in an authoritarian way. But the dialectic can go in either direction, and there is another kind of irony which is reflexive in the sense that it is turned towards an extremity, so that writing and other modes of technology are unleashed in a disseminating and uncontrollable manner which escapes the system.

The force of repetition takes over from the subject in fragmentary writing. It is the repetition enabled by modern technology, the printing press, that drives the logic behind the paperback to the point of explosion in 'The Great Reducers' (1965), which is the last mention of technology in Blanchot for fifteen years. The 'braking and stopping system' associated with modern technology and culture is transformed in this essay into 'an explosive process' (F 68). Works are so readily available following the development of the inexpensive paperback that it is as if time were abolished by mass reproduction: 'Duration, this time of maturation and patience which until now, rightly or wrongly, was considered necessary for all cultural transmission, thus tends to be abolished' (F 70). The printing press allows that interruption or fracture of which Foucault writes in 1979, outplaying the cultural limits within which it functions. Blanchot argues that one consequence of the mass reproduction of texts is that we might now better understand the reductive power associated with culture, a power that degrades works to mere values and ensures that the incalculable and enigmatic distance of the work becomes familiar, knowable and sayable. Culture is here defined by plenitude; existing within a continuous and homogeneous space without weakness or digression, an all-encompassing unity and identity are its ideals (F 71). Literature is displaced through cultural appropriation; but 'literature', questioning not only the limits of this cultural unity but also itself, challenges this continuity. Quoting Trotsky in the concluding footnote to the essay, Blanchot compares literature and art to the Revolution which turns life into a sort of bivouac, rendering everything – but itself more than anything else – strange, transitory and precarious (F 295).

A little over one year later, in 'Nietzsche and Fragmentary Writing' (1966/7), Blanchot no longer appeals to nihilism – he describes nothingness as an all-too-convenient refuge – but turns to the fragment as a means of responding to the outside indicated by this rupture. At stake is another crucial difference between Blanchot and Heidegger: Nietzsche is not the last metaphysician, the label applied by Heidegger, but a writer of fragments that gesture towards an outside which resists expression. The significance of typography to the elaboration of the fragmentary in this essay is striking. 'Language: affirmation itself, that which no longer affirms itself in reason or in anticipation of Unity. Affirmation of difference, yet never different. Plural speech' (IC 156). The account of the neuter in 'Forgetting, Unreason' echoes this unstable relationship between language and affirmation, where madness: (un)reason. And just as the telephone call in *The Madness of the Day* establishes and annuls a distance within the doubled narrator, the colon equates language to an affirmation of (in)difference which it simultaneously destabilises. This is not an isolated instance where Blanchot uses punctuation as a destabilising technique: 'We only know that the thought of the overman signifies: man disappears, an affirmation pushed furthest when it doubles as a question: does man disappear?' (IC 158); '$\pm$ $\pm$ To interpret: the infinite: the world. The world? A text? The text: the movement of writing in its neutrality' (IC 168); '$\pm$ $\pm$ Difference: the non-identity of the same, the movement of distance, that which carries by carrying off [*porte en déportant*], the becoming of interruption' (IC 170). The colons suggest a clear and stable relationship between two, sometimes three, terms; however, the relation is no sooner asserted than it is placed under erasure through the introduction of semi-colons or question marks in a sort of typographical re-enactment of the movement of distance and the becoming of interruption described in that last line quoted.

The plus-minus sign ($\pm \pm$), the mathematical symbol preceding these fragments, indicates a choice of two possible values, each of which is the suspension or deferral of the other. This symbol points to that original separation, allowing difference to speak (because what matters is the unstable answer or reversible movement between the two values) and an incalculable excess to escape this mathematical system. Blanchot notes the importance of typographical marks in the penultimate fragment of the essay:

> $\pm \pm$ [. . .] Articulating the void with the help of the void, structuring it as the void by drawing out the strange irregularity that always, and from the outset, defines it as the void, is how spatial signs [*signes d'espace*] – punctuation, accents, scansion, rhythm (disposition) –, a prior requisite of all writing, put difference into play and are drawn into its play. It is not however their function to translate this void or to make it visible, as in the case of musical notation: on the contrary, far from holding back a written text at the level of the traces it leaves or the forms it makes concrete, their distinguishing feature [*leur propriété*] is to indicate in that text the fissure or incisive breach (the invisible marking of a mark) by which the inside is forever turned outside, even as the distance that always differentiates the mark from itself [*l'écart qui toujours l'en écarte*] shows itself as the power to give meaning and seemingly constitute its origin. (IC 169–70)

These interrupting signs do not translate the void but indicate a rupture. Of course, this distance is never stable and is continually distanced from itself in a doubled movement of external reflection, which recalls the discussion of revolution and literature at the end of 'The Great Reducers' similarly enabled by the printing press. The Nietzschean fragment, Blanchot had written in his notes for the *International Review*, is linked to that roving thought which is accomplished in separate affirmations (PW 63); these signs place this discourse in relation to the fragmentary which lies outside the totality and coherence of language, enabling each fragment to think the impossible. For Derrida, analysing the significance of punctuation for Blanchot in *Michel Foucault as I Imagine Him*, such carefully selected typographical marks indicate the impossible, not fatal, experience of dying.³⁶ Any thought of dying is a deconstruction of the will in which the machine takes over.

The mechanical worklessness of fragmentary writing is further underscored by Blanchot in a fragment on Nietzsche's Eternal Return which first appeared in 1970, the year after Pierre Klossowski's *Nietzsche and the Vicious Circle*. Heidegger thinks Eternal Return as the sum of the will: by dint of the will, Nietzsche is able to overcome time, and Eternal Return is the last-ditch statement of metaphysics. Blanchot, on the other hand, following Klossowski, sees in Eternal Return a total loss of will. Klossowski reads Eternal Return on two levels: the paradoxical revelation experienced by Nietzsche at Sils-Maria (a revelation that cannot be a revelation because it has always already happened) and the presentation of the doctrine of the vicious circle.³⁷ Eternal Return as revelation represents an apprehension of the self as what it really is (a fortuitous moment) through a process of passing through previous instances of the self. The past is irretrievable, and so to will the past is to will necessity or to will what is beyond will. In this account, the self is nothing other than a discontinuous series of non-identical and fortuitous instances, and Eternal Return is a forgetting of the current self and a remembering of the others each in turn, until one returns to the inactive self that first underwent the revelation of Return.³⁸ Eternal Return is therefore a sort of deconstruction of the will, which brings us back to the machine. It is in this context that Blanchot writes in 1970:

> ♦ Let us accept that events are 'real' only in the past, as in the case of a machine functioning in such a way that, with the help of an efficient memory, though with a lingering doubt, we might recall all that the future [*futur*] promises us or makes us fear. But isn't the past always less rich than the future [*avenir*] and always other? Most certainly, except if, the past being the infinitely void and the future [*avenir*] the infinitely void, the one and the other were only the oblique way (with the screen set at a different angle) in which the void is given, simulating now the possible-impossible, now the irrevocable-revoked [*l'irrévocable-révolu*]; or again, except if the law of Eternal Return were to leave no other choice than for one to live the future in the past and the past as still to come [*vivre au passé l'avenir et à venir le passé*], without the past or the future being required however to swap places as in the circular movement of the Same, since, from the one to the other, interruption, the lack of presence, may be thought to prevent all communication other than by interruption: an interruption experienced either as what is the finality of the past or the potential of the future [*le révolu du passé ou le possible de l'avenir*], or precisely as the unbelievable utopia of Eternal Return. One cannot however believe in Eternal Return. That is its sole guarantee, its

'verification'. Such, in some far-away place [*là-bas*], is the demand of the Law. (SNB 14)

The future belongs as much to yesterday as to tomorrow when it is experienced as repetition of an irretrievable past. This is a messianic futurity void of any past or future Messiah, which, rather than hastening the end, is the patient deferral of all ending. This messianic structure is eternally open to a future which is never limited by the horizons of meaning and allows for the passage towards the other.[39] At every point in Eternal Return the present is eclipsed and interrupted: a void is opened between past and future in which what matters, like those two values indicated by the plus-minus sign in 'Nietzsche and Fragmentary Writing', is that difference that always risks slipping into indifference. But the only proof we have of Eternal Return is that we cannot believe in it: what Klossowski calls the presentation of the doctrine of the vicious circle is always describing something that escapes description. The law of interruption interrupts itself; returning to the self that first underwent the revelation of Eternal Return, the will that wills this experience is undone and Eternal Return, dehumanised, becomes an uncontrollable mechanism. The final section of this chapter considers how the shift towards a broader, more inclusive techne following the suppression of *technique* in 1965 results in an inorganic writing.

Nature Gone Haywire

The description of Eternal Return as a forgetting machine in *The Step Not Beyond* reveals the otherwise unarticulated role of techne in the privation of subjectivity. Eternal Return, preventing all communication other than by interruption, is a sort of radicalised telephone call exposing the self to its own fortuity at all moments in time. Fragmentary writing similarly disobeys all rule of identity to outplay the human. When *technique* disappears from Blanchot's idiom, technology becomes everywhere implied, and the humans, animals and insects that once populated Blanchot's writing give way to piles of rubble in *The Step Not Beyond*.

Blanchot's short contribution to a special issue of *Cahiers Confrontation* entitled *Who Comes after the Subject?* provides no answer to the interrogative pronoun 'Who?' which it takes as its title, but is an unwilled refusal to respond between the one who writes and a spectral figure hanging over their shoulder: 'Someone looking over my shoulder (me perhaps) says, reading the question: *Who comes after the subject?*: "Here you are, returned to that distant time when *you were taking your baccalaureate exam."* – "Yes, but this time I will fail."'[40] What comes after the subject is a non-identical past; there can be no facsimile when the self is destitute and the repetitive energy of fragmentary writing takes over, undoing all presence. The *who?* does not belong to an ordinary temporality – always arriving, its arrival is perpetually deferred – but to the temporality of a suspended afterwards. In this sense the *who?* is non-living and the unending dialogue that forms the bulk of this 'response' gives way to a writing affirmed as mechanistic dissemination: some of the closing lines of 'Who?' are a quotation from Claude Morali who is in fact quoting from *The Step Not Beyond*.[41]

According to Klossowski, Eternal Return as doctrine, a thought void of any content, places the entirety of individual experience under the law of repetition, non-identity and discontinuity.[42] The interrogative pronoun, having evacuated the subject of all identity, persists unanswered so that the only thing left to question is itself. The result is the echoed repetition of the *who?* which is forever differing from itself like that spectral figure looking over the shoulder of the one who writes. Interrogating the neuter is analogous to posing the question: 'Who?'

> ♦ We can inquire into the neuter, aware that the inquiry only goes as far as itself; it may already be said to be neutralised, and cannot be in the form of any 'what is . . .?', even if it then leaves the place of what is questioned empty by questioning only that empty place; perhaps because the neuter always comes into question while remaining beyond question. We can scrutinise the neuter, without the neuter ever being under scrutiny. As for the answer, the repeated echo of the neuter, this is not even pure tautology, since it scatters the speech of the same. *The neuter, the neuter*: is this repetition, or not rather something like the rebounds that, to an infinite degree, by the slipping of what slips, align themselves in multiple series: the pebble [*galet*], the force of the throw, the surface supporting it, the surface falling away, time, the straight line bending and returning to the point of the fall which then, without being part of them, results from each of these moments, and cannot therefore be isolated, even though it takes place separately from them, such that the singular point that may be thought to mark it remains, in its singularity, outside the reality of the whole: unreal and unrealised? (SNB 109)

'*The neuter, the neuter*', Blanchot writes in this extract, leaving the unspoken difference suspended over the clause that follows. This rebound produces differing unforeseen effects with each impact. Like a stone skimming across the water, the subject becomes impoverished, weakened with each glance off the water's surface, and is revealed to be nothing other than a discontinuous series of non-identical and fortuitous instances. There are echoes here of the description of Eternal Return as forgetting machine: *galet* may refer to a pebble but also to the tensioner or pulley in an engine that keeps the belt taut and the engine running smoothly; here the pulley is faulty and introduces play into the mechanism. Derrida, in his analysis of the apocalyptic tone, remarks that 'tonos' first signified everything subject to stricture: the tight ligament, cord, the braided rope, cable, strap (we could also add to this list the shoelaces in the painting by Van Gogh).[43] Changes in tone or a multiplicity of tones leads to a slackening or unravelling of the philosophical tone, a derailment that interrupts the unity of the destination, the self-identity of the addressee or sender. Fragmentary writing allows such a multiplicity of tones and proposes radical change; the neuter renders everything non-identical with itself; but this cannot take place in the here and now – the neuter can never be the object of an interrogation – and once advanced like the skimmed stone this radical change collapses and everything remains the same.

The effects of this mechanism are seen in the strange spaces and figures of *The Step Not Beyond*, in which fragments emanate from a depopulated world where non-living figures await a forever-deferred future. There is almost nothing in this text which can be identified as natural or organic: those fragments that seem to narrate a fiction are set in a cityscape littered, indoors and out, with rubble.

> ♦ *Words exchanged over the heavy marble table, going from immobility to immobility. He moved a few paces away, listening to the young murmur of the distant days and years. All around were men apparently asleep, lying on the ground, covers thrown over them like one throws earth onto an embankment, and these innumerable little knolls, thoughts of the crumbled city, were levelled to the point of becoming the bare floor of the room.* (SNB 111–12)

The stones scattered across the floor of this room signal a radical non-identity which is open to the other because it is difference itself; the doubled figure of 'Who?' and the ricocheted movement of the skimming stone and of the neuter also indicate this difference. The stones are neither dead nor alive but suspended in non-living repetition; the difference that speaks from them is also the difference that renders the subject destitute. Blankets are thrown over these figures as if they were throwing earth on an embankment; the piles of rubble are a defence or resistance comparable to the refusal explored earlier which, Blanchot had written in connection to De Gaulle's return to power in 1958, is not accomplished by an individual but 'from a very poor beginning that belongs first and foremost to those who cannot speak' (PW 7). It is in this sense that not only the stones but this movement of repetition as such are open to the other, which could be human, animal, insect or thing.

Depicted in this fragment is the echo of a politically significant event, most likely the student occupations of May 1968 in which Blanchot was heavily involved.[44] A debate takes place across the table while on the floor tired figures lying down to rest are exposed to a persistent youthful murmuring. The echo of May 1968 is also heard in the children's song in that displaced quotation at the end of 'Who?' (Blanchot quoting Morali quoting Blanchot): '"*As if this call had rung out, stifled, but a joyful call nonetheless, the cry of children playing in the garden: "Who is me today?" – "Who is taking my place?" And the joyful, infinite reply*: him, him, him [*lui, lui, lui*].'[45] Only children can give an account that is open to impossibility, Blanchot continues, and only children can sing it joyously: 'Let us be, even [*Soyons, fût-ce*] in the anguish and the heaviness of uncertainty, from time to time, these children.'[46] In the French, the first-person plural imperative commands or asserts the presence of these children, which is then suspended by the third-person imperfect subjunctive that follows, introducing uncertainty and discontinuity and eclipsing this presence. The song of the children playing in the garden simultaneously rings out and is stifled; the stress is on their presence and identity as subjects but the response is inconclusive, and the repeated impersonal pronoun indicates a ricochet, an unspoken difference, that has undone and will undo the subject. That the undoing of the subject has already begun is more apparent in the version quoted in 'Who?' in 1984, where a dash is inserted that does not appear in *The Step Not Beyond* in 1973.

The unwilled refusal to respond to the impossible question put to Blanchot in 1984 reveals a destitute subject evacuated of all identity and suspended in the temporality of non-living repetition. The subject, interrupted, gives way to an uncontrollable mechanism: fragmentary writing. The fragment behaves like a cancerous cell, proliferating beyond its own borders and undermining the stability of (Blanchot's) original text:

> ♦ What is it about the mythic or hyperbolic term 'cancer' that frightens us by its very name, as if it were the unnameable itself? The reason might be that it claims to defeat the system of codes under the authority of which, alive and accepting life, we enjoy the security of a purely formal existence, obeying a model sign according to a programme unfolding in apparently normative fashion from beginning to end. 'Cancer' may be thought to symbolise (and 'realise')

the refusal to respond: here is a cell that ignores instructions, develops outside the law, in a way said to be anarchic – but it also does more: it destroys the idea of any programme, undermining both the exchange and the message, and the possibility of reducing everything to a sign-based simulation. Cancer, in this perspective, is a political phenomenon, one of the rare ways in which the system comes to be dislocated, and its universal programming and signifying power disarticulated by proliferation and disorder – a task accomplished in former times by leprosy, then by the plague. Something we cannot understand maliciously neutralises the authority of knowledge in its position of mastery. It is not therefore because it simply represents death at work [*au travail*] that cancer may be described as a singular threat: it is as a deadly *malfunction* [*dérèglement*], a malfunction more threatening than the fact of dying itself and endowing that fact with the characteristic of not allowing itself to be counted or taken into account, in the same way that suicide disappears from the statistics supposed to keep count of it. [If the so-called cancerous cell, reproducing itself indefinitely, is timeless, whoever is dying of it thinks, and this is the irony of their death: 'I am dying of my timelessness.'] (WD 86–7)

The final sentence of the fragment quoted here does not appear in the first French edition of the text dated 18 September 1980; this sentence is a later addition that does not change the pagination of the text, which bears no acknowledgement that it is anything other than a first edition.[47] Through a sort of wayward proliferation, an uncontrollable dissemination that escapes the system, the cancerous cell works outside the law of the programme and destroys all idea of a programme. The cancerous cell is perhaps a Foucauldian resistance to the biopolitical forces that regulate and manage our lives – Foucault writes in the first volume of *The History of Sexuality* that suicide was once a crime, because the right to death was the power possessed by the sovereign over his people, but now it is a unique and individual act of resistance against forms of administering life[48] – but Blanchot goes further: cancer is mortal malfunctioning, not simply death at work. The significance of this difference is clarified in the cancerous proliferation of the fragment: the irony of this death is that it eludes the subject. Blanchot would suggest that Foucault's account of suicidal resistance is reliant on the will of a subject (we saw earlier that Blanchot understands romantic irony as an expression of poetic subjectivity); this cancerous proliferation is a different sort of incomprehensible and infinitely reflexive irony that exceeds and contests subjectivity.

A Blanchotian reflexivity marks this image of the proliferating cancerous cell: turning outwards it contests and is contested to the point that it is effaced. The fragment echoes this cancerous proliferation: beyond simple opposition, the relationship of the fragmentary to the organic is one of excess. The telephone call and stag beetle of *The Madness of the Day*, the impact of mass paperback publishing, the careful punctuation of the essay on Nietzsche, the description of Eternal Return as forgetting machine, the stones scattered throughout *The Step Not Beyond*: mechanical references in Blanchot indicate a rupture that allows an excess. In its excess the fragmentary is that techne that outplays the human; it shows that the end does not always imply a new beginning but a suspended moment where nothing is final — and there is something radically affirmative about this interruption which offers the chance to hear something other than dominion in technology.

Notes

1. Maurice Blanchot, 'Passage de la ligne', *La Nouvelle Nouvelle Revue française* 69 (1958): 468–79 (p. 477) (my translation).
2. Levinas quoted in Blanchot, 'L'Étrange et l'étranger', in *La Condition critique*, p. 287 n. 1. Levinas continues: 'Anonymous, neuter, it directs it, ethically indifferent, as a heroic freedom, foreign to all guilt with regard to the other.' Emmanuel Levinas, 'Philosophy and the Idea of Infinity' (1957), in *Collected Philosophical Papers*, trans. Alphonso Lingis (Dordrecht: Martinus Nijhoff, 1987), pp. 52–3.
3. Hill, *Maurice Blanchot and Fragmentary Writing*, pp. 6–7.
4. Ian James, *An Introduction to the Philosophy of Jean-Luc Nancy: The Fragmentary Demand* (Stanford, CA: Stanford University Press, 2006), p. 3.
5. The first reference to technology comes one page earlier: 'The substitution of rules for the law seems to be, in modern times, an attempt not only to demystify the power of prohibition but also to release thought from the One by proposing multiple and disparate technological possibilities to conventional wisdom' (WD 143).
6. See the transition traced by Michel Foucault from the sovereign power exercised in the spectacle of execution to a more subtle and dispersed disciplinary power in the opening chapter of *Discipline and Punish: The Birth of the Prison*, trans. Alan Sheridan (London: Penguin, 1991), pp. 3–31.
7. Foucault outlines how the distribution of individuals, the control of activities, the organising of geneses and the composing of forces produce a cellular, organic, genetic and combinatory individuality respectively (ibid., pp. 135–69).
8. Ibid., p. 156.
9. Michel Foucault, *The History of Sexuality*, trans. Robert Hurley, 3 vols (London: Penguin, 2020), I: *The Will to Knowledge*, p. 95.

10. Reminiscing about the 1950s with his friend Paul Veyne, Foucault is reported to have said: 'At that time, I dreamt of being Blanchot.' See Didier Eribon, *Michel Foucault*, trans. Betsy Wing (London: Faber, 1992), p. 58.
11. Michel Foucault, 'Vivre autrement le temps', in *Dits et écrits: 1954–1988*, ed. Daniel Defert and François Ewald, 4 vols (Paris: Gallimard, 1994), III: *1976–1979*, pp. 788–90 (p. 788) (my translation).
12. Ibid., p. 790 (my translation).
13. Promising a brief history of writing in the introduction to *Writing Degree Zero*, Barthes argues that writers in the nineteenth century increasingly reflected on the status of literature in an attempt to distance their work from bourgeois cultural and social dominance; this led to attempts in the twentieth century to eradicate all signs of Literature from what Barthes calls a 'colourless writing': 'in those neutral modes of writing, called here "the zero degree of writing", we can easily discern a negative momentum, and an inability to maintain it within time's flow, as if Literature, having tended for a hundred years now to transmute its surface into a form with no antecedents, could no longer find purity anywhere but in the absence of all signs, finally proposing the realisation of this Orphean dream: a writer without Literature. Colourless writing like Camus's, Blanchot's or Cayrol's, for example, or controversial writing like Queneau's, represents the last episode of a Passion of writing, which recounts stage by stage the disintegration of bourgeois consciousness.' Roland Barthes, *Writing Degree Zero*, trans. Annette Lavers and Colin Smith (New York: Hill and Wang, 1968), p. 5. On the dialogue between Blanchot and Barthes and the question of the neuter, see Christophe Bident, 'R/M, 1953', in *Blanchot's Epoch*, ed. Hill and Holland, pp. 67–83.
14. Clémence Ramnoux, *Héraclite ou l'homme entre les choses et les mots* (Paris: Les Belles Lettres, 1959), pp. 308–16.
15. See Martin Heidegger, 'Logos (Heraclitus, Fragment 50)' (1951) and 'Aletheia (Heraclitus, Fragment 6)' (1954), in *Early Greek Thinking*, trans. David Farrell Krell (New York: Harper and Row, 1984), pp. 59–78, 102–23. These essays were adapted from lectures given in 1944 and 1943 respectively.
16. Ramnoux, *Héraclite*, p. 220.
17. Lars Iyer, reading Blanchot on Heraclitus, misinterprets the neuter when he thinks of words in the neutral gender (mentioned by Blanchot in this essay) as the mark of the immediate in language, which stands for the materiality of the whole; according to Iyer this is a form of resistance to the 'great liquefaction of reality in the streaming of language'. Lars Iyer, '*Logos* and Difference: Blanchot, Heidegger, Heraclitus', *Parallax* 11, no. 2 (2005): 14–24 (p. 22). The neuter as a sort of non-concept, an impersonal force, cannot be located within any one term, concept, or text; nor is it pure indifference as Iyer suggests, but a difference always differing from itself.
18. Some critics misread the neuter as ontology in disguise. Anne-Lise Schulte Nordholt, for instance, argues that 'this ontological region

of the elementary, where everything is absent and yet by that means infinitely present, this is what Blanchot calls the neuter'. Anne-Lise Schulte Nordholt, *Maurice Blanchot: l'écriture comme expérience du dehors* (Geneva: Droz, 1995), p. 203 (my translation). Chapter 3 showed, through Blanchot's strikethrough of 'nothingness' as well as 'Being', that not just Being but potentially all words and all language can be put under erasure. Derrida similarly thinks Difference prior to ontology in 'Différance', in *Margins of Philosophy*, pp. 1–27.
19. See also Ramnoux, *Héraclite*, pp. 1–5.
20. Ibid., p. 314 (my translation).
21. See Michel Foucault, 'The Great Confinement', in *History of Madness*, trans. Jonathan Murphy and Jean Khalfa, ed. Jean Khalfa (London: Routledge, 2006), pp. 44–77.
22. Ibid., p. xxviii.
23. Derrida similarly argues that *History of Madness* is an impossible project in 'Cogito and the History of Madness' (1963), in *Writing and Difference*, trans. Alan Bass (London: Routledge, 2001), pp. 36–76.
24. This was first published in a literary journal bearing the name of the eponymous hero of Hölderlin's unfinished tragedy of 1797–99; the title of Blanchot's contribution was given as 'Un récit?' on the front cover of the journal, but appeared simply as 'Un récit' on the inner contents page of *Empédocle* 2 (1949): 13–22.
25. Hill, *Blanchot: Extreme Contemporary*, pp. 100–1.
26. Christopher Fynsk, *Last Steps: Maurice Blanchot's Exilic Writing* (New York: Fordham University Press, 2013), p. 66.
27. Jacques Derrida, 'Ulysses Gramophone: Hear Say Yes in Joyce', trans. Tina Kendall, rev. Shari Benstock, in *Acts of Literature*, ed. Derek Attridge (New York: Routledge, 1992), pp. 253–309 (pp. 271–2); see in particular the second section of this essay (pp. 265–75).
28. Leslie Hill, 'From Deconstruction to Disaster (Derrida, Blanchot, Hegel)', *Paragraph* 39, no. 2 (2016): 187–201 (p. 198).
29. Foucault argues that madness exceeds the limits of society and that, from the seventeenth century onwards, society endeavoured to protect itself by locking madness away, by making it possible and knowable, by interning and silencing the outside. See, for instance, the chapters '*Stultifera navis*' and 'The Great Confinement', in Foucault, *History of Madness*, pp. 3–77.
30. Foucault, 'Maurice Blanchot: The Thought from Outside' (1966), pp. 21–2.
31. Ibid., p. 23.
32. Ibid., p. 22.
33. 'Athenaeum Fragments', trans. P. Firchow, in *Classic and Romantic German Aesthetics*, ed. Bernstein, pp. 246–60 (pp. 248, 251).
34. Philippe Lacoue-Labarthe and Jean-Luc Nancy, 'Noli me frangere' (1982), in *Expectation: Philosophy, Literature*, by Jean-Luc Nancy, trans. Brian Holmes (New York: Fordham University Press, 2018), pp. 131–41 (pp. 132, 135–6). Other critics have also overstated the connection

between Blanchot and Romanticism: J. M. Bernstein argues that Romanticism is the primary context in which one should read Blanchot in 'Poesy and the Arbitrariness of the Sign: Notes for a Critique of Jena Romanticism', in *Philosophical Romanticism*, ed. Nikolas Kompridis (London: Routledge, 2006), pp. 143–72 (pp. 164–8); and we saw in Chapter 1 that Gerald Bruns reads Blanchot out of context when he describes him as a 'last Romantic'. On the association of Blanchot with the early German Romantics by Nancy and Lacoue-Labarthe, see Hill, *Nancy, Blanchot*, pp. 28–37.

35. The 'original' passage from which this quotation is taken reads: 'And certainly [Romanticism] is often without works [*sans œuvre*], but this is because it is the work of the absence of the work, poetry affirmed in the purity of the poetic act, affirmation without duration, freedom without realisation, a force [*puissance*] elevated in its disappearance, in no way discredited if it does not leave any trace, for this was its goal: to make poetry shine, not as nature, nor even as work [*œuvre*], but as pure consciousness in the instant' (IC 353). Blanchot's return to Schlegel in 1980 was probably prompted by the publication in French in 1978 of Philippe Lacoue-Labarthe and Jean-Luc Nancy, *The Literary Absolute: The Theory of Literature in German Romanticism*, trans. Philip Barnard and Cheryl Lester (Albany, NY: State University of New York Press, 1988).

36. Jacques Derrida, *Politics of Friendship*, trans. George Collins (London: Verso, 1997), pp. 301–2.

37. Pierre Klossowski, 'The Experience of the Eternal Return', in *Nietzsche and the Vicious Circle*, trans. Daniel W. Smith (London: Athlone, 1997), pp. 55–73.

38. See Ian James, 'Eternal Return and the "Signe du Cercle Vicieux"', in *Pierre Klossowski: The Persistence of a Name* (Oxford: Legenda, 2000), pp. 129–41.

39. The text by Blanchot which most obviously sets in play this self-deconstructive movement of the messianic (the promise that can never realise itself and in affirming itself resists the possibility of its realisation and in so doing simultaneously maintains and suspends itself) is *The Writing of the Disaster* (1980), trans. Ann Smock (Lincoln, NE: University of Nebraska Press, 1995), pp. 141–2. On the messianic in Blanchot, see Hill, *Maurice Blanchot and Fragmentary Writing*, pp. 368–91.

40. Maurice Blanchot, 'Who?' (1989), trans. Eduardo Cadava, in *Who Comes after the Subject?*, ed. Eduardo Cadava, Peter Connor and Jean-Luc Nancy (New York: Routledge, 1991), pp. 58–60 (p. 58).

41. Claude Morali, *Qui est moi aujourd'hui?* (Paris: Fayard, 1984), p. 11. The lines from *The Step Not Beyond* are quoted later in this chapter.

42. Klossowski, 'The Experience of the Eternal Return', pp. 57–8.

43. Derrida, 'Of an Apocalyptic Tone', pp. 8–9. See Chapter 2 for a discussion of the loose shoelaces in the painting by Van Gogh as questioned by Derrida in 'Restitutions of the Truth in Pointing'.

44. On Blanchot's involvement in May '68, see Bident, *Maurice Blanchot*, pp. 375–85.
45. Blanchot, 'Who?', p. 60. This extract, without the dash, appears in *The Step Not Beyond* (1973), trans. Lycette Nelson (Albany, NY: State University of New York Press, 1992), p. 7.
46. Blanchot, 'Who?', p. 60.
47. Blanchot says this in a letter to Pierre Madaule dated 2 March 1981: 'I can tell you this: the first edition of *The Writing of the Disaster* having gone out of print (how? I don't know, almost no one spoke about it), I added only one single sentence which ends with these words: "I am dying of my timelessness".' Maurice Blanchot and Pierre Madaule, *Correspondance: 1953–2002*, ed. Pierre Madaule (Paris: Gallimard, 2012), p. 29 (my translation). That this was the only change he made to the text makes it all the more significant.
48. Foucault, *The History of Sexuality*, I, p. 139.

Conclusion

This book began by noting that literature and criticism, the one being always already implied in the other, are associated with the task of liberating thought from the notion of value and of opening up history to an entirely different and still unforeseeable affirmation. This is, in Blanchot's words, 'one of the most difficult but important tasks of our time' (LS 6). Blanchot recognises that nostalgic thought which aims to combat nihilism by restoring value to the highest values offers no solution. Instead, he seeks to go beyond nihilism by affirming the nothingness of values and the force of nothingness. Blanchot offers a radical alternative to traditional and habitual ways of thinking when he accepts that embracing the future as affirmation is, if not the solution, at least all that remains.

Blanchot shares the reference to nihilism and the view of literature as techne with Heidegger, but any point of convergence between these literary and philosophical attitudes is always displaced by the resistance of literature or writing to any totality or absolute. The difference stems from a reading of Mallarmé, who propels Blanchot's view of literature in the direction of the bottomless abyss and endless self-reflexivity, and it is echoed in their divergent readings of Hölderlin, Rilke, Nietzsche and Heraclitus. The claim that literature radicalises a feature inherent to all language not only undermines the opposition between the aesthetic and the technical, it also provides Blanchot with a critical strategy and a syntax that displaces the totalising discourse of Heidegger. At every stage of his engagement with Heidegger, he reveals that a closer attention to the movement of language undermines the foundations of this thought, which relies on truth as revealing. Art or literature for Blanchot is not a vehicle of truth or non-truth but otherwise than truth. This is why writing offers a response to nihilism which is radically different from the appeal made by Heidegger, in his explication of Nietzsche and in the context of modern technology perceived as the unrivalled nihilistic situation, to restore to value Being and the Holy.

Perhaps surprisingly, it is in an eclectic selection of texts published over the course of the 1950s and brought together in the first half of *Friendship* several years later alongside essays on paperback publishing and the atomic bomb – on Malraux's imaginary museum, Ulysses' encounter with the Sirens, Lévi-Strauss's anthropological project – where the view of writing as a mode of techne is clearest in Blanchot. The Sirens' song in particular expresses this view when it is described as the reproduction of an always forgotten original and at once what is most human and inhuman. The song is an invocation to come spoken from an origin that resists all mediation and structures our experience of writing and modern technologies. (Blanchot here anticipates what Derrida will later name iterability as the condition of possibility of writing that undermines the possibility of any 'original' copy.) 'Modern man' is no different to Ulysses who – tied to the ship's mast by crewmen whose ears are stuffed with wax – is foolish for thinking himself an all-powerful conqueror and master of technology; the encounter with the Sirens may be impossible, but their song persists and reaches beyond the limits of the text. The song is the event that never arrives because always arriving, what Blanchot refers to in relation to the atomic bomb as the apocalypse that disappoints.

Reflecting on the fear induced in him by modern technology, Heidegger argues that humans no longer have any agency in a hopeless world where they are uprooted from earth and left only with purely technical relationships – the danger for Heidegger is tellingly felt more keenly in images sent from space than in the murderous capacity of the atomic bomb. Technology thought in its relationship to art in Blanchot reveals that the background hum that reminds us of our powerlessness was always already there (and could be heard in the work of Hölderlin, Mallarmé, Beckett). Between Blanchot and Heidegger there is, then, a marked difference in their response to modern technology: Heidegger is fearful; Blanchot is cautious, recognising the dangers but seeing an opportunity for a different way for thought. The question posed by modern technology turns on nihilism, or how to think other than value, and the response in this mechanistic writing that outplays the will of the subject takes on inhuman proportions.

Blanchot complains that we dismiss the abstract shadow of the apocalypse 'as if it were an irritating fly' when we persevere with the habits, traditions, expressions of old ways of thinking while nonetheless calling for change (F 108). The fly might seem a strange and surprising reference, but this is the mark of what Derrida would call the *arrivant*. The fly is an example of what Blanchot writing on Kafka in 1949 had called a symbol: it is the reversal of the world in its totality through the imagination – Blanchot writes in relation to the bomb that our understanding, which takes us to the limits of comprehension, helps us to imagine that we will 'elude the knowledge of this universal death and [end] up in the platitude of an end devoid of all importance' (F 107) – and it represents a moment of extreme instability for thought, which is, both here and in the essay on Kafka, triggered by a technological device (the atomic bomb and the telephone call).

Elsewhere in Blanchot's fictional writing a fly at the end of *The Most High* is a further indication of how we might embrace the unknowable future. At a heightened moment of tension in the closing pages of the novel – just before Jeanne returns with a gun which she fires at the narrator Sorge – a small fly distracts and mesmerises Sorge as it crawls up curtains and bats against walls. The fly emits an excessive buzzing that it seems unable to contain, and its vibrating wings fascinate Sorge as a reminder of his physical existence that makes him feel a giddiness comparable to hunger (MH 250). The description of Jeanne in this passage is interrupted or derailed by this fly as it flits and turns around the room:

> I started whistling quietly. I whistled a little louder and the slight clicking of wings was set off; when she leaned over me the insect took flight, whirled around, and fell backwards heavily onto the sheet. For a moment, it did not move; only one of its legs was trembling, and I saw it. Then the legs started moving slowly, and again the buzzing arose, quiet but persistent, coming through the sheet; the side legs clung to the fabric, they pulled gently on the linen, moistening it, and with a single bound it turned over with such force that it lay flat and did not move. I heard [her or it] yelling [*Je l'entendis crier*], 'I'll be your creature. Never, never will you get away from me.' The insect was running with insane speed, constantly changing direction, dodging the same danger in front and behind. I got up to get a better view and it stopped, overwhelmed [*suffoqué*], then fled like an arrow, blindly blindly. She threw herself at me, then jumped back. I lay flat against the wall. My teeth were grinding, so tight and tense was my jaw. A moment later, she knocked over the stool and ran out of the room. I slowly opened my mouth so as not to suffocate. (MH 252)

This scene complicates limits more than once. The limit between the insect and Jeanne is contested in this appeal to creatureliness, a point further underscored in the French, where the contraction of the direct pronoun before the verb in the introduction of the statement, 'I'll be your creature', introduces an irresolvable ambiguity. Jeanne might say these words but, given Sorge's fascination with this insect, it is not far-fetched to suggest that the fly might also speak in a sort of reworking of the Sirens' song. Coming just before the firing of the gun at the end of the novel, the scene also complicates the limit between life and death and the limit of the work, not only because the fly seems to drop dead twice only to return to life with a remarkable vigour, but also because Sorge is unable to narrate his death once Jeanne fires the gun in the following pages and so the narration begins again. The last line of the novel is placed in quotation marks: 'Now, now I am speaking' (MH 254). This closing citation has been described as an interruption that forces the work to acknowledge what exceeds its limits in a mute gesture made towards the unspeakable.[1] The fly in the previous pages is just such a gesture: fleeing 'like an arrow', in the same way that we dismiss or swat the shadow of the nuclear apocalypse 'like an irritating fly', its presence is similarly withdrawn from being and non-being (we do not learn if it leaves the room or if it dies). The fly cannot be confronted head on because to do so would be an attempt to overcome the nihilistic situation narrated at the end of *The Most High* and in 'The Apocalypse is Disappointing', and to restore value to both 'endings'.

The 'entirely different affirmation' of which Blanchot writes will always remain unforeseeable because all modes of techne contest historical limits. Roger Laporte recognises the prophetic nature of Blanchot's writing, which looks towards and welcomes an uncertain future: 'Blanchot, contrary to what some have thought, does not open a new religious space: not only does he not feel any nostalgia for a former world, he announces, even prophesises, an epoch when atheism would be a thing of the past, because the concern with God and the absence of God would have finally passed.'[2] In rejecting the binary between theism and atheism, Blanchot recognises something profoundly affirmative in a future where nothing is predetermined, neither by an all-powerful God nor by the teleological progress of history. Those often italicised fragments in *The Step Not Beyond*, situated in the temporality of a suspended afterwards, reveal the patient deferral of the possibility of ending in Blanchot, marking the step beyond belief and disbelief which is precisely never a step, because *pas*, in its double meaning in French as 'step' and 'not', suspends or withdraws itself. The emphasis placed by Derrida on the 'to come' [*à-venir*] was no doubt prompted by Blanchot's invocation of the future: unlike the 'future' [*futur*] – which is predictable, programmable, foreseeable and will be at a later date – the 'to come' [*à-venir*] in Derrida is the totally unpredictable coming of the other.[3] Derrida insists on how far Blanchot is still ahead of us: 'I have never imagined him so far in front of us as I have today. Awaiting us, still to come [à venir], to be read, to be reread by those very same ones that do it ever since they knew how to read and *thanks* to him.'[4] It is as though this Blanchotian thought resonates from an unknowable future and our response to it can only ever be inadequate.

The uncertainty that undermines any claim that we are undergoing a change of epoch signals not that writing has fallen into timeless eternity, but a withdrawal from presence which is simultaneously a radical interruption of the present, demanding a new perspective. It resonates in some ways with eco-criticism while nonetheless suggesting that by thinking the end otherwise, by embracing something unknowable in the future, we might change the structures and ways of thinking that have so far condemned us to repeat the errors of the past and respond in platitudes to impending catastrophe.[5] Blanchot remains relevant today because his priority is to insist how, with danger, comes also a chance. This is his version of what Hölderlin says in 'Patmos': 'But where danger threatens | That which saves from it also grows [Wo aber Gefahr ist, wächst | Das Rettende auch]'.[6] The chance for something other than destruction is heard in the call of the impossible which insistently appears throughout Blanchot's work in forms that contest the limit between nature and technology, and between human and inhuman. Blanchot's is a radical nihilism which is no longer nihilism in the sense of nostalgia for values, but an embrace of the impossible, beyond being and non-being, that is the future, and by that token is inseparable from responsibility for the future and justice for the many, both dead and to come. The end does not always imply a new beginning, but a suspended moment where nothing is final – 'the end is beginning' (MD 10).

Notes

1. Hill, *Bataille, Blanchot, Klossowski*, pp. 204–6.
2. Roger Laporte, 'L'Ancien, l'effroyablement ancien', in *Études* (Paris: P.O.L., 1990), pp. 9–50 (p. 12) (my translation).
3. Derrida's analysis of the 'Come' that features in what would become, once the third section was suppressed, the closing line of *Death Sentence* signals his indebtedness to Blanchot. See Derrida, 'Pace Not(s)', in *Parages*, pp. 11–101.
4. Ibid., p. 43.
5. See, for instance, Timothy Morton's call for us to think ecology without Heideggerian world in 'Coexistants and Coexistence: Ecology without a World', in *Ecocritical Theory: New European Approaches*, ed. Axel Goodbody and Kate Rigby (Charlottesville, VA: University of Virginia Press, 2011), pp. 168–80. Blanchot would most likely be resistant to

the notion of the Anthropocene as it is described by Timothy Clark: '[the Anthropocene represents] for the first time, the demand made upon a species consciously to consider its impact, as a whole and as a natural/physical force, upon the whole planet – the advent of a kind of new, totalizing reflexivity as a species'. Timothy Clark, 'Nature, Post Nature', in *The Cambridge Companion to Literature and the Environment*, ed. Louise Westling (Cambridge: Cambridge University Press, 2014), pp. 75–89 (p. 86).
6. Hölderlin, *Poems and Fragments*, p. 462.

Bibliography

Books by Maurice Blanchot, in order of original publication

Thomas l'Obscur (Paris: Gallimard, 1941)
Faux pas (Paris: Gallimard, 1943)
Le Très-Haut (Paris: Gallimard, 1948)
L'Arrêt de mort (Paris: Gallimard, 1948)
La Part du feu (Paris: Gallimard, 1949)
Lautréamont et Sade, rev. edn (Paris Minuit, 1949)
Thomas l'Obscur, nouvelle version (Paris: Gallimard, 1950)
L'Espace littéraire (Paris: Gallimard, 1955)
Le Dernier Homme (Paris: Gallimard, 1957); *Le Dernier Homme: nouvelle version* (Paris: Gallimard, 1977)
Le Livre à venir (Paris: Gallimard, 1959)
L'Attente L'Oubli (Paris: Gallimard, 1962)
L'Entretien infini (Paris: Gallimard, 1969)
L'Amitié (Paris: Gallimard, 1971)
La Folie du jour (Montpellier: Fata Morgana, 1973; Paris: Gallimard, 2002)
Le Pas au-delà (Paris: Gallimard, 1973)
L'Écriture du désastre (Paris: Gallimard, 1980)
La Communauté inavouable (Paris: Minuit, 1983)
L'Instant de ma mort (Montpellier: Fata Morgana, 1994; Paris: Gallimard, 2002)
Les Intellectuels en question: ébauche d'une réflexion (Paris: Fourbis, 1996; Tours: Farrago, 2000)
Chroniques littéraires du Journal des débats: avril 1941–août 1944, ed. Christophe Bident (Paris: Gallimard, 2007)
Écrits politiques: 1953–1998, ed. Éric Hoppenot (Paris: Gallimard, 2008)
La Condition critique: articles 1945–1998, ed. Christophe Bident (Paris: Gallimard, 2010)
Correspondance: 1953–2002, with Pierre Madaule, ed. Pierre Madaule (Paris: Gallimard, 2012)
Chroniques politiques des années trente: 1931–1940, ed. David Uhrig (Paris: Gallimard, 2017)
Thomas le Solitaire, ed. Leslie Hill and Philippe Lynes (Paris: Kimé, 2022)

Other works by Maurice Blanchot cited

'Un récit[?]', *Empédocle* 2 (1949): 13–22
'Tu peux tuer cet homme', *La Nouvelle Nouvelle Revue française* 18 (1954): 1059–69
'Le Mal du Musée', *La Nouvelle Nouvelle Revue française* 52 (1957): 687–96
'Nietzsche aujourd'hui', *La Nouvelle Nouvelle Revue française* 68 (1958): 284–95
'Passage de la ligne', *La Nouvelle Nouvelle Revue française* 69 (1958): 468–79
'L'Attente', *Botteghe oscure* 22 (1958): 22–33
'Lettre de Maurice Blanchot à Roger Laporte du 22 décembre 1984', in Jean-Luc Nancy, *Maurice Blanchot: passion politique, lettre-récit de 1984 suivie d'une lettre de Dionys Mascolo* (Paris: Galilée, 2011), pp. 47–62

Works by Maurice Blanchot in English translation, in order of French publication

Faux pas [1943], trans. Charlotte Mandell (Stanford, CA: Stanford University Press, 2001)
'*Days of Hope* by André Malraux' [1946], trans. Michael Holland, in *Blanchot's Epoch*, ed. Leslie Hill and Michael Holland = *Paragraph* 30, no. 3 (2007): 5–12
The Most High [1948], trans. Allan Stoekl (Lincoln, NE: University of Nebraska Press, 1995)
Death Sentence [1948], trans. Lydia Davis (Barrytown, NY: Station Hill Press, 1978)
The Work of Fire [1949], trans. Charlotte Mandell (Stanford, CA: Stanford University Press, 1995)
Lautréamont and Sade [1949, rev. 1963], trans. Stuart Kendall and Michelle Kendall (Stanford, CA: Stanford University Press, 2004)
Thomas the Obscure [new version 1950], trans. Robert Lamberton (Barrytown, NY: Station Hill Press, 1988)
'The Beast of Lascaux' [1953], trans. Leslie Hill, in *Disastrous Blanchot*, ed. Timothy Clark, Leslie Hill and Nicholas Royle = *Oxford Literary Review* 22 (2000): 9–18
The Space of Literature [1955], trans. Ann Smock (Lincoln, NE: University of Nebraska Press, 1982)
The Last Man [1957], trans. Lydia Davis (New York: Columbia University Press, 1987)
The Book to Come [1959], trans. Charlotte Mandell (Stanford, CA: Stanford University Press, 2003)
Awaiting Oblivion [1962], trans. John Gregg (Lincoln, NE: University of Nebraska Press, 1997)

The Infinite Conversation [1969], trans. Susan Hanson (Minneapolis, MN: University of Minnesota Press, 1993)

Friendship [1971], trans. Elizabeth Rottenberg (Stanford, CA: Stanford University Press, 1997)

The Madness of the Day [1973], trans. Lydia Davis (New York: Station Hill Press, 1981)

The Step Not Beyond [1973], trans. Lycette Nelson (Albany, NY: State University of New York Press, 1992)

The Writing of the Disaster [1980], trans. Ann Smock (Lincoln, NE: University of Nebraska Press, 1995)

The Unavowable Community [1983], trans. Pierre Joris (Barrytown, NY: Station Hill Press, 1988)

'Michel Foucault as I Imagine Him' [1986], trans. Jeffrey Mehlman, in *Foucault, Blanchot*, by Michel Foucault and Maurice Blanchot, trans. Jeffrey Mehlman and Brian Massumi (New York: Zone Books, 1987)

'Who?' [1989], trans. Eduardo Cadava, in *Who Comes after the Subject?*, ed. Eduardo Cadava, Peter Connor and Jean-Luc Nancy (New York: Routledge, 1991), pp. 58–60

'Allow me to reply briefly . . .' [1992], trans. Michael Holland, in *Blanchot's Epoch*, ed. Leslie Hill and Michael Holland = *Paragraph* 30, no. 3 (2007): 43

'The Instant of My Death' [1994], in *The Instant of My Death/Demeure: Fiction and Testimony*, by Maurice Blanchot and Jacques Derrida, trans. Elizabeth Rottenberg (Stanford, CA: Stanford University Press, 2000), pp. 2–11

Into Disaster: Chronicles of Intellectual Life, 1941 [2007], trans. Michael Holland (New York: Fordham University Press, 2013)

Desperate Clarity: Chronicles of Intellectual Life, 1942 [2007], trans. Michael Holland (New York: Fordham University Press, 2013)

A World in Ruins: Chronicles of Intellectual Life, 1943 [2007], trans. Michael Holland (New York: Fordham University Press, 2016)

Death Now: Chronicles of Intellectual Life, 1944 [2007], trans. Michael Holland (New York: Fordham University Press, 2018)

Political Writings [2008], trans. Zakir Paul (New York: Fordham University Press, 2010)

For a full bibliography of books and essays by Maurice Blanchot, which lists original dates and places of publication for all essays, see the *Espace Maurice Blanchot* webpage: www.blanchot.fr/bibliographie

Selected works on Blanchot

Bident, Christophe, *Maurice Blanchot: A Critical Biography*, trans. John McKeane (New York: Fordham University Press, 2019)

Bruns, Gerald L., *Maurice Blanchot: The Refusal of Philosophy* (Baltimore, MD: Johns Hopkins University Press, 1997)

Buclin, Hadrien, *Maurice Blanchot ou l'autonomie littéraire* (Lausanne: Antipodes, 2011)

Clark, Timothy, *Derrida, Heidegger, Blanchot: Sources of Derrida's Notion and Practice of Literature* (Cambridge: Cambridge University Press, 1992)

—— 'Maurice Blanchot and the End of Nature', *Parallax* 16, no. 2 (2010): 20–30

De Man, Paul, 'La Circularité d'interprétation dans l'œuvre critique de Maurice Blanchot', *Critique* 229 special issue 'Maurice Blanchot' (1966): 547–60

Derrida, Jacques, *Parages*, trans. Tom Conley, James Hulbert, John P. Leavey and Avital Ronell, ed. John P. Leavey (Stanford, CA: Stanford University Press, 2011)

Foucault, Michel, 'Maurice Blanchot: The Thought from Outside' [1966], trans. Brian Massumi, in *Foucault, Blanchot*, by Michel Foucault and Maurice Blanchot (New York: Zone Books, 1987), pp. 7–58

Fynsk, Christopher, *Last Steps: Maurice Blanchot's Exilic Writing* (New York: Fordham University Press, 2013)

Gill, Carolyn Bailey, ed., *Maurice Blanchot: The Demand of Writing* (London: Routledge, 1996)

Hart, Kevin, ed., *Clandestine Encounters: Philosophy in the Narratives of Maurice Blanchot* (Notre Dame, IN: University of Notre Dame Press, 2010)

—— *The Dark Gaze: Maurice Blanchot and the Sacred* (Chicago: University of Chicago Press, 2004)

Hart, Kevin, and Geoffrey H. Hartman, eds, *The Power of Contestation: Perspectives on Maurice Blanchot* (Baltimore, MD: Johns Hopkins University Press, 2004)

Hill, Leslie, *Bataille, Blanchot, Klossowski: Writing at the Limit* (Oxford: Oxford University Press, 2001)

—— 'Blanchot and Mallarmé', *MLN* 105, no. 5 (1990): 889–913

—— *Blanchot: Extreme Contemporary* (London: Routledge, 1997)

—— *Blanchot politique: sur une réflexion jamais interrompue* (Geneva: Furor, 2020)

—— '"A Form that Thinks": Godard, Blanchot, Citation', in *Forever Godard*, ed. Michael Temple, James S. Williams and Michael Witt (London: Black Dog Publishing, 2004), pp. 396–415

—— 'From Deconstruction to Disaster (Derrida, Blanchot, Hegel)', *Paragraph* 39, no. 2, special issue 'Resounding *Glas*' (2016): 187–201

—— *Maurice Blanchot and Fragmentary Writing: A Change of Epoch* (London: Continuum, 2012)

—— *Nancy, Blanchot: A Serious Controversy* (London: Rowman and Littlefield International, 2018)

Hill, Leslie, and Michael Holland, eds, *Blanchot's Epoch* = *Paragraph* 30, no. 3 (2007)

Hill, Leslie, Brian Nelson and Dimitris Vardoulakis, eds, *After Blanchot: Literature, Criticism, Philosophy* (Newark, DE: University of Delaware Press, 2005)

Holland, Michael, *Avant dire: essais sur Blanchot* (Paris: Hermann, 2015)
—— 'From Crisis to Critique: Mallarmé for Blanchot', in *Meetings with Mallarmé in Contemporary French Culture*, ed. Michael Temple (Exeter: University of Exeter Press, 1998), pp. 81–106
—— 'Towards a New Literary Idiom: The Fiction and Criticism of Maurice Blanchot from 1941 to 1955', unpublished doctoral thesis, University of Oxford, 1981
Hoppenot, Éric, and Dominique Rabaté, eds, *Blanchot*, Cahiers de l'Herne, 107 (Paris: Herne, 2014)
Iyer, Lars, 'Logos and Difference: Blanchot, Heidegger, Heraclitus', *Parallax* 11, no. 2 (2005): 14–24
Lacoue-Labarthe, Philippe, *Ending and Unending Agony: On Maurice Blanchot*, trans. Hannes Opelz (New York: Fordham University Press, 2015)
Lacoue-Labarthe, Philippe, and Jean-Luc Nancy, 'Noli me frangere', in *Expectation: Philosophy, Literature*, by Jean-Luc Nancy, trans. Brian Holmes (New York: Fordham University Press, 2018), pp. 131–41
Laporte, Roger, 'L'Ancien, l'effroyablement ancien', in *Études* (Paris: P.O.L., 1990), pp. 9–50
—— 'Le Oui, le non, le neutre', *Critique* 229 special issue 'Maurice Blanchot' (1966): 579–90
Levinas, Emmanuel, *Sur Maurice Blanchot* (Montpellier: Fata Morgana, 1975)
Limet, Yun Sun, *Maurice Blanchot critique: essai* (Paris: La Différence, 2010)
Maclachlan, Ian, *Marking Time: Derrida, Blanchot, Beckett, des Forêts, Klossowski, Laporte* (Amsterdam: Rodopi, 2012)
McKeane, John, and Hannes Opelz, eds, *Blanchot Romantique: A Collection of Essays* (Oxford: Peter Lang, 2010)
Mehlman, Jeffrey, 'Blanchot at Combat: Of Literature and Terror', *MLN* 95, no. 4 (1980): 808–29
Nancy, Jean-Luc, 'The Confronted Community', trans. Amanda Macdonald, *Postcolonial Studies* 6, no. 1 (2003): 23–36
—— *The Disavowed Community*, trans. Philip Armstrong (New York: Fordham University Press, 2016)
—— *The Inoperative Community*, trans. Peter Connor, Lisa Garbus, Michael Holland and Simona Sawhney (Minneapolis, MN: University of Minnesota Press, 1991)
—— *Maurice Blanchot: passion politique, lettre-récit de 1984 suivie d'une lettre de Dionys Mascolo* (Paris: Galilée, 2011)
Schulte Nordholt, Anne-Lise, *Maurice Blanchot: l'écriture comme expérience du dehors* (Geneva: Droz, 1995)
Sheringham, Michael, 'Attending to the Everyday: Blanchot, Lefebvre, Certeau, Perec', *French Studies* 54, no. 2 (2000): 187–99
Smith, Douglas, 'The Burning Library: Hubert Damisch, Maurice Blanchot and the "Paperback Revolution"', *French Studies* 72, no. 4 (2018): 539–56
Surya, Michel, *L'Autre Blanchot: l'écriture de jour, l'écriture de nuit* (Paris: Gallimard, 2015)

—— ed., *Les Politiques de Maurice Blanchot: 1930–1993*, Revue Lignes, 43 (Paris: Lignes, 2014)
Syrotinski, Michael, 'How is Literature Possible?', in *A New History of French Literature*, ed. Denis Hollier (Cambridge, MA: Harvard University Press, 1989), pp. 953–8
Watt, Calum, 'The Uses of Maurice Blanchot in Bernard Stiegler's *Technics and Time*', *Paragraph* 39, no. 3 (2016): 305–18
Weller, Shane, 'Voidance: Linguistic Negativism in Maurice Blanchot's Fiction', *French Studies* 69, no. 1 (2015): 30–45
Zarader, Marlène, *L'Etre et le neutre: à partir de Maurice Blanchot* (Lagrasse: Verdier, 2001)

Other works cited

Agamben, Giorgio, *Remnants of Auschwitz: The Witness and the Archive*, trans. Daniel Heller-Roazen (New York: Zone Books, 2002)
Allemann, Beda, *Hölderlin et Heidegger*, trans. François Fédier, 2nd edn (Paris: PUF, 1987)
Baer, Ulrich, *The Rilke Alphabet*, trans. Andrew Hamilton (New York: Fordham University Press, 2014)
Barthes, Roland, *Writing Degree Zero*, trans. Annette Lavers and Colin Smith (New York: Hill and Wang, 1968)
Bataille, Georges, 'Letter to X, Lecturer on Hegel', in *The College of Sociology, 1937–1939*, ed. Denis Hollier, trans. Betsy Wing (Minneapolis, MN: University of Minnesota Press, 1988), pp. 89–93
Beistegui, Miguel de, *Heidegger and the Political: Dystopias* (London: Routledge, 1998)
Benjamin, Walter, 'The Work of Art in the Age of its Technological Reproducibility', trans. Edmund Jephcott and Harry Zohn, in *Selected Writings*, ed. Howard Eiland and Michael W. Jennings, 4 vols (Cambridge, MA: Belknap Press of Harvard University Press, 2004–06), III: *1935–1938* (2006), pp. 101–33
Bernstein, J. M., ed., *Classic and Romantic German Aesthetics* (Cambridge: Cambridge University Press, 2003)
—— 'Poesy and the Arbitrariness of the Sign: Notes for a Critique of Jena Romanticism', in *Philosophical Romanticism*, ed. Nikolas Kompridis (London: Routledge, 2006), pp. 143–72
Boa, Elizabeth, 'Revoicing Silenced Sirens: A Changing Motif in Works by Franz Kafka, Frank Wedekind and Barbara Köhler', *German Life and Letters* 57, no. 1 (2004): 8–20
Bowie, Malcolm, *Mallarmé and the Art of Being Difficult* (Cambridge: Cambridge University Press, 1978)
Bradley, Arthur, *Originary Technicity: The Theory of Technology from Marx to Derrida* (Basingstoke: Palgrave Macmillan, 2011)
Carroll, David, *French Literary Fascism: Nationalism, Anti-Semitism and the Ideology of Culture* (Princeton, NJ: Princeton University Press, 1998)

Caygill, Howard, *Walter Benjamin: The Colour of Experience* (London: Routledge, 1998)
Clark, Timothy, 'Nature, Post Nature', in *The Cambridge Companion to Literature and the Environment*, ed. Louise Westling (Cambridge: Cambridge University Press, 2014), pp. 75–89
Compagnon, Antoine, *Literature, Theory, and Common Sense*, trans. Carol Cosman (Princeton, NJ: Princeton University Press, 2004)
Critchley, Simon, *Very Little . . . Almost Nothing: Death, Philosophy, Literature* (London: Routledge, 1997)
Damisch, Hubert, 'La Culture de poche', *Mercure de France* 1213 (1964): 482–98
—— *Ruptures/Cultures* (Paris: Minuit, 1976)
De Man, Paul, *Allegories of Reading: Figural Language in Rousseau, Nietzsche, Rilke, and Proust* (New Haven, CT: Yale University Press, 1979)
—— *Blindness and Insight: Essays in the Rhetoric of Contemporary Criticism*, 2nd edn (London: Routledge, 1983)
Derrida, Jacques, *Acts of Literature*, ed. Derek Attridge (New York: Routledge, 1992)
—— *Aporias*, trans. Thomas Dutoit (Stanford, CA: Stanford University Press, 1993)
—— *Dissemination*, trans. Barbara Johnson (London: Athlone, 1981)
—— 'Geschlecht II: Heidegger's Hand', trans. John P. Leavey, in *Martin Heidegger*, ed. Stephen Mulhall (London: Routledge, 2006), pp. 431–66
—— *Margins of Philosophy*, trans. Alan Bass (New York: Harvester Wheatsheaf, 1982)
—— 'Of an Apocalyptic Tone Recently Adopted in Philosophy', trans. John P. Leavey, *Oxford Literary Review* 6, no. 2 (1984): 3–37
—— *Of Grammatology*, trans. Gayatri Chakravorty Spivak (Baltimore, MD: Johns Hopkins University Press, 1997)
—— *Of Spirit*, trans. Geoffrey Bennington and Rachel Bowlby (Chicago: University of Chicago Press, 1989)
—— *Points . . . : Interviews, 1974–1994*, trans. Peggy Kamuf et al. (Stanford, CA: Stanford University Press, 1995)
—— *Politics of Friendship*, trans. George Collins (London: Verso, 1997)
—— *Spectres of Marx*, trans. Peggy Kamuf (New York: Routledge, 1994)
—— *The Truth in Painting*, trans. Geoffrey Bennington and Ian McLeod (Chicago: University of Chicago Press, 1987)
—— *Writing and Difference*, trans. Alan Bass (London: Routledge, 2001)
Djebar, Assia, *Ces Voix qui m'assiègent: . . . en marge de ma francophonie* (Paris: Albin Michel, 1999)
Eribon, Didier, *Michel Foucault*, trans. Betsy Wing (London: Faber, 1992)
Fóti, Véronique M., *Heidegger and the Poets: Poïēsis, Sophia, Technē* (Atlantic Highlands, NJ: Humanities Press, 1992)
Foucault, Michel, *Discipline and Punish: The Birth of the Prison*, trans. Alan Sheridan (London: Penguin, 1991)

—— *Dits et écrits: 1954–1988*, ed. Daniel Defert and François Ewald, 4 vols (Paris: Gallimard, 1994)
—— *History of Madness*, trans. Jonathan Murphy and Jean Khalfa, ed. Jean Khalfa (London: Routledge, 2006)
—— *The History of Sexuality*, trans. Robert Hurley, 3 vols (London: Penguin, 2019)
Genette, Gérard, *Narrative Discourse*, trans. Jane E. Lewin (Oxford: Blackwell, 1980)
Haar, Michel, *The Song of the Earth: Heidegger and the Grounds of the History of Being*, trans. Reginald Lily (Bloomington, IN: Indiana University Press, 1993)
Heidegger, Martin, *Basic Writings*, ed. David Farrell Krell, rev. edn (London: Routledge, 1993)
—— *Being and Time*, trans. John Macquarrie and Edward Robinson (Oxford: Blackwell, [1962] 1988)
—— *Early Greek Thinking*, trans. David Farrell Krell (New York: Harper and Row, 1984)
—— *Elucidations of Hölderlin's Poetry*, trans. Keith Hoeller (Amherst, NY: Humanity Books, 2000); *Approche de Hölderlin*, trans. Henry Corbin et al. (Paris: Gallimard, [1963] 1973)
—— *The Fundamental Concepts of Metaphysics*, trans. William McNeill and Nicholas Walker (Bloomington, IN: Indiana University Press, 1995)
—— *Gesamtausgabe* (Frankfurt am Main: Vittorio Klostermann, 1975–)
—— *Nietzsche*, trans. David Farrell Krell, 4 vols (San Francisco: Harper and Row, 1979–87)
—— *Off the Beaten Track*, ed. and trans. Julian Young and Kenneth Haynes (Cambridge: Cambridge University Press, 2002)
—— *Parmenides*, trans. André Schuwer and Richard Rojcewicz (Bloomington, IN: Indiana University Press, 1992)
—— *Pathmarks*, ed. William McNeill (Cambridge: Cambridge University Press, 1998)
—— *What is Called Thinking?*, trans. J. Glenn Grey (New York: Perennial Library, [1976] 2004)
Hewson, Mark, *Blanchot and Literary Criticism* (London: Continuum, 2011)
Hill, Leslie, 'On the Persistence of Hedgehogs', in *Philosophy and Poetry: Continental Perspectives*, ed. Ranjan Ghosh (New York: Columbia University Press, 2019), pp. 235–47
Hölderlin, Friedrich, *Hölderlin's Sophocles*, trans. David Constantine (Highgreen: Bloodaxe, 2001),
—— *Poems and Fragments*, trans. Michael Hamburger (London: Routledge and Kegan Paul, 1966)
Hollier, Denis, *The Politics of Prose: Essay on Sartre*, trans. Jeffrey Mehlman (Minneapolis, MN: University of Minnesota Press, 1986)
Husserl, Edmund, *The Crisis of the European Sciences and Transcendental Phenomenology: An Introduction to Phenomenological Philosophy*, trans. David Carr (Evanston, IL: Northwestern University Press, 1970)

Inwood, Michael, *A Heidegger Dictionary* (Oxford: Blackwell, 1999)
James, Ian, *An Introduction to the Philosophy of Jean-Luc Nancy: The Fragmentary Demand* (Stanford, CA: Stanford University Press, 2006)
—— *The New French Philosophy* (Cambridge: Polity, 2012)
—— *Pierre Klossowski: The Persistence of a Name* (Oxford: Legenda, 2000)
Janicaud, Dominique, *Heidegger en France*, 2 vols (Paris: Albin Michel, 2001)
Joyce, James, *Ulysses* (Oxford: Oxford University Press, 1998)
Kafka, Franz, *The Castle*, trans. Willa and Edwin Muir, additional material trans. Eithne Wilkins and Ernst Kaiser, definitive edn (London: Secker and Warburg, 1953)
—— *The Complete Stories*, ed. Nahum N. Glatzer (New York: Schocken Books, 1983)
—— *Das Schloss*, ed. Max Brod (Frankfurt am Main: Fischer Taschenbuch, [1963] 1983)
Klossowski, Pierre, *Nietzsche and the Vicious Circle*, trans. Daniel W. Smith (London: Athlone, 1997)
Kojève, Alexandre, *Introduction to the Reading of Hegel: Lectures on the Phenomenology of Spirit*, ed. Allan Bloom, trans. James H. Nichols (Ithaca, NY: Cornell University Press, 1980); *Introduction à la lecture de Hegel: leçons sur la 'Phénoménologie de l'esprit' professées de 1933 à 1939 à l'École des Hautes Études*, ed. Raymond Queneau (Paris: Gallimard, 1947)
Lacoue-Labarthe, Philippe, *Heidegger and the Politics of Poetry*, trans. Jeff Fort (Urbana, IL: University of Illinois Press, 2007)
Lacoue-Labarthe, Philippe, and Jean-Luc Nancy, *The Literary Absolute: The Theory of Literature in German Romanticism*, trans. Philip Barnard and Cheryl Lester (Albany, NY: State University of New York Press, 1988)
Levinas, Emmanuel, *Collected Philosophical Papers*, trans. Alphonso Lingis (Dordrecht: Martinus Nijhoff, 1987)
—— *Difficult Freedom: Essays on Judaism*, trans. Seán Hand (London: Athlone, 1990)
—— *Existence and Existents*, trans. Alphonso Lingis (The Hague: Martinus Nijhoff, 1978)
—— *God, Death and Time*, trans. Bettina Bergo (Stanford, CA: Stanford University Press, 2000)
—— *Time and the Other*, trans. Richard A. Cohen (Pittsburgh, PA: Duquesne University Press, 1987)
Lévi-Strauss, Claude, *Tristes tropiques*, trans. John Weightman and Doreen Weightman (London: Penguin, 2011)
Lloyd, Rosemary, *Mallarmé: The Poet and His Circle* (Ithaca, NY: Cornell University Press, 1999)
Maclachlan, Ian, *Roger Laporte: The Orphic Text* (Oxford: Legenda, 2000)
Mallarmé, Stéphane, *Collected Poems and Other Verse*, trans. E. H. Blackmore and A. M. Blackmore (Oxford: Oxford University Press, 2006)
—— *Divagations*, trans. Barbara Johnson (Cambridge, MA: Belknap Press of Harvard University Press, 2007)

—— Œuvres complètes, ed. Bertrand Marchal, 2 vols (Paris: Gallimard, 1998–2003)
Malraux, André, Anti-Memoirs, trans. Terence Kilmartin (New York: Holt, Rinehart and Winston, 1968)
—— Œuvres complètes, 6 vols (Paris: Gallimard, 1989–2010)
—— The Voices of Silence, trans. Stuart Gilbert (St Albans: Paladin, 1974)
Mehlman, Jeffrey, Genealogies of the Text: Literature, Psychoanalysis, and Politics in Modern France (Cambridge: Cambridge University Press, 1995)
Morali, Claude, Qui est moi aujourd'hui? (Paris: Fayard, 1984)
Moran, Dermot, Husserl's Crisis of the European Sciences and Transcendental Phenomenology: An Introduction (Cambridge: Cambridge University Press, 2012)
Morton, Timothy, 'Coexistants and Coexistence: Ecology without a World', in Ecocritical Theory: New European Approaches, ed. Axel Goodbody and Kate Rigby (Charlottesville, VA: University of Virginia Press, 2011), pp. 168–80
Nietzsche, Friedrich, The Gay Science, ed. Bernard Williams, trans. Josefine Nauckhoff (Cambridge: Cambridge University Press, 2001)
—— Thus Spoke Zarathustra, trans. Graham Parkes (Oxford: Oxford University Press, 2005)
Paulhan, Jean, The Flowers of Tarbes, or Terror in Literature, trans. Michael Syrotinski (Urbana, IL: University of Illinois Press, 2006)
Pearson, Roger, Mallarmé and Circumstance: The Translation of Silence (Oxford: Oxford University Press, 2004)
—— Stéphane Mallarmé (London: Reaktion, 2010)
Polt, Richard, Heidegger: An Introduction (London: UCL Press, 1999)
Ramnoux, Clémence, Héraclite ou l'homme entre les choses et les mots (Paris: Les Belles Lettres, 1959)
Rilke, Rainer Maria, Duino Elegies, trans. Martyn Crucefix (London: Enitharmon, 2006)
—— The Notebooks of Malte Laurids Brigge, trans. M. D. Herter Norton (New York: W. W. Norton, 1992)
Robert, Marthe, The Old and the New: From Don Quixote to Kafka, trans. Carol Cosman (Berkeley, CA: University of California Press, 1977)
Rockmore, Tom, Heidegger and French Philosophy: Humanism, Antihumanism and Being (London: Routledge, 1995)
Sartre, Jean-Paul, What is Literature?, trans. Bernard Frechtman (London: Routledge, 1993)
Savage, Robert, Hölderlin after the Catastrophe: Heidegger, Adorno, Brecht (Rochester, NY: Camden House, 2008)
Schapiro, Meyer, 'Still Life as Personal Object: A Note on Heidegger and Van Gogh', in Theory and Philosophy of Art: Style, Artist and Society: Selected Papers (New York: George Braziller, 1994), pp. 135–42
Sheringham, Michael, Everyday Life: Theories and Practices from Surrealism to the Present (Oxford: Oxford University Press, 2006)

Sternhell, Zeev, *Neither Right Nor Left: Fascist Ideology in France*, trans. David Maisel (Princeton, NJ: Princeton University Press, 1986)

Stiegler, Bernard, *Technics and Time*, 3 vols (Stanford, CA: Stanford University Press, 1998–2010); *La Technique et le temps* (Paris: Fayard, 2018)

Trawny, Peter, *Heidegger and the Myth of a Jewish World Conspiracy*, trans. Andrew J. Mitchell (Chicago: University of Chicago Press, 2015)

Valéry, Paul, *The Collected Works of Paul Valéry*, ed. Jackson Mathews, 15 vols (Princeton, NJ: Princeton University Press, 1957–75)

Wolin, Richard, ed., *The Heidegger Controversy: A Critical Reader* (Cambridge, MA: MIT Press, 1993)

Index

Adorno, Theodor, 55, 96n, 141n
Agamben, Giorgio, 80, 145n
Algerian War of Independence, 5, 112, 114
Allemann, Beda, 71–3, 96n
animal *see* inhuman
Antelme, Robert, 138
apocalypse, 100–1, 108, 122, 125–7, 134–5, 164, 173, 175
Apollinaire, Guillaume, 20
atomic bomb *see* nuclear weapons

Barthes, Roland, 112, 150, 152, 168n
Bataille, Georges, 37
Baudelaire, Charles, 105
Beckett, Samuel, 39, 150, 173
Benjamin, Walter, 7, 99, 105, 112, 123, 139n
Bident, Christophe, 139n, 145n
Blanchot, Maurice
  'L'Attente', 119
  Awaiting Oblivion, 151, 156
  'The Beast of Lascaux', 5, 6, 14n, 111–12, 121
  The Book to Come, 5, 75, 105–8, 150–1
  Death Sentence, 79–82, 86–7, 109, 176n
  Faux pas, 2, 22–7, 31–2, 38, 42n, 46, 52, 78–80
  Friendship, 4, 39, 100, 101–5, 108–11, 113–14, 123–7, 135, 136, 138–9, 141n, 158–9, 173–4, 175
  The Infinite Conversation, 5, 7, 14n, 28, 114–21, 123–5, 127–32, 133, 138, 142n, 144n, 146–7, 151–3, 156–7, 159–60, 170n
  The Instant of My Death, 104, 141n
  The Last Man, 12, 134–9, 145n
  Lautréamont and Sade, 2–5, 9, 11, 82–3, 87–8, 118–19, 133, 172

  The Madness of the Day, 154–6, 159, 167, 176
  The Most High, 31, 174–5
  The Space of Literature, 8, 37–40, 63–7, 69–73, 76–7, 83–5, 140n, 143n
  The Step Not Beyond, 30, 147, 151, 161–5, 167, 175
  Thomas le Solitaire, 29, 98n
  Thomas the Obscure, 18, 29–30, 37, 55–6, 88–90, 98n, 109
  'Who?', 162–3, 165
  The Work of Fire, 32–8, 56–7, 101, 132–3, 140n
  The Writing of the Disaster, 2, 41n, 64, 67–8, 75–6, 130–1, 147–9, 151, 158, 165–6, 167n, 170n, 171n
Bowie, Malcolm, 21
Brasillach, Robert, 55
Brecht, Bertolt, 55, 144n
Bruns, Gerald L., 27–8

Camus, Albert, 18, 41n, 42n, 121, 168n
Cézanne, Paul, 105
cinema, 9, 105, 150
Clark, Timothy, 91, 177n
Clavel, Maurice, 148
Curtius, Ernst Robert, 110

Damisch, Hubert, 113
Daniel-Rops, Henri, 10
Darrieussecq, Marie, 11, 16n
death, 2, 6, 8, 40, 46–7, 51, 58–9, 61–77, 79–83, 85, 87, 89–90, 99, 104–5, 111, 115–16, 120, 125–6, 129, 131–2, 134–5, 138, 145n, 160–1, 166, 174–6

189

Derrida, Jacques, 1, 2, 11, 40, 43n, 44n, 50–2, 68–9, 73–4, 78, 86, 87–8, 91–2n, 93–4n, 95n, 97n, 100–1, 126–7, 134, 139n, 155, 160–1, 164, 169n, 173, 175–6
Djebar, Assia, 1, 13n
Drieu La Rochelle, Pierre, 18
Duthuit, Georges, 110

Einstein, Albert, 108
Eliot, T. S., 20
Éluard, Paul, 55
end of history, 4, 115–16, 118, 125, 139n
Eternal Return, 119–20, 161–4, 167

Flaubert, Gustave, 25, 128–9
Fóti, Véronique, 61–2
Foucault, Michel, 2, 147–9, 152–3, 156–7, 159, 166, 168n, 169n
fragmentary, 12, 30, 39, 41n, 117, 119, 123, 146–52, 156–67
Fynsk, Christopher, 155

Gagarin, Yuri, 122–4, 126, 128–30
Gasché, Rodolphe, 37–8
de Gaulle, Charles, 5, 102, 104, 112, 122, 155, 164
Genette, Gérard, 129
Gide, André, 25
Godard, Jean-Luc, 105

Haar, Michel, 81–2
hands, 12, 49, 51, 69, 82–3, 84–7, 89–91, 92n, 99, 109, 135, 141n
Hegel, G. W. F., 28, 35, 37, 43n, 63, 93n
Heidegger, Martin, 1–7, 9–12, 17, 38, 40, 42n, 46–72, 80, 81–2, 83, 84 89–91, 93n, 96n, 99, 100, 110, 117–22, 124–6, 146, 156, 159, 161, 172–3, 176n
 Being and Time, 1, 2, 46–8, 49, 63–4, 67, 74
 The Black Notebooks, 5, 14n
 Early Greek Thinking, 151–2
 Elucidations of Hölderlin's Poetry, 2–3, 23–5, 31, 46, 48, 56–7, 72, 93n
 The Fundamental Concepts of Metaphysics, 77–8
 'Letter on "Humanism"', 52
 'Nietzsche's Word, "God is Dead"', 117
 '"Only a God Can Save Us"', 121–2
 'On the Question of Being', 118
 'The Origin of the Work of Art', 48–52, 54, 112
 Parmenides, 59

 'The Question Concerning Technology', 5–6, 47, 54, 60, 94n, 108, 112–13, 118, 142n
 What is Called Thinking?, 49, 85–6, 92n, 108, 112, 135–7
 'Why Poets?', 57–62, 69–71, 74–6, 94n, 112
Heraclitus, 112, 151–2, 168n, 172
Hill, Leslie, 15n, 97n, 105, 140n, 146, 154, 156
Hitler, Adolf, 5, 9, 53–4
Hölderlin, Friedrich, 2–3, 5–6, 23–5, 31, 42n, 46, 48, 52–8, 59, 61–2, 64, 71–4, 76, 90, 93n, 94n, 96n, 150, 169n, 172, 173, 176
Holland, Michael, 126, 143n
Hollier, Denis, 36
Homer, 106–7
Husserl, Edmund, 29–30, 37, 42n

inhuman, 11–12, 22, 47, 49, 52, 58–61, 68–70, 73–4, 76–82, 84–91, 98n, 99, 107–8, 109, 121–2, 125, 127, 132–5, 136–9, 143n, 145n, 146, 150, 154–5, 157, 162, 165, 167, 173–6
International Review, 123, 127, 130, 144n, 160
iterability, 87–8, 173; *see also* repetition

James, Ian, 146–7
Jaspers, Karl, 42n, 116, 125–7
Joyce, James, 20, 21, 23, 25, 155
Jünger, Ernst, 115–16, 117–18

Kafka, Franz, 12, 67, 101, 127–34, 136, 149, 150, 154, 173–4
Klossowski, Pierre, 139n, 161–3
Kojève, Alexandre, 35, 37, 43n

Lacoue-Labarthe, Philippe, 53–4, 96n, 141n, 157–8, 170n
Laporte, Roger, 18, 121, 175
Lautréamont (Isidore Ducasse), 11, 21, 23, 42n, 82–4, 87–8
Levinas, Emmanuel, 2, 6, 37, 46, 79, 83–4, 93n, 95n, 146, 167n
Lévi-Strauss, Claude, 102, 108–10, 173
Limet, Yun Sun, 39
Linder, H. R., 88
literature
 relation to everyday language, 3, 12, 17–40, 44n, 46, 48, 52, 54, 57, 140n
 relation to philosophy, 46–7, 55–7, 66, 70–1, 83, 94n

relation to politics, 4, 18, 21, 27–8, 40, 41n, 55–6, 113–14; *see also* politics, refusal
role of criticism, 1–5, 9, 11, 17, 31–5, 38, 40, 87–8, 118–19, 130–1, 144n, 172
Madaule, Pierre, 171n
Mallarmé, Stéphane, 5, 12, 18–28, 31–4, 38–40, 41n, 42n, 46, 52, 55–6, 76, 90, 105, 150, 172, 173
Malraux, André, 101–5, 107, 110, 141n, 173
de Man, Paul, 93n, 95–6n
Mascolo, Dionys, 4–5, 144n
Mauron, Charles, 24
Maurras, Charles, 55
May 1968, 144n, 165
Mehlman, Jeffrey, 15n, 27
Melville, Herman, 21, 22–3, 106–7
Mondor, Henri, 25
Morali, Claude, 163, 165
Morton, Timothy, 176n
myth, 20, 22–5, 40, 53–4, 59, 61–2, 94n, 101, 105, 106–7, 133, 141n, 165

Nancy, Jean-Luc, 9–10, 15n, 147, 157–8, 170n
Nerval de, Gérard, 23
the neuter, 46, 75, 90, 93–4n, 100, 110–11, 114, 117, 120–34, 136–8, 139n, 146, 150, 152–3, 157, 163–4, 168n, 169n
Nietzsche, Friedrich, 58, 59, 63, 65, 116–18, 120, 125, 135–6, 142n, 159–62, 167, 172
nihilism, 57, 115, 117–22, 125, 135, 147, 159, 172–3, 175–6
Novalis, 25, 28
nuclear weapons, 4, 5, 7, 9, 62, 100, 112, 114–16, 122, 125–7, 135, 138, 173–4, 175

the Occupation, 18, 24, 40, 41n, 102
the Open, 47, 49, 51–2, 56–61, 64, 69–71, 73–7, 89
Oppenheimer, Julius Robert, 108

paperback, 113–14, 158, 167, 173; *see also* printing press
Paulhan, Jean, 18, 26–8, 30, 33
Pearson, Roger, 20–1
Pétain, Philippe, 18
photography, 102–3, 105, 110–11
Plato, 1, 110, 111, 136
Poe, Edgar Allan, 23

politics: Blanchot's relation to, 9–10, 15n, 18, 27–8, 43n, 55, 90, 104–5, 112, 140–1n; *see also* literature, relation to politics; refusal
printing press, 5, 9, 100, 113–14, 117, 123, 125, 158–9, 160; *see also* paperback

radio, 9, 150
Ramnoux, Clémence, 151–2
refusal, 12, 18, 27, 155–6, 162, 164–6; *see also* literature, relation to politics; politics
repetition, 1, 7, 65, 76, 87–8, 90, 99, 103, 105, 107–8, 123, 133, 139n, 140n, 150, 158, 163, 165
Rilke, Rainer Maria, 12, 46, 47, 49, 57–67, 69–71, 74–7, 80, 83, 85–7, 90, 95–6n, 99, 125, 172
Robert, Marthe, 130
romanticism, 23, 26–8, 91, 146, 166
  Jena Romantics, 28, 48, 53, 73, 157–8, 170n
Rosenberg, Alfred, 54

Sade, Marquis de, 113
Sartre, Jean-Paul, 3–4, 18, 32, 35–6, 41n, 43n
Scève, Maurice, 55
Schapiro, Meyer, 50–1
Schlegel, Friedrich, 73, 96n, 157, 170n
Sheringham, Michael, 125
Socrates, 110, 121
solitude, 78, 81–5
spaceflight, 5, 9, 100, 122–26, 129–30; *see also* Yuri Gagarin
Sternhell, Zeev, 27–8, 43n
Stiegler, Bernard, 1, 6–8, 14n, 92n, 139n, 142n
stone, 11–12, 49, 52, 68–9, 77–8, 89, 98n, 146, 162–5, 167; *see also* inhuman
Surya, Michel, 9

Teilhard de Chardin, Pierre, 115–16
telephone, 9, 11, 82, 86, 101, 133–4, 150, 154–6, 159, 162, 167, 174
television, 114
there is [il y a], 37, 79–80, 83–4, 90
translation, 123, 130, 151
Trotsky, Leon, 113, 159
typography, 8, 66, 118, 120, 123, 143n, 151, 159–60, 165, 167

Valéry, Paul, 32, 34–5, 42n, 44n
Van Gogh, Vincent, 50–1, 69, 164

EU representative:
Easy Access System Europe
Mustamäe tee 50, 10621 Tallinn, Estonia
Gpsr.requests@easproject.com

www.ingramcontent.com/pod-product-compliance
Lightning Source LLC
Chambersburg PA
CBHW051126160426
43195CB00014B/2365